Praise for

Ghost

Named One of the Best National Security Books of 2008
by Family Security Matters

"In many ways, this book reads like a le Carré spy novel.... Fascinating."
—*Booklist*

"In this startling memoir, [Burton] recounts his strategies, successes and
failures in tracking down some of the world's most wanted and elusive
criminals." —*The Sacramento Bee*

"In *Ghost*, Burton has taken his decades of counterterrorism and security
experience and boiled it down to a fast-paced narrative of an undercover
agent who was plunged into a murky world of violent religious extrem-
ism spanning the streets of Middle Eastern cities and the informant-
filled alleys of American slums. Riveting ... an entertaining ... journey
into the heart of U.S. counterterrorism. Burton, it would seem, is one of
the closest things we have to James Bond."

—*Risk Management*

"Illuminating ... This memoir is all at once hard-hitting, well-researched,
and an easy read. It recounts aggressive actions taken to protect our nation's diplomats—actions in a campaign that almost cost Burton his mar-
riage and family." —*SmallWarsJournal.com*

ghost

RANDOM HOUSE TRADE PAPERBACKS / NEW YORK

ghost

CONFESSIONS OF A COUNTERTERRORISM AGENT

Fred Burton

This book is dedicated to Special Agent Brad Smith, deceased, Counterterrorism Division, Diplomatic Security Service, U.S. Department of State

LIBRARY OF CONGRESS CATALOGING-IN-PUBLICATION DATA
Burton, Fred.
Ghost: confessions of a counterterrorism agent / Fred Burton.
p. cm.
ISBN 978-0-345-49425-2
1. Burton, Fred.   2. Intelligence officers—United States—
Biography.   3. Terrorism—United States—Prevention.   4. United
States. Dept. of State. Diplomatic Security Service.   I. Title.
JK468.I6.B89 2008
363.28—dc22
[B]   2008000073

Book design by Susan Turner

contents

preface

I carry a list of names with me at all times. It is written in the black ink of a fountain pen in a hardback black Italian moleskin journal, and it travels with me around town in my weathered Ghurka shoulder bag or, when I'm on the road, in my small Zero Halliburton aluminum case, right next to my Smith & Wesson Model 637 five-shot revolver.

There are about fifteen names on the list at any given time, but really the number varies, depending on the speed of justice in the world. Some of the names on the list are known actors, while others are aliases or secret code names. I classify some as UNSUB, spook language for an unidentified suspect. A few are rogue intelligence operatives who have carried out assassinations and bombings over the years.

Mostly the names are those of the so-called puzzle makers: the tactical commanders who put together terrorist operations and dispatch the foot soldiers to carry them out. They are the brains behind the attacks. Every attack has a cycle of planning and execution, and I have always been fascinated by the planners who can put it all together.

A few of the names on my list are those of the watchers, a phrase stolen from John le Carré's stories about George Smiley of British intelligence. The watchers conduct the preoperational surveillance—the crucial first phase of the attack cycle. Lurking in the shadows, or operating openly with a laptop perched at a Starbucks table, they study a target in detail to find openings to attack. The good ones move like a gentle breeze, are never noticed, and rarely leave a trail.

Others on my list have been trigger pullers in an assassination operation, placed a bomb on a plane, or attacked a building containing innocent children. These are the cold-blooded knuckle draggers, the shooters. In the bloody aftermath of most of these things, a political group will claim credit under the banner of jihad. But in my mind, the prime responsibility goes to the one who squeezed the trigger or connected the detonator's wires. They are special to me.

Each name on my list has eluded pursuit and is still out there, on the loose. There is a story behind every one. Images of their victims still hover in my view. Some are frozen in time, forever young, with loved ones and family members and children standing by grave sites, left, sometimes forever, to wonder what happened.

I have been told that it is normal to forget. That time heals. For some reason, that has not been true for me. Some nights, after the kids are in bed, I sit and look at the list and pick up my Parker rollerball pen to make updates, add new names, or relish the opportunity to finally cross one off when he has been arrested or slain. The fate of some will never be known. That troubles me the most of all.

I don't need the list to remember their names, for they are all burned into my memory like the sharp flash of a revolver in a dark alley. I close my eyes and recall the sophisticated street dances of surveillance, the code names and radio traffic chattering in my earpiece while my feet ached from standing so long on post, the sharp smell of a lit time fuse, the feel of an Uzi bucking in my hands, or the satisfying final crimping of a blasting cap. The shadow work, the attack cycle, safe-house meetings, eyes-only back-channel cables, black diplomatic passports in various names, cash reward payments in standard-issue black Samsonite briefcases, hotel rooms with signed receipts under code names, airplane fuselages split by explosions, and kidnapping victims chained to radiators. I remember the bodies of children made unrecognizable by the blast of a truck bomb, embassies lying in rubble, body bags on an airport tarmac. Unfinished business, all of it.

I have been told that James Jesus Angleton, the legendary CIA spy-master known by the code name of "Mother," kept such a private, hand-written list. Upon his death, Mother's list was cremated along with his body by the old boys at the Agency, letting him take his secrets to his grave.

My own list remains as current as today's headlines. Most of the names have long been forgotten by the public, but not by me. I take it personally when justice has not been done, and I intend some day to catch up with every one of them, to help in some way to bring them down. Only then will I remove them from my list.

I have been fortunate enough to have had a hand in scratching off a number of those names. I helped create and lead the Counterterrorism Division of the Diplomatic Security Service of the U.S. Department of State. Very few people have ever heard of us. My training for that work was as a street cop back when terrorism was in its infancy.

In the old days, we cataloged what we knew about terrorists by hand on index cards. Today the agencies collect, sort, and store a daily avalanche of information and analysis with a state-of-the-art data-management system. But raw data does not bring wisdom. Information alone cannot distill experience. Computers do not go into the weeds after the bad guys. That is where guys like me come in.

People have always been intrigued by what I do, particularly since most of it was so shrouded in secrecy. Counterterrorism special agents do not court publicity. We have no wish to become targets instead of hunters. We seek the shadows, using secure telephones and untraceable license plates to keep us hidden. Before I left public service, I wore a necklace of laminated identity cards that granted entrance to the inner recesses of the intelligence agencies. My special black passport whisked me past customs officers abroad. My bag was kept packed at all times to answer calls that would have me heading for the other side of the world within hours.

But the rules have changed. It was once thought that security matters and knowledge of the inner workings of terrorism were best kept quiet and left to specialists within the intelligence trade. Now everyone needs to know more, for knowledge is always power. Be it a multinational cor-poration, a government agency, or an individual citizen, the more you know, the safer you can be.

With this book, I hope to let readers walk in my shoes for a while, to go behind the curtain to look at the "how" as well as the "why" of what I call "the Black World." I'll explain the nuts and bolts of how terrorists plot, stalk, and kill, and how counterterrorism agents try to bring the perpetrators to justice. The difference between failure and success can depend upon tiny things: a piece of pocket litter or an offhand boast by an interrogation subject. The truth is often elastic, the process of seeking it like aiming a telescope through a rotating glass prism.

This book is partly a personal catalog of balls dropped, leads not followed, opportunities missed and the ensuing cover-ups. I also have some successes to report and some conclusions that might surprise you, just to show that good things can happen when everything comes together the right way. All too often, success is not quantifiable, and many stories go untold because of the need to protect ongoing operations.

The personal payoff for me comes when we bring down one of the terrorists. I never really care if he's captured in handcuffs or loaded dead on a stretcher. I don't care whether the takedown was the result of hard work, bravery, or pure luck. Whenever we take a bad guy off the board, I feel good. I can justify relaxing for a moment and spending time with my wife and children without a second thought. I can take a long jog with my trusty canine partner. I can watch a game of football or visit an old friend.

But for a great many years, during my whole tenure in government service, I found that no matter how much I wanted to leave the Dark World's burdens behind, the call of the next operation always seemed to bring me back. I couldn't ever stop thinking that how hard we terrorist hunters worked would determine the speed of justice in the world. And I couldn't wait for the next opportunity to scratch another name off my list.

PART I: ROOKIE YEAR

one

THE BURIED BODIES

0500
February 10, 1986
Bethesda, Maryland

On my morning run through February's chilly darkness, my chocolate Lab, Tyler Beauregard, sets the pace. This is our routine together, though we always vary our route now. At agent training, which I just completed, they drilled into us the notion that in our new lives, routines will get us killed. When you join the Dark World, you must become unpredictable. Erratic. We must strip away all the conventions of our old lives and fade into the background. We've been trained. We've practiced. Today, I begin my life as a ghost.

These morning runs will be my one tip to the old life I'm leaving behind. Still, today I take new precautions, such as the snubby Smith & Wesson Model 60 .38-caliber revolver tucked away under my belt.

I love these morning runs with Tyler. She is a remarkable animal, my familiar, a canine that intuits more about loyalty and honor than most of the people I encountered as a police officer in Montgomery County, Maryland. She pads along, tongue lolling, breathing steady. She's a pro. She could run marathons of her own.

My footfalls echo across the empty Bethesda neighborhood. The tidy brick houses and apartments are dark. In my new life, I'll be spending a lot of time in darkness. I've learned to be paranoid. I've learned to look around corners and watch my back. Our instructors warned us that the KGB opens a file on every one of us new agents as soon as we graduate. Then they probe our lives and backgrounds in search of weaknesses, skeletons, or any sort of leverage by which to exploit or co-opt us. Sooner or later, they will make contact with an offer. Or a threat.

I glance behind me, half expecting to see some Eastern Bloc thug in a trench coat shadowing me. But all I see is a thin layer of fog and an empty suburban block.

I look behind me a lot these days. It goes with the job. Situational awareness is essential if we are to stay alive. I don't run with a Walkman banging out Springsteen's *Born to Run* anymore. My ears are unbound and tuned to the street. Every little sound, every shuffle or distant downshift of an automobile on MacArthur Boulevard registers with me. I file each new noise away in my mind, cataloging it so I'll notice anything out of the ordinary. I've been trained to be an observer. Since I started my training last November, I hone and refine this skill on every morning run.

Tyler picks up the pace. She's taking me toward Glen Echo, a small town on the Potomac. We reach a little jogging trail that runs along Reservoir Road. Here, we escape the suburbs and plunge into the woods. Just before we enter the tree line, I steal a sidelong glance behind me again. I practice this move every day; it is something we learned in training. The trick is to be unobtrusive, to not reveal that you're clearing your six. It has become automatic for me now.

No tails. We're not being followed.

Today my life changes forever. I have no idea what is in store for us new guys. I just know that a year ago, I was a Maryland cop. I protected my community. I loved law enforcement, but I wanted something more. So I applied for federal service, and the Diplomatic Security Service offered me a job. Until last fall, I'd never even heard of the DSS.

I started my training in November 1985, just a few weeks after terrorists hijacked the cruise liner *Achille Lauro* and executed Leon Klinghoffer for the crime of being an American citizen—and a Jew. They shot him then dumped him overboard in his wheelchair.

The world needs more cops.

Only one out of every hundred who start the training get to the finish line. I felt lucky just to be there. After the ceremony, we stood in alphabetically arranged lines waiting to receive our first assignments. Our class coordinator, Special Agent Phil Whitney, began reading off our names and telling us what we'd be doing for the next phase of our lives. Some of us picked up overseas assignments in our embassy field offices. Some landed protective security tours, guarding our diplomats and the secretary of state. Whitney told a few they'd be assigned as diplomatic couriers, where they would carry our nation's most-guarded secrets from one place to another all around the globe.

When he got to me, Whitney paused. He stared at his clipboard for a moment before saying, "Burton, Counterterrorism Branch."

I'd had no idea what that was. When Whitney reached the middle of the alphabet he called out, "Mullen, Counterterrorism Branch."

I looked down the rows of agents to John Mullen. His flaming red hair was easy to spot. I could see him searching me out. We were the only two to be sent to this puzzling assignment. We exchanged confused glances. What had we gotten into?

At least I'd be going into it with a rock-steady veteran. Before he joined the DSS, Mullen had been an agent with the Drug Enforcement Administration, battling the growing narco-criminal element and co-caine cartels on the streets of New York City. Legend had it that he'd been in a nasty shoot-out and had run out of ammunition in the midst of the fray. After that, he always carried two guns. One he tucked away in a shoulder holster. The other he wore strapped to his ankle. He prepared for the worst and trusted in firepower. I swear we all thought he slept with those weapons. They were his pacifiers.

A light rain drizzles down on us now. Tyler shakes her coat in mid-stride, sending water droplets flying. I wish I could do that. We're still on a course that is taking us away from our little redbrick apartment, a fact that I sense is starting to disappoint my dog. I hurry forward until I'm even with her and bend down to run my hands through her damp fur. She looks up at me with pure love. I've already told my wife that when I die, Tyler's ashes will be buried with me.

Back home, my wife, Sharon, is probably just getting up to face her own Monday. We were high school sweethearts and have known each other most of our lives. Up until now, we've lived an average DINK life (Double Income, No Kids). She's an accountant, a damned good one. She's aggressive and driven and works long hours. Now, I'm a spook. Se-

crecy is our watchword. I realize with a grin that we'll have nothing to
talk about at cocktail parties.

Tyler Beauregard dashes ahead of me again until she reaches a narrow
footbridge. She waits for me to catch up. She knows this bridge. We've investigated it before. It is top on the list of Dark World sites to see in Washington, D.C. Of course, there are no plaques or markers noting this piece of
spy history. To the average workaday American—guys like me until four
months ago—it was just a little bridge over a small creek.

But now I know its dark side. This was Kim Philby's dead-drop point.
Philby was the KGB's first true superspy, a British intel operative who
embraced Communism while at Cambridge in the thirties. He compromised hundreds of agents, destroyed scores of operations, and sold out
the lives of countless patriots. When his cover was finally blown in the
sixties, he escaped to Moscow and got what he deserved: a hellish life
under the regime he had helped sustain. In the dingy concrete apartments he later called home, he devolved into a bitter, broken alcoholic
given to frequent bouts of complete incoherence. His conscience became
his enemy. He died in shame, his name a byword for treason.

In the late 1940s, Philby was posted to Washington, D.C. It was said
that he somehow learned the true size of our atomic stockpile, which was
not large at the time. He passed that vital tidbit of national security on to
the KGB by taping a tube full of documents under this bridge. Legend
has it that the information the Russians retrieved here emboldened
Stalin to blockade Berlin in 1948.

This is my world now. The days of chasing speeders, driving drunken
high school kids home, and taking down burglars is over. At least for me.

Tyler senses I'm brooding and sets off again. This is her way of telling
me it is time to return to the warmth of our apartment. I trail along behind
her, my breathing easy. As I watch her galloping for home, it strikes me
that she too has a connection to the Dark World. She's from Winchester,
Virginia. I bought her from a breeder there in town when she was just a
pup. That's John Mosby country. He was a Confederate colonel, a rene-
gade guerrilla nicknamed the "Gray Ghost" who struck terror into the
hearts of Union rear-area types during the height of the Civil War.

Now I'm counterterror. Whatever that means. I suppose like every
American who watches the evening news, I've seen Americans abroad
fall victim to political violence. One terror attack after another has dark-

ened the nightly broadcasts—the *Achille Lauro,* plane hijackings, car bombings, Beirut. We're a nation still scarred by the Iran hostage crisis and that 444-day nightmare. Will I be fighting against this sort of criminal now? I'm not sure, but I hope so.

Time to find out. We run through the morning, never retracing our steps. Periodically, I check my rear. No KGB agent picks up my tail. When we reach the apartment, we're still alone. A half hour out in the neighborhood and we never saw another soul. It is refreshing to have such privacy.

A quick shower and a hastily downed breakfast soon follow our arrival home. I dress carefully. I toss my Casio watch onto the nightstand. I use it only for running. In its place, I strap on a black-faced Rolex Submariner. There's no way I could afford such a luxury at retail price on my salary. A government special agent makes $22,000. But on our honeymoon to the Virgin Islands a few years ago, I snagged this one for $750.

In the closet, I find my Jos. A. Bank suit. Brown. Standard spook issue. The company gives us agents a discount. I button up a white dress shirt and throw on the one thing that will give me any distinction among my colleagues: a duck-patterned Orvis tie. No sense in totally obliterating my identity with my government threads.

Finally, I reach down to find my Johnston & Murphy lace-up shoes. I used to wear loafers when I wore a suit, but that's a no-no in the Dark World. Our instructors taught us to always wear lace-up shoes. Why? If you have to kick someone while wearing loafers, chances are your shoe will fly off. Lace-ups stay on through hand-to-hand combat.

I wonder who I'll need to kick in the months to come.

I slip a Parker rollerball into my shirt pocket, then check my briefcase. Inside is a small black pouch with the Holy Grail of our business: five little pins designed to be affixed to our left lapels. Each one is color-coded: black, red, blue, green, and gold. Depending on the day and the mission, they denote to other agents that the wearer is on protective security duty. That's basically bodyguard detail, like what the Secret Service does for the president. In agent training, we were told that if we lose these pins, it would automatically trigger an internal affairs investigation.

In the briefcase next to the pouch is my custom-made radio earpiece. It was molded specifically for me and my left ear. When in the field, this will be my lifeline to my fellow agents.

I pull my credentials out of the briefcase. They look like an average wallet until you open them. Inside, they're marked "This special agent holds a Top Secret clearance and is worthy of trust and confidence." Our gold badge sits next to those words. I fold the creds up and tuck them into my left jacket pocket. I'm agent number 192.

Last, I strap on my belt holster. It holds two speed loaders for my Smith & Wesson Model 19 .357 Magnum. I slide the ebony weapon into its sheath and snap the strap in place. With the two speed loaders, I've got eighteen rounds. That should be enough. If you can't get the job done with eighteen shots, you'd better run.

I'm ready for work. Well, almost. It's a cold day and I'll need a jacket. Inside my closet hangs a green Barbour Beaufort. This is a standard-issue piece of cold-weather gear for the British MI5 and several other intelligence services. They're warm and have inner pockets that are perfect for hiding an extra revolver or a small radio. The pockets are lined and keep hands toasty, even on a snowy day. This allows us to forgo gloves, making it easier to draw our weapons.

Or so the veteran spooks have told me.

Back in the day, special agents preferred tweed. Look around D.C. in the sixties and seventies, and the spooks from Langley and the Hooverite FBI agents all wore brown tweed with elbow patches. They looked a bit like college professors, only cooler and in better shape. And well-armed.

That's old-school now. We new guys go with the Barbour Beauforts. One of my instructors told me just before graduation that in a pinch, if you need help while out on the street during an assignment, look for the Barbour Beaufort jackets. Chances are they'll be keeping a spook warm.

But for which side?

By now it's almost six. Sharon's coiffed and ready for work. We kiss and both of us depart, leaving the apartment to Tyler. She'll take good care of it.

My gold Jetta awaits. It is not James Bond's Aston Martin, just the best we could do on our salaries. I climb aboard and head for MacArthur Avenue. I check my rearview mirror every few seconds, memorizing the cars behind me. Are any following? I merge onto Canal Road and pass along the outskirts of the Georgetown University campus.

It seems like such a normal commute in an average part of America. Yet I know that today is going to be different. The life here on the surface, the life 90 percent of us lead, is going to be a mere reflection from now on for me. Already there have been changes. I have a false driver's license. I'm Fred Booth to people in the normal world. We keep our first names so we respond naturally when somebody uses it. I stole my uncle's last name for my pseudonym.

There's another distinction. The plates on my Jetta are standard-looking Maryland issue, but they are blanks in the state's computer system. If anyone runs a trace on them, the Maryland DMV will alert our office. If the KGB wants info on us newbies, our license plates will be a dead end.

Through the predawn darkness, I drive and watch my tail in the light traffic. Seventeen minutes later, I reach the Harry S Truman Building. This is the State Department's home base. Located a short ways off the National Mall, it is an imposing edifice.

I flash my creds to the guard. He nods. I'm new; he recognizes it. I ask him where the Counterterrorism Branch is located. He shrugs. Even the guards don't know where it is. It takes me a few minutes to find my way down to the investigations section, located deep inside the bowels of the building. I find myself underground. No windows, poor air circulation. Government-issued desks abound. Someone takes pity on me and leads me to a narrow corridor, past a set of restrooms, where I am left in front of an oversized wooden door, painted blue. Embedded inside the wood is an S&G combination lock. I knock tentatively.

The door opens, and I come face-to-face with...not James Bond. Medium length, salt-and-pepper hair, mustache, ruddy, rugged features make this man look more like a patrol sergeant than James Bond. For a moment, I'm rooted in place with astonishment. All I can do is stare as he swings back out of the doorway and sits behind a weather-beaten old desk, cigarette dangling from his lips. He ignores me and picks up two phones, sticking one in each ear. Piled on the desk in front of him are stacks of paper. He seems to be reading as he talks. Using a red pen, he scribbles something across a piece of paper even as he shouts into one of the phones. Then he slams it down, takes a long drag on the smoke, and stares up at me.

I look around the room. The walls are bare. The office is tiny, made even smaller by the fact that there are three oversized wooden desks in it. Not Bond's sits slightly off to one side, but the other two are back-to-back. Mullen is perched in an ancient chair that looks like it could have gone government surplus sometime before the Spanish-American War.

He appears completely dumbfounded. He's already surrounded by stacks of paperwork and file folders. He's gamely making an effort to read something, but I can tell his attention is really on Not Bond, who has returned to chewing somebody out over the other phone while crushing his cigarette out in an overflowing ashtray. He nods at me and points at the remaining desk. Apparently, I get to sit face-to-face with Mullen all day. Privacy is not a luxury we will enjoy here.

A couple of fans blow the dusty air around. Already, it carries a whiff of body odor, tinged with that musty smell yellowing documents give off. They mingle to create a totally new sort of odor, one part locker room, one part dingy, dank document repository, like a high school football team has set up shop in the basement of the National Archives.

Mullen gives me a weak grin, as if to say *Welcome to Oz, Burton.*

I step to my desk. Around it, in every nook and cranny, tan burn bags are stacked and double stacked. Apparently, we'll be turning much of the paperwork in here into ashes at some point or another. More burn bags slump against a series of five paint-flecked, industrial gray file cabinets. I wonder what those contain. I glance over at Not Bond. He waves at me and points to my chair. Dutifully, I sit in it. He's jabbering a mile a minute. Words spill out of his mouth, but I can't understand what he's saying. He seems to have his own language. I hear him use *Fullback, POTUS, Eagle 1, LIMDIS,* and *NODIS* all in the same series of sentences. Is this English or is Not Bond a Navajo code talker? And will I have to learn all this stuff, too? Who starts a new job that requires a new language?

I try not to stare by keeping my eyes on the file cabinets. It takes me a minute to realize that stacked around us are piles of plastic explosives, some of which are labeled in Russian Cyrillic.

Not Bond lights another cigarette and sticks another phone in his ear. I wonder if smoking around stuff that blows up is all that wise of an idea.

One of the fans blows a big waft of tobacco smoke across my desk. I try not to cough. Mullen studiously avoids eye contact. He looks like a frazzled redheaded college student cramming for a midterm.

Not Bond slams one of his phones down onto its cradle. It's an old rotary, like something from the seventies. Minutes later, he cradles the other one. This is a mixed blessing. Now all his multitasking attention is riveted on me. We stare at each other. I try not to look panicked, but the truth is I can already see I'm in way over my head. I'm in an office full of bombs.

"Steve Gleason," says Not Bond. "Sorry about that. Talking with the Folks Across the River."

I give him a blank look.

"The CIA. This is an unsecured line. We have to talk around things." He guffaws, takes a deep drag on his smoke, then adds, "As if the Reds couldn't figure out who the 'Folks Across the River' are."

I stay silent. It seems like the prudent thing to do.

"See those cabinets?" He points his cigarette at the line of gray boxes on the far wall.

I nod.

"That's where the bodies are buried."

I hope that's not literal. At this point, given the plastique, the burn bags, the smells, all bets are off.

He reaches over his desk and grabs a couple of files. He tosses them at me. They slide across my desk. "Beirut I and II. Read them." I look down. The files are coded with numbers and letters. They offer me no clue as to what they contain.

He lunges for more paperwork. "Open a case number on these two. Then go draw some travel money. We take turns running to FOGHORN to pick up the latest cables."

I don't understand any of this. I want to ask what FOGHORN is, but I decide it would be more prudent to remain silent.

"Look, what we do here is very secret. Hardly anyone here at State knows what we do. Keep it that way. What we do here stays in this room, clear?"

"Yes."

"Read these." He launches a raft of diplomatic cables my way. The top ones are marked "SECRET" in red letters. I'd never read a secret document in my life. Now, I'm trapped in a blizzard of them. It'll take me hours to read this stuff.

"Check out the cold cases. Dissect them. Find ways we can keep our people alive in the future, okay?" He stabs the air with his cigarette, pointing at the file cabinets again.

His phone rings. He snatches it up, his attention on me broken. It is time to get to work.

I look down at the pile of paper and wonder where to start.

two

"CT03." That's what the outside of one oversized brown file folder says. It was written with a black Magic Marker in spiky hand lettering. I untie the folder and open it up. Sitting inside are more legal-sized green file folders. They're worn and ragged and look decades old. Each one has a label. I sort through them looking at the subheadings: "Intelligence," "Unsolved Leads," "Unanswered Questions," "Witness Statements." In the back is another one marked "Evidence."

My cop instinct leads me to pull out the evidence folder first. It seems awfully thin. When I open it up, I find only a single sealed plastic bag. On the outside it reads, "Department of State—Evidence—SRG." I assume those are Gleason's initials. I lift it up and examine its contents. Whatever is inside looks like a dried-up mushroom.

"What is this?" I ask myself softly.

Gleason overhears me and replies, "An ear."

First day on the job, and I'm holding a human body part. The Alice in Wonderland experience is complete. I've gone down the rabbit hole.

I continue to hold the ear. Miss Manners doesn't cover this sort of scenario. What should I say? How should I react? I'll wing it.

"So, did you cut this off a suspect?" I ask Gleason.

He is not amused. He just looks at me with a *You have no idea what you've gotten yourself into here* sort of expression. Then he goes back to scribbling on more paperwork. Almost as an afterthought he says, "That's what's left of the suicide bomber."

Suicide bomber? As in kamikaze? I better start at the beginning. I tuck the ear away and pull out the first file. The sheaf of papers becomes my gateway to the world we Americans don't want to know about. I read the stilted words, mesmerized by the meaning behind them.

April 18, 1983. Beirut was chaos—it is even worse now. The city, once known for its Westernized and cosmopolitan atmosphere, had long since become a battleground. As the various factions dueled for control, spooks and terrorists played a game of cat and mouse amid the ruins. On April 18, the anniversary of Paul Revere's ride, the terrorists scored their first decisive victory against the United States.

At 1300 hours local time, a van passed through a security checkpoint and drove up to the front of the embassy. The driver parked under a portico, then detonated the two thousand pounds of explosives stuffed into the back.

Now I understand why there is only an ear left.

The explosion tore apart the entire front of the U.S. Embassy, killing sixty-three people and wounding a hundred more. I vaguely remember hearing about it on the news three years ago. I never heard who carried out the attack.

What possesses a man to blow himself up while murdering scores of innocents at the same time? What is the motivation? I suspect those are questions I'll be wrestling with for a long time.

The attack was orchestrated by Islamic Jihad, which has been in the news a lot lately. The "Intelligence" folder has plenty on Islamic Jihad, and before lunch I learn that it is really just a name. The real player is Hezbollah, and the power behind that name is Iran.

The Iranians blew up our embassy in Beirut. Hezbollah—controlled, directed, and supported by Iranian intelligence—provided the foot soldiers for the attack.

How was this not an act of war?

I sit back and take a breath, then I press on. The witness statements are the worst. The grim, bloody retelling of broken bodies, the rubble, the misery—even the formal, objective language used in these documents can't conceal the trauma of this attack. It was the worst one ever against a U.S. embassy. Nothing in our history compares to it. That much is clear to me just from the initial reading.

I delve further, flipping through well-worn pages, many of which were written by Gleason himself. One thing begins to stand out. The timing of the attack was peculiar. As it happened, the CIA's entire Middle East contingent was hunkered down in a meeting room toward the front of the embassy. When the bomb exploded, the CIA's Near East director, Robert Ames, and seven other CIA officers were killed.

Was the CIA meeting compromised? I open the "Unanswered Questions" file. There's no evidence to show that Hezbollah knew of the meeting. Then again, with all the foreign nationals working in the embassy, it is quite possible that word of the meeting had been leaked. This question is a loose end, one of many stemming from the attack.

Coincidence or cunning? In the Dark World, our instructors told us, there are no coincidences. Nor will all the puzzle pieces ever fall into place. The best you can do is assemble what you have and try to divine the rest. This first file reinforces that training lesson.

Just before lunch, Gleason tells us the combination for the big blue door. "Don't write it down. Just memorize it," he says. Then he gives us the combinations to the safes under our desks. I hadn't noticed mine until he mentioned it. They are for storing top-secret files we're using. Every time we leave the office, the material on our desk needs to be locked up in these safes or returned to the dead bodies cabinets.

With those combination numbers rattling around in my head, I decide to take a short break. I head for the restroom out in the hallway on the other side of the big blue door. When I get there, Mullen is just coming out. As he slides through the doorway, he grimaces at me and mentions, "Gleason told me the Weather Underground blew this bathroom up back in '75. Took out three entire offices."

I'm working at ground zero of a terrorist attack. I hurry into the restroom as Mullen starts spinning the combo lock on the big blue door. I make a mental note not to spend too much time in this place—just in case.

Back in the office a few minutes later, I find Gleason eating and smoking at his desk. He manages to multitask in ways I've never seen before. He alternates stuffing a sandwich into his mouth between puffs on his smoke while writing notes on a cable. Periodically, he grabs a phone and barks at somebody in that foreign language of his.

I sit back down and begin reading again. Gleason asks, "Have you opened those two cases yet?"

"No, I'm still studying the files you gave me."

"Beirut One or Two?"

"One."

Gleason grunts and goes back to work.

There was a second attack in Beirut. I close the April 18, 1983, case folder and untie the other one Gleason had given me when I first came in. Sure enough, a year after the first bombing, Islamic Jihad scored another big victory against us. Already, Hezbollah and the Iranians had crippled our military effort in Beirut with another suicide bomb attack, this one aimed at the marine barracks near the airport. That was in October 1983. Two hundred and forty-one marines died in that attack. The destruction prompted the Reagan administration to pull our troops out of Lebanon. Hezbollah: 2, United States: 0.

A year later, Hezbollah hit the American embassy annex in northeast Beirut. This was where our diplomatic staff had been operating. Although the fixed-site security had been beefed up, another Hezbollah suicide bomber managed to breach the outer perimeter. This time the guards unloaded their weapons at the speeding vehicle, but the suicide bomber still managed to reach his target and detonate himself.

Twenty-four people, including two Americans, died. Hezbollah: 3, United States: 0.

Each of these cases is so complex that every file leads to more reading. I feel like I'm peeling an onion. Each layer reveals more layers, more information that I will have to know for my new life. I discover that Hezbollah's tactics derived from the true pioneers of terror: Black September. Known as BSO, or Black September Organization, in the files, these fanatical Palestinians assassinated eleven members of the Israeli Olympic team in Munich back in 1972.

Gleason tells me, "To understand terrorism today, you must understand Black September."

I put down the Beirut I and II files and delve deeper into the dead bodies cabinets. I find thick folders devoted just to Black September and its evil genius, the erudite, impeccably dressed mass murderer known as the Red Prince. The Red Prince was the archterrorist, the mastermind behind countless hijackings, bombings, and assassinations. He liked to keep things simple and used brute force whenever possible.

Gleason's right. Hezbollah is only the latest iteration of terror. Same with all the other alphabet-soup terror groups. They are only evolutions on BSO's heyday in the 1970s.

I start taking notes. I find some three-by-five index cards and return to the Beirut I file to start jotting down the basics of the attack. Suicide bomber. The van breached all the outer security and was able to get right next to the main embassy building. This was vital to the success of the attack. Had the outer security perimeter stopped the van, the damage would have been minimized.

I underline a lesson here. I have no idea what I'm doing, but it just appears to me to be common sense. *Stand-off distance.*

I grab another index card and write out the basic facts and lessons learned. Again, the outer security ring was obviously deficient. Was I even supposed to be noticing these things? I glance over at Gleason, wondering if I should ask for guidance. He's buried in paperwork, a phone growing out of one ear. He looks irritated and overwhelmed.

The attacks in Beirut sparked a congressional inquiry into the safety of our overseas diplomatic missions. Headed by Admiral Bobby Inman, the commission reported a long list of security deficiencies in embassies all over the globe. Among the laundry list of recommendations, the Inman Commission sought millions of dollars to build new facilities, plus additional money to hire more State Department agents. In 1985, in response to the Inman recommendations, Congress created the Bureau of Diplomatic Security and the DSS. Mullen and I are the first wave of agents resulting from that piece of legislation. In agent training, they called us "Inman Hires."

I glance over at Gleason again. He's off the phone now. He sees me looking at him and tosses me a few more files. "Lebanon." "Beirut." "Hostages." "Look these over. See what you can piece together."

My stack of first-day reading just got even larger. As I flip through the new material, Gleason says, "Mullen, you're going to cover South

America. You've dealt with the cartels. You know the ground. There's plenty there to keep you busy. Colombia. FARC. Shining Path."

Our new boss pauses long enough to toss another butt in the growing morass in his ashtray. He pulls out a fresh smoke and lights it up.

"Burton, you've got the Sandbox. But you'll both help out where needed."

I'm not sure what that means. He sees that right away and adds, "Anything related to the Middle East. That's your turf. You will become the subject-matter expert."

I don't know anything about the Middle East. The files on my desk right now are the tip of the iceberg. In the months to come, I'm going to be doing a lot more reading.

"We don't have a mission statement. I don't have time to write one. Just know that our job is to keep our embassy personnel alive. Take a look at the cold cases. Think about how the attacks were carried out. Who did them, the mechanics, the tactics. Then we've got to figure out ways to counter them. Ways to prevent them. Right now, we're playing catch-up. We're reactive and always undermanned. We need to figure out how to get in front of things. Understood?"

Two new agents nod dutifully. This is why Gleason handed me Beirut I and II right off the bat. They are the big ones, the attacks that reshaped the security landscape for our diplomats.

I wonder how I'm supposed to figure out how to stop such catastrophic events like those two. Six months ago, I was a Maryland cop. The worst I'd seen were homicides and car wrecks. I've never encountered anything on the scale of Beirut I.

I guess in my gut I realized that when I joined the DSS, I would not be working a run-a-day nine-to-five job. Now, I've glimpsed the scope—and the stakes. This isn't a job or a career, it is a way of life. Lives are at stake. The moves we make in the weeks and months to come will mean the difference between a thwarted effort and a lead story on CNN.

No pressure or anything.

Gleason disappears through the big blue door. Mullen and I work on in silence. I read through more cases, more carnage, more destruction. The same names keep popping up: Hezbollah, Imad Fayez Mugniyah, Abu Nidal. I discern that there are three major players in the Middle East terror game: Iran through Hezbollah and its cohorts, Libya through its own intelligence service and its surrogates, and the Palestinians through the Palestine Liberation Organization (PLO), its splinter groups, and Black September. I have much to learn. The curve is steep.

Gleason returns and hands me more files that he's taken from the dead bodies cabinets. They land on my desk with a heavy thump. I'm getting a crash course in human depravity. It is tough to take, and after a while, all the human misery resident within these pages starts to blur together. The parade of violence, the car bombings, the suicide attacks, the machine gunning of civilians, hostage takings, hijackings—file after file describes horrific events. It leaves me numb.

The world is on fire. And I had no idea.

Late that afternoon, Gleason leaves the office again. Mullen and I work on in silence, continuing our crash course in world terror. A few minutes later, he returns with another raft of diplomatic cables. "Okay, this is the latest from FOGHORN, our communication center. All incoming messages are sent there and prioritized. I'll show you where it is later."

As he squeezes by my desk, Gleason says, "Burton, we've got a source who says our ambassador to Chile is about to get assassinated. You're meeting the informant tomorrow in Charlottesville. When you're done there, write it up, then get up to Philadelphia."

"Philadelphia?"

"Yeah, we've got a source who says his family is Hezbollah. He says he knows where the hostages are in Beirut. For a hundred and fifty grand, he'll spill his guts. Go see if he knows anything."

He hands me two more files on these informants. "Get familiar with them tonight. In the meantime, you'll be traveling on a moment's notice from here on out. Keep an overnight kit packed, okay?"

So much for on-the-job training. Tomorrow, the real game begins.

three

February 13, 1986
Outside of Philadelphia

The Amtrak coach rolls and sways as we clatter along the old tracks between D.C. and Philadelphia. Most of the passengers around me are trying to doze, but a few are busy reading under spotlights clicked on from the overhead panel above each seat. Periodically, we stream past a freight train, and I watch scores of boxcars swish past my window.

I love train travel. It harkens back to a more genteel time, when manners and style reigned unchallenged by the speed and utility of modern airliners. Indeed, this short voyage tonight on Amtrak's rails should be a chance for me to relax far away from the rush-rush-rush of my new office.

But I am not relaxed. Tonight, when I exit this car at the 30th Street Station, along Philadelphia's Schuylkill River, I will meet with a source I know nothing about. Gleason merely told me the rendezvous point and the recognition signal. Since I'll be alone on this mission, I'm mimicking Mullen's habit of carrying extra firepower. Before I left D.C., I strapped my Smith & Wesson Model 60 into the ankle holster now riding on my right shin.

The source says he knows something about our hostages in Lebanon.

For the past few years, Hezbollah and criminal gangs have snatched American citizens off the streets of Beirut. The gangs sell their catches to Hezbollah. Right now, there are dozens of hostages in their hands, including one very special one: William Francis Buckley.

Before I left for Charlottesville and my first rendezvous with an informant on Tuesday, I read through the Buckley file. He was grabbed as he left his house in Beirut. For him, it had started out as any other day. His pattern rarely varied, which was an obvious mistake. He'd get up, get dressed, have breakfast, and walk out to his car. A short drive through the city and he'd be at the U.S. Embassy. A typical commute story, only this one went through the middle of a civil war. Somebody took notice of this well-dressed, dapper-looking American. Somebody like Hezbollah.

On March 16, 1984, a four-man snatch team rolled up in front of his house, surprising Buckley before he could reach his car. The terrorists seized him and dragged him back into their ride. In seconds, it was over. Buckley had been armed, but he'd stuck his pistol inside his briefcase. The abduction happened so fast he never had time to go for it.

File that one away in the lessons-learned category. After that, word went out to every American in the Dark World: Carry your weapon on you at all times. Don't stuff it in a bag and expect to be safe.

It happened that quickly. A matter of seconds and Hezbollah—the Iranians—had triumphed again. There had never been a worse defeat for us within the Dark World. William Buckley had not been an ordinary embassy employee. He was the CIA's station chief.

Another freight train thunders past, and our coach car rocks in its slipstream. A few of the dozers pop an eyelid, look around, then return to their naps. They sleep in blissful ignorance. Do they understand what a luxury that is? I wonder if I'll ever enjoy that sort of unencumbered sleep again.

When Hezbollah nabbed Buckley, they brought down every current operation and operative in the entire Middle East. Nothing like this had ever happened. Even the KGB had never dared to seize a station chief. With Buckley in enemy hands, the Agency had to assume that all the information inside his head would be compromised. Hezbollah and the Iranians were not known to abide by the Geneva Convention. Torture, intimidation, beatings—those were how they debriefed their captives. Certainly, Buckley would not be spared their worst.

It was a catastrophic blow to our intelligence efforts in the hottest spot on the planet. After he was grabbed, we basically had to start from scratch, building new networks, running new agents. In the meantime, we operated with almost no HUMINT—human intelligence. All the gadgets, satellites, and eavesdropping our technology affords us cannot compare to one good agent in the right place and time. Hezbollah poked our eyes out with Buckley's abduction. What are we missing? What won't we see coming? It is chilling to realize how vulnerable we are.

Our train rounds a gentle curve and hits the industrial outskirts of Philadelphia. I stare out the window at a parade of rusting factories and wrecking yards. The darkness makes the scene particularly bleak.

Before I left the office today, Gleason took me aside and gave me one other directive: Find out if this informant knows where Buckley is. He is our priority. The Agency, furious, humiliated, and loyal, is desperate to get him back. They have unleashed a massive effort to find him. So far, every tip has been a dry hole. But each one must be checked out.

The train begins to slow, and the dozers around me sense the change in speed. A few yawn and reach for their bags. A few gaze out the windows, and I can see their faces reflected in the tinted glass. Average Americans. These are the people I'm sworn to protect. Our job is to keep the Dark World from their doorsteps.

Just this week, Gleason, Mullen, and I found almost a dozen credible threats in the cable traffic that landed in FOGHORN's claustrophobic recesses. A dozen a week. Year after year after year. It doesn't take a rocket scientist to know the odds are stacked against us. The CIA, the FBI, the DSS—they can have tens of thousands of field agents and all the money any hungry bureaucracy can burn and still some of these plots will escape our attention. It takes only one terrorist to bring tragedy and trauma—and lots of media coverage. Thinking about those long odds has kept me awake this week. We can't be 100 percent right forever. But we have to try—and therein lies the weight of the world that has sagged Gleason's shoulders and worry-worn his face these past few years. He's handled this staggering load by himself until now. I can't imagine how he's done it.

We roll into the 30th Street Station. Around me, the coach bustles with activity as passengers grab their briefcases and detrain. I step onto the passenger concourse and marvel at the rectangular windows that make this station such a spectacular architectural achievement. The concourse glows gold from the lantern-style lights suspended overhead.

I walk outside and pass the six thick columns that stand watch over the station's entrance. They give the station a sort of ancient Greek temple look from this side. It is bitterly cold, and I pull my jacket tight around my collar as I make my way toward the line of cabs on the street.

I gesture to one of the cabbies, and he pops a door open for me. I give him the address of the motel that will be our rendezvous point and ask him to drop me off a few blocks short. I want to be able to scope out the territory before I go in. Also, I don't want anyone watching to know that I'm alone. There will be no backup if things get rough.

Charlottesville was an easy assignment compared to this one. That's probably why Gleason had me warm up with it. I took one of our State Department Jeep Wagoneers, the kind with the faux wood finishing on the sides, and drove down through blue-blood country until I reached a horse farm set back from the road. The house had been built on a hill, giving anyone inside a clear field of vision to see a visitor's approach. Well-manicured landscaping surrounded it, but none of the bushes were tall enough to mask intruders from the house. The place gave off a strange vibe—it was too neat, too picturesque. An Agency safe house? George Smiley's summer home? Whoever owned it clearly had money.

When I rang the bell, a stunningly attractive Latina in her midthirties answered. Her white blouse accentuated her tan, and she'd pulled her dark hair back into a ponytail that gave her an athletic look. She invited me in and we drank coffee. The day before, FOGHORN had received an incoming cable from Santiago, Chile, regarding a potential hit on our ambassador there. This woman knew one of the names mentioned in the cable. My job was to get as much information on him as possible.

It did not take long. She didn't know much. She was a grad student at the University of Virginia who had had minimal contact with the individual named in the cable. She spoke openly of what she knew, and I dutifully took notes so I could write it all up for Gleason when I returned to the office. I enjoyed the coffee and the company, left my business card, and drove back to D.C. Easy. This spy stuff didn't seem all that hard.

Until tonight. The cabbie plunges us deep into an urban jungle. Rundown row houses, abandoned warehouses, and garbage on the streets mark my descent into Philadelphia's dark side. We finally stop a few blocks from the motel. I'm in dangerous waters now. I hand the cabdriver a few bucks, then climb out.

A transient lies in a doorway across the street. Nearby, drug addicts are sprawled around a set of stairs leading up to a row house. One's shooting up as the others watch. The cabbie, clearly uncomfortable, speeds off the moment my feet hit the sidewalk.

I shouldn't have worn a suit.

As I start walking toward the motel, the local wildlife locks on to me. Red-rimmed eyes size me up, calculating whether or not I'd be easy to roll.

On the next corner, I move through a small squadron of prostitutes. Tube tops and miniskirts abound, though a few have on leg warmers, too—a *Taxi Driver* meets *Flashdance* sort of fashion statement. A few call to me. I ignore them and press on, wondering how they can endure the almost freezing temperature in such dress.

One more block through the human flotsam and I reach the motel's parking lot. The place is a dive, and I'm sure the proprietor is happy to charge by the hour—fresh sheets extra, of course.

Time after time, our instructors pounded into our heads that observant agents are live agents. Every day, I practice taking everything in, memorizing the things unfolding around me so that I can write them up later if necessary. It pays off now. I sweep the motel with my eyes. Metal stairs on either end give access to the second floor. The building itself is L-shaped. The parking lot is full of older junk cars. I scan the license plates. Most are Pennsylvania, some sport long-expired tags. At the far end of the lot, a prostitute struts toward the motel, a john in tow. They stare at me before disappearing up one set of stairs. A few seconds later, they're out on the second floor, moving along the catwalk until they come to their room. The john casts a wary glance back over at me before closing the door to the night.

What a miserable place.

I take a few steps through the parking lot, still searching for clues as to who I'm supposed to meet. Is he a local? Is one of these beat-up cars his? Then I spot a shiny new sedan. New Jersey plates. It sticks out as badly as I do in this neighborhood. A rental car perhaps? Did my informant drive it over from the airport? I walk over to examine it. It is covered with water drops. Dew? The other cars are dry. This one's been in the lot for a while, probably overnight. I peer inside the car. It is clean, though the ashtray's open and full of cigarette butts.

The bums and hookers on the street are still watching me. Could any of them be backup for the informant? Is this a setup? I can't tell. If anyone is covering the informant's back, I can't make him. All I see is a street dotted with human wreckage.

The rendezvous room is on the second floor. I climb the stairs warily, right hand inside my Barbour Beaufort jacket, fingers tight around my revolver's handle. I feel like a cop again. It is the same tension I used to feel when responding to a burglary call.

I reach the door and tap quietly while standing to one side. Just in case it is a setup, I'm not going to get shot through the door. A few seconds tick by, but the door doesn't open. I can hear someone moving around inside the room. I wait. The door cracks open a few inches.

Silence.

"Are you a friend of Steve's?" I ask. This is the recognition signal.

"Yes, I'm Steve's friend," comes the accented reply.

The door swings open to admit me. I slip through inside the room and close the door behind me.

The informant sits on the bed. There's a nightstand with an ancient lamp on it, and I study it briefly, looking for any potential threats. Nothing. The room is narrow with a chair and a small, scarred table rounding out the furniture. I run my eyes over everything, searching for weapons, recording devices, or anything else that could tip me off that this is a trap. I can't see into the bathroom. Is someone in there? I'll have to keep an eye on that door.

The informant fires up a Marlboro and waits. He seems jittery. His hands are shaking. He's backlit by the only available light in the room—the nightstand lamp—but I can still see that he has an olive complexion, a stocky build, and is perhaps in his midthirties. His eyes dart between me and apparently random points in the room. He won't stay focused on me, won't look me in the eyes.

"I . . . know where the hostages are. My family is from Beirut. I was just there," he tells me in a voice full of nerves. I don't say anything. Better to let the informant talk, especially if there's a listening device planted somewhere out of sight.

He studies me as if he's trying to outlast my silence. He takes a long drag on his smoke, then exhales in frustration.

"I'll give you their location, but I want money."

There it is.

"How much?" I ask. In this meeting, I will measure my words. Less is best.

"One hundred and fifty thousand."

I back against the wall across from the bed. A quick glance toward the bathroom door, then my attention refocuses on Steve's friend. He stares at the frayed carpet at my feet. Is he ashamed, or afraid?

"For that kind of money, you'll need to give us something first."

"What do you mean?"

"How do we know you know where the hostages are?"

He deliberates for a few seconds, eyes meandering. Then he reveals, "They are in southern Beirut."

"How do you know this?"

He launches into a long story about his family in Beirut. He claims he's ex-Hezbollah, but that several of his relatives are still in the organization.

"While I was in Beirut, my relative told me he'd seen them."

"Who is your relative?" I ask. A subsource is already in play here, which diminishes the value of the information. The further you go from the source, we were taught, the less likely the information will be accurate. It is sort of like a Dark World game of Telephone.

Steve's friend won't tell me who his relative is or even what the connection is between them.

"What about money?" he asks again. "I want a hundred and fifty thousand."

"Okay, look, it is premature to be talking money at this point," I reply. He looks disappointed and even more edgy. I tell him to walk me through his story again. This time, I pull out a notebook and start scribbling.

Two hours later, he's told me everything he's willing to give up. He says nothing about specific hostages—no mention of Buckley. He rambles on about his family, his association with Hezbollah, and Beirut. In the process, he actually tells me very little. His family lives in West

Beirut. Somehow, this relative of his saw hostages in the southern part of the city. No information on how many hostages or who they were. No more specifics, no more details. I press him, but he doesn't divulge anything else and makes it clear he won't until he has been paid off.

"I'll report this to Steve and he'll get in touch with you." The informant looks disappointed. I think he expected me to shovel bags of cash at him.

I let myself out. He remains on the bed, smoking with a still-shaky hand. That's the last I see of him. I head down the stairs and hit the street again, hooker and junkie eyes following my every move. I feel like a goldfish with a pack of cats peering into my bowl. The night is even colder now. Steam billows up from the manhole covers. The scene is bathed in darkness.

I walk through this moribund neighborhood, keenly aware of everything around me. The addicts remain on their steps. The transient is still passed out in the doorway. The prostitutes on the corner shiver and rub their arms. A drunk staggers past, swathed in a corona of foul odors. I take this all in, eyes alert for any potential threat.

At the same time, my mind stays fixed on the case at hand. The cop in me wants to dismiss Steve's friend as little more than a sleazy huckster looking for a big score. His information is secondhand. I don't think he has much more than what he's already told me.

On the other hand, he must have been on the level to some degree, otherwise Gleason never would have sent me out here. Some basic check into the informant probably confirmed he'd just returned from Lebanon. To be thorough, I'll check out his story and cross-check as much of it as possible. If it does look like he is legit, maybe some money will come his way.

All in all, my gut tells me this was a waste of time. We're not going to find Buckley or the others through this guy. The thought depresses me. The CIA's Beirut station chief in Iranian hands. Perhaps I was hoping for the break that would bring him home. That was naïve of me. Thousands of tips come in every day. Most are like this guy: a dry hole.

Then again, it only takes one.

four

March 24, 1986

The search for William Buckley will never stop—not until he's found—but right now, we've got trouble brewing with the Libyans. Serious trouble.

For reasons that are above my pay grade, Muammar al-Qaddafi has been provoking us for years. Using their diplomatic missions (they call their embassies "People's Bureaus") as bases of operations, the Libyans have attacked American and British targets all over the world. They are not shy about their targets, either. They once sniped at a crowd of anti-Qaddafi protesters from their consulate in London, killing a British policewoman in the fusillade. In the dead bodies cabinets the other day, I discovered a file on a 1980 assassination plot against President Ronald Reagan. Nobody is out of bounds.

In January, a couple of navy F-14s shot down two Libyan MiGs during a dustup over the Gulf of Sidra. Qaddafi considers the gulf Libyan territory. The rest of the world considers the gulf international waters. The U.S. Navy is the only force capable of challenging Qaddafi on this point of law. President Reagan has sent three carrier battle groups into the Mediterranean Sea to drive home to Qaddafi the seriousness of our objections. The Libyan dictator has proclaimed a "line of death" across the northern boundary of the Gulf of Sidra. Cross it, he says, and he will strike.

He did, too. Yesterday, March 23, we crossed the line of death. The Libyans launched missiles at our aircraft. We blew up several of their radar installations in response. After that, the Libyans sent out several patrol boats to attack a three-ship surface task force we'd pushed into the gulf. A combination of A-7 Corsair IIs and A-6E Intruders blasted two patrol boats out of the water and crippled a third.

Today, Qaddafi called on Arabs to form suicide squads, turn themselves into human bombs, and go blow Americans up wherever they can be found. "Make everything American a military target!" he exhorted during his speech.

Behind the scenes, in the Dark World, much worse is going on. Our intelligence reports are full of bad news. Orders went out from Tripoli to thirty of their diplomatic missions to initiate attacks on American targets.

We're going to get hit. It is not a matter of if, but how hard, where, and when. The DSS is on high alert. We've sent messages to every embassy to be extra vigilant and to tighten security. Our diplomats and DSS agents overseas are hunkering down, waiting for what is sure to come.

Behind the big blue door, Gleason, Mullen, and I spend the day trying to read the tea leaves coming into FOGHORN. We don't want to absorb this attack. We want to stop it. My worst nightmare is to disregard a threat or misread a signal, then watch as an attack unfolds and people die. I would be responsible for their deaths. My judgment has to be perfect. This is the fear I live with every day; it both motivates me and keeps me awake at night.

As the day progresses, Mullen looks increasingly haggard. I steal occasional glances at him and can tell he's feeling the same pressure I do. Call it a hazard of the job.

All the incoming news is bad and getting worse. One intel report shows that the Libyans have an operational plan calling for ten simultaneous attacks on targets all over the world. This could be a bloodbath.

Our embassies in Europe and South America report suspicious sightings of Libyans. Some are seen eyeballing our diplomatic missions. Others are seen lurking near overseas military bases. As we sift through all this raw intel, we try to separate overreactive paranoia from legitimate threats.

It is plodding work, made more difficult by our means of communicating with our agents in the field. In order to send messages back up through FOGHORN, we must type them on a special coded typewriter. We use an IBM Selectric with an optical character recognition (OCR) element. It takes me forever to hunt and peck the messages together. Of course, if I make a mistake, I have to start over—we can't use Wite-Out. As we try to get follow-up questions answered, the lag time grows longer and longer. What if by the time we get our answer, it is too late?

Sooner or later, we must streamline this process.

For now, this crisis gives me a crystal-clear view of exactly who and what we are as an organization. Federal law mandates that the State Department takes the lead role in any investigation into an international terrorist attack against American citizens. Within the Department of State, it falls to the Diplomatic Security Service to get into the field and figure out what happened. Sometimes we step back and let the FBI or CIA or a foreign agency take point, but even when that happens, we stay very involved in the process. Every American embassy has a small cadre of DSS agents. We're the only law-enforcement force that's in every country on the planet. Yet, hardly anyone outside the Beltway has ever heard of us.

We like it that way.

The DSS got its start in 1916 when it was formed to serve as a counterintelligence and counterespionage section of the State Department. Known then as the Office of the Special Agent, we predated the FBI, the Office of Strategic Services (OSS), and the CIA. As an organization, the DSS's spying days ended after World War II with the establishment of the CIA. In the war's aftermath, we got a new name—Office of Security, or SY for short—and a host of new roles. We protected our ambassadors and our embassy staffers. We covered the secretary of state like the Secret Service does the president. We also guarded foreign heads of state and visiting dignitaries when they came to the United States. And, of course, we investigated crimes against Americans overseas, passport fraud, visa fraud, and other issues involving foreign nations, such as illegal arms sales. We still do most of these things today, though the Secret Service now handles protection for heads of state. We still protect foreign diplomats and dignitaries, including Prince Charles and Princess Diana whenever they come to the United States.

Over the years, the FBI and CIA have become the heavyweights. This means we do a lot of liaisoning with our counterparts at the two agencies. This can either be a bureaucratic chore, or it can go smoothly, depending on who we deal with in each office. Like any other profession, cultivating contacts where it counts helps get the job done. So far, I've experienced the extremes. There are times nobody at the FBI wants to see me. Our evidence-analysis requests tend to get lost in the shuffle. Lab time is at a premium at the FBI, and every organization has high-priority issues that need to be addressed. The DSS sometimes ranks low on their list of agencies to please.

The CIA is a different matter. It is like our younger cousin who's grown up into the six-foot-six star football player we never were. My first visit to Langley will never leave my memory. I stood in the entrance, my CIA badge around my neck. I stuck it into a slot next to a turnstile and was granted access into the inner sanctum of America's intelligence nerve center. To the right of the doors stands a statue of Nathan Hale, the Revolutionary War spy who went to a British hangman's noose with the immortal words "I only regret that I have but one life to lose for my country" on his lips.

Along the walls in the lobby are gold stars. Each one represents a fallen agent, killed in the line of duty. Not one star has a name attached. The stars ensure their sacrifices will never be forgotten, but their names and deeds will remain anonymous.

Carved into the granite wall next to the stars are the biblical words "And ye shall know the truth and the truth shall make you free."

Beyond the lobby, the CIA looks and functions much like any other government agency. Mazes of cubicles, stacks of paper, and rows of cramped offices with people running back and forth compose the everyday scene. On those first few trips, I learned that the bureaucracy there is much like every other. They're protective of their turf, don't like it when they feel infringed on, and the only way to keep a smooth line of communication flowing between them and us is to focus on building personal relationships. It is a touchy situation, partly because of the CIA's inherent internalizing of information. Sharing does not come naturally to the CIA. They're protective of their assets and their information, which is understandable in this line of work. There is also some friction between the DSS and the Agency because we overlap in places overseas, especially during counterterror investigations. We have the same goals—

usually—but our methods and motives are different. The CIA wants to find the *who* and *why* in every attack. We want to find out the *how* so we can prevent it from happening again. For the most part, I've found that the Agency does play well in the Sandbox with us; we just need to manage that relationship carefully.

After Beirut I and II, the Inman Commission set the stage for another major reorganization. The Office of Security became the Diplomatic Security Service. Our numbers swelled, and our focus on counterterror increased. Back in the day, the old DSS agents were offensive-minded. They'd root out spies and networks in the United States and take them down. Today, the FBI does that. Overseas, it is the CIA that carries the fight to the enemy. Today, in 1986, the DSS is the most defensive-minded of America's agencies. Our job is protection, keeping people alive. To do that, we have our own network of informants, our own sources of intelligence, and our own means to thwart attacks or apprehend terrorists. After all, the best defense is frequently a good offense. More often than not, though, we work hand in hand with the other agencies to make those things happen. The FBI, CIA, and National Security Agency (NSA) all have more people and more resources than we do.

In many ways, we're America's Dark World redheaded stepchild. We maneuver in the cracks and crevices between the other agencies. It is a tough place to operate.

Here in the counterterrorism (CT) office, behind the big blue door, we are supposed to see the overall picture. All the overseas threats and the reports from our embassies and field agents flow into our little corner of the Harry S Truman Building. That intel merges with information disseminated from the FBI, NSA, CIA, foreign intelligence agencies, local police departments, and the International Criminal Police Organization (Interpol), among other places. We face a mind-numbing mountain of paper every day, but here in D.C., we're supposed to have perspective, which is no easy task when we're inundated with so much raw information.

The agents overseas are focused on their immediate surroundings and host country. They see the trees. We see the forest. At least we're supposed to see it. And it is our job to figure out which sections of the forest are ripe for attack.

Over the past month, I've seen all sorts of threat indicators and sent those back out into the field. A tip from Bangkok comes in via FOGHORN. The source there says an embassy in the Middle East is going to be hit with a car bomb. We route that to our regional security officers (RSOs)—the senior agents in charge at our embassies—with a flash warning to pay particular attention to vehicular traffic and unattended automobiles.

Behind the big blue door, we are the trip wire. The threats come in. We figure out the best way to handle them and send out warnings. In a sense, this makes Mullen, Gleason, and I managers and filters for all the incoming chaos. At the same time, while keeping our eye on the big picture, we must also delve into the field.

Already, I've had to investigate several terror attacks on American interests overseas, including the bombing of our embassy in Lisbon, Portugal. A radical group planted a bomb on a marine's personal vehicle. Somehow, it escaped notice when the car was searched by the embassy security force manning the front gate. The bomb went off a short time later. Fortunately, nobody was killed.

The gate guards were local nationals. Was it an inside job? Gleason gave the case to me. It turned out they had just missed the bomb during the search; there was no conspiracy. We put together a revised set of security procedures for the guards so that such an attack could not happen again.

Hopefully not, anyway.

If we can't stop an attack before it happens, before the smoke clears over the target we open a CT investigation. Once a counterterror investigation is opened, our office has one major objective: Find out what went wrong. Again, it is a defensive role; we want to study the attack—break it down into its individual components to see how the terrorists carried it out. Once we figure out how they succeeded, our security flaws become evident. This knowledge will save lives in the future, as we can devise new security tactics that fill the gaps the attack exploited in the first place. Frankly, we're way behind the ball right now, struggling to catch up to our enemies. That is what makes us vulnerable.

That's also why our trip-wire efforts are so important. If we can divine the target of the next attack, we can warn our men in the field. They can counter the threat and hopefully deter the terrorists. One month into my job and this much is obvious: If we miss the warning signs, it'll be too late. Once the truck bomber starts his mission, the chances of it succeeding are almost 100 percent. The only sure way to prevent an attack is to stop it before he gets behind the wheel. There are two ways to do that: Find and bring down his network, or change tactics and security around the target in such a way that the terror cell aborts the attack.

All day long, Gleason, Mullen, and I work feverishly to find those little nuggets, those genuine threat indicators we can pass along to our agents overseas. Dinner is forgotten. The cafeteria closes at six, and I didn't have time to get up there anyway. I eat a granola bar at my desk and plow through more incoming cables.

Close to midnight, I'm exhausted and need a break. I finally work my way to the parking garage and find my Jetta. A short drive home, and I fall facedown into my waiting pillow.

I sleep with a portable phone next to my ear and a code card on my nightstand. In the event of flash cable traffic, FOGHORN will call me with the news. Flash is the highest-priority cable we can receive. They demand immediate attention, even at four in the morning. Other times, we get NIACT cables. These are flagged "Night Action," and are also cause for a call in the dead of night. Over the past month, I've not gone more than one night a week without being woken up by FOGHORN's night-duty officer, telling me in cryptic phrases that something bad has happened again.

I hardly fall asleep when the phone rings. "Venus has reported a threat in Crowbar." I grab my code card and start scanning for Crowbar. The code words change frequently, and I don't have the time to memorize them. I know Venus is the FBI. Crowbar eludes me.

"Can you help me out here. City?"

He gives me an elliptical clue. I figure it out. Beirut. I have to deal with this one. Sleep forgotten, I start making phone calls.

Morning. A quick run with Tyler Beauregard fails to shake me loose from the bone weariness I feel. Even when I want to sleep—need to sleep—I have a hard time. Tyler senses how stressed I am, and she stays close to me today. She lopes along right by my side, and I feel the comfort of her fur as she brushes against my legs every few strides. Did I say I love this dog? She's doing her best to take care of me.

I reach the office before 0600, and it is already a madhouse. Mullen appears unwashed and unslept. Has he been here all night? Probably.

Gleason looks more than ever like an over-tasked patrol sergeant. Eyes bulging, he's already chewing somebody out over the phone. A stack of incoming traffic awaits me on my desk. I get to it.

March 25, 1986, looks to be another really bad day. The U.S. Navy and the Libyans are still fighting in the Gulf of Sidra. Everyone is jittery. The Italians are almost apoplectic, as this is unfolding right in their own backyard. The French are playing coy, which doesn't surprise me. Rumor has it that the French have cut a deal with various terror groups, including the Palestinians and the many-striped jihadists. France will leave them alone if they do not attack the French homeland. As a result, many of our terrorist enemies have started camping out in Paris, using it as their home base for strikes elsewhere in Europe. That our erstwhile ally would do something like this shocked me at first. Then, over lunch at our desks one day, Gleason mentioned that the French intelligence service has spent much of the seventies and eighties engaged in economic espionage against us. They've done plenty of black-bag jobs—breaking and entering—and eavesdropping in an effort to give the likes of Airbus a leg up over Boeing. Hearing things like that quickly knocks the naïveté out of young agents like me.

So in this tussle with the Libyans, the French are off the board. The Italians are spooked. The Germans are quiet. So are the Brits, though I know they'll offer support when needed. Elsewhere around the Med, we're catching plenty of flak from the Greeks. The Eastern Bloc allies are all denouncing us. No surprise there. Meanwhile, Radio Tripoli issued a call to arms today, urging supporters to storm American targets in the Arab world.

And then the scary stuff arrives. First, we get a flash message warning that the Libyans are recruiting Palestinian and European assassins to be proxies in attacks against our interests. That's concern enough, but then the U.S. Embassy in Ankara, Turkey, reports a disturbing development. Turkish police uncovered a plot to strike at a U.S. officers' club in Ankara. We have to deal with this one right away. We increase security at all our bases in Turkey and warn all personnel there to take extra precautions on and off base. Meanwhile, the Turkish authorities are tracking down the terror cell involved in planning the attack. I check in with them during the day, but the Turks are keeping the investigation close to the vest, and I don't learn much more than we already know.

The threats keep stacking up. I'm heartsick. Which ones should we focus on? We can't cover everywhere at once. We need to marshal our assets. We don't have enough agents. In crises like this, it would be terrific if we had a strategic reserve of counterterror teams ready to fly to a regional hot spot at a moment's notice. Right now, Mullen, Gleason, and I are the strategic reserves, and just handling the incoming traffic has us totally committed in D.C.

The afternoon brings a report that the Libyans plan to strike at Sixth Fleet headquarters in Naples, Italy. Follow-up questions from us reveal that the Libyans have assassins poised to strike at our senior Sixth Fleet naval officers. Apparently, they know where our people in Naples live. This tells me the Libyans have done their homework and have been watching our naval personnel very closely for quite some time.

As the threats mount, one basic fact becomes clear: The Libyans have been watching a lot of places for a long time. They must have built target profiles of key installations and vulnerable locations months ago. They have done their homework and their legwork. Until now, nobody has noticed. And now it is too late. We're chasing the bus at this point, not building the roadblocks we need to stop it.

Later in the day, news of the first attack comes in. Beirut. A Libyan-aligned group tries to shell our embassy. Fortunately, they are bad shots and miss. A few hours go by and a flash cable arrives from Tokyo. The embassy and the Imperial Palace grounds have been rocketed.

I spend the rest of the day and evening chasing this one down, coordinating the investigation with the agents in Tokyo. It doesn't take long to conclude that the Japanese Red Army, a terror organization sponsored, supported, and sheltered by Libya, carried out the attack.

Two o'clock in the morning comes before I'm aware of it. I sit, bleary-eyed, at my desk, fatigued like I've never been in the past. I've got to get home and get some sleep. I'm no good in this condition. But before I shut off the lights behind the big blue door, I pull out my three-by-five card file box and dutifully record these new attacks. My makeshift database is growing fast.

Not long after I get home and collapse on the bed, FOGHORN wakes me up again. There's been an attempted hit on the secretary of state.

five

CHASING SHADOWS

Back in the office long before sunrise, the scene is more chaos. I'm getting used to it now. The burn bags have piled up and we've now got piles on piles cascading around our desks. We'll have to make some runs down to the basement incinerator today to clear some room in here.

Gleason's busy trying to get the details of what's happened to the secretary of state. Mullen has the thousand-yard stare that I had a few hours before. Do I still have it, too? Probably.

Our embassy in Athens gives us sketchy details of the attack. Secretary of State George P. Shultz had flown to Greece to sit down with Prime Minister Andreas Papandreou, who had declared the unfolding conflict in the Gulf of Sidra nothing less than the "armed enforcement of a new Pax Americana" and "the attempt for a holocaust in the Mediterranean."

While Shultz was in Athens, a car with U.S. plates exploded in a gas station a short distance from his hotel. Was it a car bomb? Was there a connection to Shultz's arrival? It seems a logical conclusion.

While we wait on more information, I open up a CT case on the attack and enter it into my card file. More traffic flows in. It was no car bomb; terrorists threw a bomb of some sort at the car. Another bomb is found on a diplomat's vehicle and defused. Perhaps the security changes we devised after Lisbon helped catch that one.

The day grinds on. Mullen gets bad news from Bolivia. Somebody threw a stick of dynamite onto the roof of our embassy there. Fortunately, it caused little damage and nobody was hurt.

Sporadic fighting continues in the Gulf of Sidra. Anti-American protests flare in Italy, Greece, Syria, and elsewhere in Europe. Everyone is edgy. Will this conflict blossom into full-scale war? Nobody is sure. The *Times* of London reports that Qaddafi has earmarked six million dollars for attacks on American and British interests in Lebanon. Apparently, Libyan intelligence agents are talking with militia leaders in Beirut, offering them cash payments to carry out attacks.

A rare piece of good news finally reaches FOGHORN. The Turks have arrested two individuals working for Libyan intelligence. They've already confessed to planning attacks on American targets in Turkey. We need more help like that overseas.

And then Qaddafi steps squarely onto my turf. The Libyans are pulling out all the stops in Beirut. A source reports that their agents are offering vast sums of money to Hezbollah to buy the American hostages they're holding. No word yet on what Hezbollah's response is, but it is clear the Libyans want some sort of leverage to get the navy to back off in the Gulf of Sidra. Or maybe they just want revenge and plan to simply execute the hostages they're able to buy.

The master terrorist Abu Nidal weighs in on Qaddafi's side. His organization vows revenge for the Gulf of Sidra. That's a very serious threat. Abu Nidal has perpetrated countless acts of murder and mayhem around the globe, but he is most reviled for his attacks in Europe just after Christmas a few months ago. With the assistance of Libyan intelligence agents, Abu Nidal sent two hit squads into the Rome and Vienna airports to attack El Al passengers waiting to fly to Israel. In Rome, the gunmen killed sixteen people and wounded another ninety-nine at El Al's check-in counter. Simultaneously in Vienna, the hit squad struck at a crowded El Al gate, killing two more people with grenades and wounding another thirty-nine.

Abu Nidal's group, which uses a number of different names, has a history of striking at airlines and air travel. A vow of revenge from him is no idle boast. His psychological profile in the dead bodies cabinets labels him as a clear psychopath. There have been reports that he is so violent he has tortured his own followers out of paranoia that they've become double agents. One report I've seen detailed how a suspected double agent in his organization had his testicles seared in skillets of burning-hot cooking oil. Even the PLO reviles him and his methods.

This is a new threat we must try and counter. Airport security must be tightened. Unfortunately, airports all over Europe have slipshod screening practices. We can't control those potential points of attack, which makes this a gaping weakness in our security armor.

Sometime around six, Gleason puts down whatever he's reading and suddenly gives his full attention to me. I sense his eyes, and look over to see him glowering through a cloud of cigarette smoke. I wonder if I'm in trouble.

He exhales suddenly, leans forward in his chair, and says, "Burton, go home. Go take a break."

I can't see how I can possibly do that. Not with all the things that are happening.

"If you don't take breaks every now and then, this job will eat you alive. Go home. Forget about everything for a couple of hours."

I try to protest, but he's serious. "There's always going to be another crisis. There's always going to be more threats." He pauses to snub out his cigarette and light another one. "This is what we do. And you've got to learn to handle the pace and know when enough is enough. Otherwise, you'll burn out."

I don't have any more energy to protest. Besides, I realize he's giving me valuable advice.

"Go home, Fred. You look like hell."

I gather up some papers, stuff them in my briefcase, check my beeper, and depart without saying a word. When I guide my Jetta out of the parking garage, I realize that this is the first time in weeks I've actually seen the sun.

I head down MacArthur Boulevard, not looking forward to the apartment that awaits me. It isn't even seven o'clock yet. Sharon won't be home from her accounting firm for another hour at least, which means the place will be dark and empty. That's not what I need now. Even with Tyler Beauregard there it will be terminally lonely.

On a whim, I make a quick right turn and speed off toward the National Naval Medical Center. It almost isn't a conscious decision, just instinct really. I realize as I drive that I'm fleeing into my past life.

Brandt Place. That's where I need to be right now.

I gun the Jetta past Wisconsin Avenue and duck into an open parking slot right across the street from the hospital. A short walk finds me in front of a white brick stand-alone house, set back from the road and screened by oak trees and bushes.

This is Fred Davis's house. In our crazy youth, we were known as the Two Freds. We served together on the Bethesda–Chevy Chase Rescue Squad, a volunteer department that covered the streets and highways of our old neighborhood.

I step to the front porch. A mangy old dog is curled up on the welcome mat, snoozing away. I rap on the door, and Fred throws it open with a big surprised grin on his face. I haven't been by in a long time, but once this Brandt Place tract house was the center of my social life. Those nights out, driving around in a big 1965 GMC Rescue responding to car wrecks and other disasters, had bonded us together. I feel relief at his warm welcome, guilt that I haven't seen more of him recently, and fear that perhaps we've grown apart now that we've gone in different directions.

"Come on in, ya want a beer?"

"No. Got any coffee?"

"I'll put some on."

In his cluttered, bachelor's kitchen, Fred brews up a pot of coffee. He's dressed in jeans and tennis shoes, but he's still wearing his badge and pistol. I take off my coat, revealing my shoulder holster and the Smith & Wesson tucked inside.

A few minutes later, we settle into a couple of chairs on the front porch. We shoot the breeze, just like the old days when we'd come off shift.

The rescue squad was a pivotal time in both our lives. We recognize that now. The volunteers who staffed the place were cops and EMTs and firefighters from the local departments. Working alongside them left an indelible mark on both Fred and me. The experience led us both into a life of law enforcement.

Fred put himself through EMT night school by working construction during the day. After he graduated from the University of Maryland, he joined the U.S. Park Police in D.C.—the guys who patrol our national landmarks, like the Washington Monument. It is an elite bunch, and from what I heard when I was a cop, Fred had fit right in.

"How're things going with the Park Police?" I ask.

"They're good, but nothing like the old days, you know what I mean?"

I nod. Back then, our only worry was our next call. Next accident. Or catastrophe.

Fred leans back in his chair and takes a drink from his longneck. "I'm applying for flight school soon."

"That's great, Fred!" I'm genuinely excited for him. The Park Police includes an aviation division. Fred's always wanted to be a cop and has always wanted to fly.

"If I get the slot, they'll send me to Fort Rucker for training."

"Isn't that where the army trains its helo pilots?"

"Yeah."

I haven't seen Fred in months. Between the training I went through after I joined the DSS and the craziness since I landed in the CT office, I have been absent from this porch. I've missed the comradeship. That sort of close-knit bond we had on the rescue squad just doesn't exist over at Foggy Bottom, as the State Department is known. We're all too busy and the pace is too intense for much of that. I've never been one to make friends easily anyway. Fred's both a link to my old life and one of the few genuine friends I've ever had. He stood up for me at my wedding a few years ago.

"Do any fishing recently?" I'm stretching here. Have we run out of small talk already? Have we let our friendship atrophy to the point that it's beyond reviving?

He offers a guttural laugh. Fred's got a gravely voice and looks like a cross between Al Pacino and Robert De Niro. I notice with a start that his short, dark hair is hidden by a blue ball cap that reads "BCCRS RES-CUE-1." We used to wear those around the station. We had the Friday-night shifts. I was the acting lieutenant and Fred was my sergeant. We slept upstairs in an old barracks-style bunk room. Whenever a call woke us up in the middle of the night, we'd leap onto a polished brass pole and slide down to that old '65 GMC. He'd drive; I'd ride shotgun. Those were glorious days, full of adrenaline rushes and lots of excitement.

Fred shakes his head sadly. "I don't understand it. Every time you and I drop a line in the Potomac, there isn't a fish for miles. Whenever I go out by myself, I catch the limit. You must scare the fish away."

"You know, it's been a long time since we've gone fishing together."

"That is true. We need to do something about that."

I detect a tone of regret in his voice. He's probably struggling with the same things I am right now. Neither of us is big on sharing a whole lot of emotion. In the past, we've just jawed about work, our cases, and the rescue squad. We don't do heavy. We don't do philosophical.

Back when I was a cop, I used to swing by Brandt Place after my night shifts. Fred was working nights, too, and we'd take off together and go play golf at six in the morning. The local courses would let us in free, sort of a thank-you perk to us for being in law enforcement.

We haven't golfed together in over a year.

I can't really talk about all the things going on in the office. Most of it is classified secret or above, and with the Park Police, Fred's cleared up to top secret. So even though I could discuss all this stuff going down in the world, the thought of rehashing it churns my stomach. I'm here to get away, not indulge.

We limp on with the small talk, each of us searching for a way to re-connect. Then Fred's roommate, a lawyer, steps onto the porch. He sits down and joins in the conversation. The limping devolves into a crawl. Lawyers and cops aren't usually a good mix, and I've never really understood why Fred lives with this guy.

At one point, the lawyer asks how we know each other. Out come the old rescue squad stories. Suddenly, the ice breaks. We enthrall our third wheel with tales from the firehouse. We responded to all sorts of incidents back in the early eighties before we'd even grown into men.

In '82, a man drove his car through the front of the local IBM plant, then opened fire and killed two people and wounded several more during a seven-hour standoff. We responded to that and carried away some of the injured in our rigs.

In January 1982, an Air Florida jetliner crashed into the Potomac after skipping off the 14th Street Bridge. Scores of people were in the water, and rescue crews were hampered by a sudden blizzard that swept the area. My crew was staged nearby, and we carried some of the survivors to the local trauma center.

We had two political assassinations in our neighborhood as well. One was an Iranian, the other an Israeli fighter pilot who worked at Israel's embassy in D.C. In fact, I've been thinking that someday, now that I'm with the DSS, I'd like to reopen both cases. Our outfit responded to both incidents, though the hit on the Israeli took place in '73, two years before I joined the squad. I was at the station when the Iranian was killed.

As I hear these old war stories again, they sound just like the chaos I'm dealing with at work right now, only on a micro level. The litany of accidents, violence, and mayhem—it didn't seem so overwhelming at the time. We rolled out of the station and never knew what to expect, but we were always in the moment. I guess it is all a matter of perspective. Maybe that's what I need right now, just a little perspective.

We've warmed up to the subject, the initial awkwardness of our conversation long left in the dust. Fred's chatting now with his usual animation. Quick swipes of his hand emphasize the points he makes. He likes to talk with his hands. It makes watching him very entertaining. He's a terrific raconteur.

And then we come to the big one, the story we love to tell outsiders most of all. Fred looks at me and winks, and says, "Twilight Zone."

"Twilight Zone," I echo back. We've told this one so many times we're starting to sound like an old married couple.

"Yeah. That was un*believable*."

"What happened?" the lawyer-roommate asks. He needn't have bothered. Once we get rolling on this road, the whole thing comes out in all its spooky splendor.

"Never seen anything like it. Never hope to again," I add.

"We were out in Rescue 18, the old GMC squad truck. I was driving," Fred begins.

I cut in, "Fred needed the hours behind the wheel. I was the truck trainer. We were just driving around late one Friday night."

"Funny how that worked out, isn't it?" Fred asks.

"Makes me want to believe in fate."

"Yeah, me, too."

"So we're up on Wilson Lane, just driving and shooting the bull," Fred continues, "when we get the call."

"The call?"

I chime in, "Dispatch tells us there's been an accident with one pinned near River Road and Wilson Lane."

"We were only a few blocks away," Fred says.

The lawyer looks puzzled. "What's 'one pinned' mean?"

"Somebody's stuck in the car."

"Anyway"—I'm talking now—"I radio in and say, 'Rescue 18 copy and en route.' Flip on the sirens and we start using the air horn to clear cars out of our way."

"God, I'd forgotten that thing," Fred interjects as he polishes off the last drops in his longneck. "Pull a cable and it rocked your world. That air horn was something else."

I cut in. "We get to the scene in minutes. Both of us jump out of the truck...."

"Creepy vibe." Fred's now really animated. One hand sweeps across his chest as he says, "Fog hugging the ground. Dark. Looked like a *Twilight Zone* episode."

"Yeah, and dead quiet, too."

"One minute, we're blazing away with lights, sirens, and the air horn. The next minute—nothing. Total silence."

"Creepy, all right."

The lawyer is rigid. We have him hooked.

Fred plays to our one-man audience, building the drama. "We look around and find this little Honda sedan upside down in a gully off the right side of the road."

I explain. "The driver had hit a pole and slid off the embankment. Flipped over. Landed at the bottom of the gully on its back. Wheels still turning, broken glass everywhere."

"Antifreeze was pouring out of the radiator. And we saw smoke."

"I ran back to the truck and called HQ, 'Rescue 18 on the scene with a rollover.'"

"I followed Fred back to the truck. Suddenly, we hear something that breaks the silence."

Fred pauses for effect. The lawyer comes out of his seat. "What? What?"

We both smile and simultaneously say, "'Stairway to Heaven.'"

"What?"

" 'Stairway to Heaven.' You know," Fred says, "that old Zeppelin song."

"You're kidding?"

"No," I say, "it was coming from the car's radio. Only sound we could hear. Fred and I just stared at each other, chills running up and down our spines."

"You got that right, brother."

"We couldn't even move for a second or two, the music was so surreal. Then, in the distance, we heard more sirens coming to us."

"We both climb down into the gully to see what we can do. Car's beat to hell. Smashed—totaled. Inside, there's the driver. He's totaled, too. He was just a kid—our age at the time."

"About nineteen," I interject.

"Yeah, nineteen. Drunk driver. Threw his life away," Fred says with a bitter smile. "Dead on the scene. Nothing we could do for him. Blood everywhere inside the car. Even on the radio, but it still worked."

"It sure did."

"And there we stood at the bottom of this gully, dead kid, smell of booze and blood in the air, listening to 'Stairway to Heaven.' "

"Totally surreal," I manage. Hearing Fred tell the story again brings me right back there to the fog. That was a horrible scene. In our old life with the rescue squad, we saw a lot of ugly things. I didn't used to think it got to me, but now I think maybe it affected me a lot deep down. I never got jaded enough to get used to such sights. Perhaps this is why I am so moved by the files in the dead bodies cabinets. I can relate, and I don't need a vivid imagination to envision the horrors that befell those innocent victims in Beirut.

The evening rolls on unfettered by stilted small talk. The gates are open, and the stories pour out. The *Twilight Zone* night was the foundation for our relationship at a time when we were brothers coming of age together in this unique and terrifying world.

I relax for the first time in months. I slump deep into my chair, put my feet up, and try to soak up every bit of this moment. It seems like old times as Fred and I regale each other with tales of the macabre. Cop stories. Rescue stories. They spill out one after another, but we never discuss the DSS. That's off-limits. Before I know it, three hours have gone by and I've got to get home.

With Mullen and Gleason, life is all business. Here, on this porch with Fred, it is all about old friends. Though we never even mentioned Libya or Qaddafi or terror attacks, I feel refreshed. Gleason was right: Sometimes you just have to get away, lest the Dark World eat your soul.

Brandt Place is my defense against that.

"Hey, Burton," Fred calls as I walk through his yard toward the street. I stop and turn.

"Don't be a stranger, okay?"

"Don't worry about that."

Later that night, the phone rings me out of the first sound sleep I've had in weeks.

six

April 4, 1986

The bodies fell out of the sky and plummeted into a shepherd's field. A Greek peasant, minding his flock of sheep, discovered them battered and smashed almost beyond recognition. Before this horrible day, the trio had been a family: one grandmother, one daughter, one infant granddaughter. These were terror's latest targets.

A fourth body was later found in some bushes, still strapped into seat 10F of TWA Flight 840.

I sit at my desk behind the big blue door and stare at the photos. They fell from eleven thousand feet. How long did it take? Probably long enough to know the awful fate that had consumed their lives. Did they have time to make their peace with God? Did they shriek and cry until the impact came? My imagination roams. I know that I won't be able to sleep tonight. The images play in my mind like I was there. The infant is the worst. Nine months old. She died in her mother's arms. I want to cry.

I turn next to a small folder of photos that have just come into the office. They show the damage to Flight 840, which was a Boeing 727. A ragged hole, roughly the size of a wheelbarrow, scars the starboard side of the fuselage just forward of the wing. Tattered aluminum strips flower out from the hole, making it clear that the explosion that befell this jet-liner came from inside the cabin.

Flight 840 was en route to Athens from Rome when the bomb went off. The pilot had already started the descent for Athens and was counting on about fifteen more minutes before touching down. A blast, then chaos. People watched as their fellow passengers got sucked out of the cabin by explosive decompression. According to the press accounts of the attack, the cabin filled with smoke and swirling debris, which the slipstream whipped around the surviving passengers with such force that several received gashes and cuts. A stewardess handed out linen napkins to the wounded, who used them to stanch the bleeding while the captain told everyone to remain calm. He promised to have the plane down in ten minutes. It took thirteen, and he executed a perfect emergency landing.

Who pulled this off? The truth is we don't know, and that's a real issue right now. The administration wants a smoking gun that points to Libya. If this is retaliation for the Gulf of Sidra, Reagan will strike back hard. But the evidence needs to be overwhelming. So far, we have a few clues, but nothing that implicates the Libyans. In fact, Qaddafi denounced the attack, calling it "an act of terrorism against a civilian target, and I'm totally against it."

It was hard not to laugh when we heard that one.

On the day of the attack, the press in Beirut reported they'd been given a handwritten statement from a group called the Ezzedine Kassam Unit of the Arab Revolutionary Cells. Kassam was a Palestinian cleric who led a revolt against the British in 1935 and subsequently died in the fighting.

The Arab Revolutionary Cells is a front name used by Abu Nidal's organization. A few days before this attack, it took credit for kidnapping two academics in West Beirut. Leigh Douglas, a British professor of political science, and Philip Padfield, the director of the language center at American University of Beirut.

The communiqué, if we could get the original, might reveal some further details. The handwriting and verbiage can be analyzed, and we might be able to connect Flight 840 more directly to Abu Nidal. In this case, however, trying to pry loose the original from the media outlet in Beirut may just prove impossible. The press is not fond of us over there.

We are forced to rely on the Greeks, who do not have a very robust intelligence service. Nor do they have a first-rate counterterror group that can investigate Flight 840 as well as we can. We offered to assist. They froze us out. The Greeks don't like us much, and they've stonewalled our efforts to assist in the investigation. It is terribly frustrating, but the root of this ill will goes back eleven years to the 1975 assassination of the CIA's Athens station chief, Richard Welch. A radical Greek group called 17 November executed the hit, and the subsequent investigation led to very bad blood between the U.S. and Greek authorities. A Colt .45 pistol was used in that assassination, and in the years to come, the same weapon was used in numerous assassinations and assaults.

Earlier today, the Greeks did provide us with some details of what they've found in the Flight 840 investigation, but there's little more there than what's already been reported in the news. Seat 10F had been occupied earlier by a woman named May Mansur, sometimes known as Elias May Mansur. She's a Lebanese radical with ties to various terror groups. She's been associated with Abu Nidal in the past, as well as the Palestinian terror group 15 May. She boarded the plane on the morning of April 2 in Cairo. The 727 flew on to Athens, where Mansur exited the plane. According to the Greeks, she waited in the international lounge for seven hours before taking a flight to Beirut. Meanwhile, the 727 flew to Rome, where it became Flight 840, then headed back for Athens. It was supposed to terminate in Cairo, but of course it never made it back there.

Our own intelligence sources show that Mansur flew from Beirut to Cairo a few days before the attack. She arrived late at the airport and the Egyptians actually drove her out to the plane in a car so she wouldn't miss the flight. The Egyptians are adamant that she went through a thorough screening. Somehow, I doubt it was thorough enough.

Her own movements that day are circumstantial evidence to her involvement. Yet, according to the media, she has denied all responsibility for the attack.

I wish we could get a team in there to dissect what happened. What kind of bomb was it? How did it get past security? What security changes can we implement to ensure this never happens again?

We don't know any of this. The truth is, we're lucky to even have these photographs spread out on my desk. The one sop the Greeks threw to us was to ask for the Federal Aviation Administration's assistance. The FAA sent one of their best investigators to Athens, and he snapped these images of the 727.

Gleason asked me to open a CT file on the attack. It is a woefully thin folder right now. I pick up the regional security officer's report from Athens. It contains the names of the victims. Alberto Ospino, age thirty-nine, had taken 10F, a window seat, in Rome. How did fate pick this average Colombian-American for this cruel end? Given the FAA's photographs, the bomb must have exploded directly beneath him, probably at his feet. As the blast tore the fuselage open, the sudden decompression sucked him out of the cabin along with Demetra Stylianopoulu, age fifty-eight. She was the grandmother. As she spun out into the void beneath the starboard wing, her daughter Maria Klug, clutching her infant, Demetra, followed her. Falling. Falling.

I've come full circle and cannot escape the image of how these innocents met death. The guilty must pay for this crime. Justice must be served. But if history is any judge, the forces of terror will likely escape their punishment. It is remarkably difficult to catch any of these killers. They have too many safe havens—too many places to hide and too many countries that protect them.

In the meantime, a few miles up the road in Annapolis, Warren Klug, a grieving husband, father, and son-in-law, awaits the return of his shattered family.

I cannot bring back the dead. I cannot balm the grief of those who survive such attacks. But here at Foggy Bottom, I swear that I will do everything in my power to see that these killers pay. Vengeance and justice are one and the same in this case. With terrorism, there is never any gray. The visions I have of the Klug family's fate will always remind me of that.

Falling. Falling. *Falling.* There will be no sleep tonight.

seven

THE MAD DOG OF THE MIDDLE EAST

April 5, 1986

The Libyans are running us ragged, and thanks to their plots every nerve in the intel world is lighting up with warnings. They're coming in from every conceivable corner of the globe, from informants in dozens of countries. Police agencies, foreign intel services—they're all adding to the chatter. It's like being in a crowded dance hall with everyone talking at once, and our job is to find the one person we need to listen to. We don't know who that is, so we've got to listen to everything. The trouble is, we're being buried by all the incoming information.

Historically, this happens all the time. After an event like Pearl Harbor, Beirut I, or the marine barracks bombing, it is easy to sift through all the traffic and find the smoking gun that warned us of the impending disaster. Hindsight is always twenty-twenty, and knowing what to look for separates the chaff right away. In real time, though, we don't have that luxury, we don't have that vision. All we see are mountains of cables and thousands of clues, all of which must be checked out lest the one valid warning go unheeded.

On top of all this, word has spread throughout the DSS network that a true CT office is now up and running. Agents have been sending us all sorts of stuff beyond the usual intel. Shell casings, bomb fragments, plastic explosives, timing devices, and photographs have been piling up, sent from embassies all over the world. The office behind the big blue door is starting to look like an evidence locker. We shuttle this stuff over to the FBI and the Bureau of Alcohol, Tobacco, and Firearms (ATF) labs for analysis, and riding herd on it all is taking more and more of our day.

The phone rings. I pick it up.

"Burton," I answer.

"Yeah, this is Wyatt at FOGHORN," comes the response. I reach for my code card. Turns out I don't need it.

"We've had an attack in Berlin."

"I'm on my way."

I grab my car keys and rush out to my Jetta. Ten minutes later, I'm hurrying through the hallways at Foggy Bottom, my stomach in knots. Something bad has happened again. What did we miss?

We missed a big one. At 0149 this morning, a bomb blew up a German disco in West Berlin. Casualties are catastrophic. The situation is chaotic. The Bundeskriminalamt—the German federal police, otherwise known as the BKA—is already sifting through the rubble. Gleason tells me to get over to the German Embassy and find out what they know. Before I leave, I open a counterterror case, CT03–0486–235–0011. CT, of course, means Counterterror, 03 denotes a bombing. The second series of numbers gives us the month and year. The next set is the country code where the incident took place. And the last set of numbers is the total number of bombing investigations opened so far this year. It has been a busy four months.

The West Germans are all over this, and the decision's been made to let them take the lead in the investigation. The BKA is the German equivalent of the FBI. These federal cops have an outstanding reputation and rank as one of the world's best law-enforcement agencies. The investigation is in good hands. When I reach the embassy, I'm ushered into the office of the staff's BKA liaison agent. He proves to be exceptionally helpful.

The attack hit a popular nightclub called La Belle Discotheque in the Schoenburg district of West Berlin. It is a well-known hangout for American GIs assigned to the Berlin Brigade who, in their off-duty hours, want to enjoy a little of Berlin's celebrated nightlife. The BKA agent tells me there were at least five hundred people inside when the bomb exploded.

The blast buckled walls and caused part of the ceiling to collapse. Chaos and panic ensued; wounded by the dozen staggered out. A Turkish woman and her GI date were killed. Another American soldier is in critical condition.

"Right now, we are being told that there are two hundred injured," the BKA agent tells me.

Two hundred? I wonder how many of them are American soldiers. My mind flashes back to the barracks bombing in Beirut. Two hundred and forty-one marines dead. Could this be as bad?

"The American wounded are being transported to military hospitals at Landstuhl and Wiesbaden."

As the agent talks, I scribble notes in my pocket-sized spiral-ringed notebook. The German tells me they already suspect the Libyans. Their agents had detected an uptick of Libyan activity in West Berlin the previous week, which included the sightings of several Libyan diplomatic-types who have been suspected of being involved in past terror operations. Shortly before the bomb detonated a Libyan agent left East Germany, bound for Tripoli on an airliner.

That was our needle in this pile of needles we've been searching through.

We wrap things up, and I drive down to Langley to coordinate with the Agency. By the time I get there, more developments have taken place. First, it turns out we had received a warning last night of an impending attack. The Libyan People's Bureau in East Berlin had sent a message to Tripoli announcing an operation was now under way against U.S. soldiers in Berlin. That piece of intel was routed immediately to the U.S. Army, and they were in the process of getting the word out on the street when the bomb exploded. We were fifteen minutes too late to head off the attack.

In those fifteen minutes at least two lives hung in the balance. We have got to do better next time.

By late afternoon, the picture comes into focus. Two hundred and twenty-nine people suffered injuries from the bomb blast or falling debris inside the club. The bomb itself had been planted near the DJ's booth. It was a simple device, composed of only a small amount of plastic explosives with a timing device to detonate it. More than fifty American soldiers are among the victims. Many have ruptured eardrums and shrapnel wounds. Sergeant Ken Ford, a twenty-one-year-old noncommissioned officer, was killed in the blast. His girlfriend, twenty-nine-year-old Nermin Hannay, was the second victim. Another American GI, Staff Sergeant James Goins, a North Carolinian, is in critical condition. The docs aren't sure if he will make it.

Back at Foggy Bottom, I report back to Gleason and tell him what I've learned. He says there's been a lot of traffic between the Libyan Embassy in East Berlin and Tripoli. One message, shortly after the attack, bragged that the operation was a success. Tripoli responded with a "job well done" communiqué.

We still aren't certain who was behind Flight 840. This one, on the other hand, looks cut and dried. The Libyans did it.

"Okay, Fred, we know enough of what happened to get the word out. Push out the MO to our agents in the field so they can help review off-post security."

"I'm on it." I hit the old IBM typewriter and start hunting and pecking away. Maybe we can prevent a rerun of this disaster.

The day and evening pass quickly. A quick run home Saturday night, and I'm back in the office Sunday morning. President Reagan just got back into town after spending the week in Santa Barbara for Easter. He's furious, and the administration wants confirmation that the Libyans were behind La Belle. A response must be in the works.

We spend the next week chasing down leads and getting further details on the bombing. Gleason has me monitor the status of the wounded at Landstuhl and Wiesbaden. Our intel agencies work overtime, putting together a case against Colonel Qaddafi. It is as airtight as a Dark World case can get. We're all convinced the Libyans pulled this one off. There is some evidence to show there were Palestinian and Syrian agents involved, but the genesis behind the attack clearly originated in Tripoli.

In the meantime, more threats pour in. Mullen and I deal with a report that a sedan with Libyan tags tailed a busload of American schoolkids in South America. Our embassy in Beirut comes under attack again. This time, rockets are fired at it. Two more bombings, one in Bangkok, the other in Stockholm, take place against American targets. We get word that the Libyans are planning to hit our consulate in Munich, kidnap an American ambassador somewhere in Africa, and bomb more embassies. Another report comes in warning that Tripoli has ordered attacks on American airliners.

No wonder President Reagan recently denounced Qaddafi as "the Mad Dog of the Middle East."

Washington starts leaking like a sieve. Press reports hint that we've been able to break Libya's diplomatic code. The Libyans read that and change their ciphers. Such reporting is flagrantly irresponsible, but our news agencies seem to care less about their national responsibilities than about getting a scoop.

Other reports show up in *The Wall Street Journal* and *Washington Times* claiming we're about to attack Libya. One media outlet even names a potential target, Bab Al Azizyah, a sprawling compound near Tripoli that's part terrorist training base, part headquarters for Qaddafi's regime. He even uses it from time to time as his personal residence. The story doesn't escape Qaddafi, who mentions it in an interview with reporter Marie Colvin.

The international press, including American TV reporters, flock to Tripoli. Flights into the potential war zone are suddenly booked solid. More hints and innuendo flow from "highly placed sources within the administration." The American ambassador to West Germany, Richard Burt, is interviewed on the *Today* show and says, "There are clear indications that there was Libyan involvement" in the La Belle attack.

Later in the week, an Italian bishop and four Franciscans are kidnapped in Tripoli. Qaddafi, knowing something is afoot, starts rounding up foreign workers and placing them under guard at high-value military targets. He's using them as human shields.

On Monday morning, we all know something is about to happen. Senator Richard Lugar tipped off the media yesterday that President Reagan has called for a meeting with congressional leaders at four o'clock today. The press took that as a sign that military retaliation is imminent.

Behind the big blue door, Gleason is quieter than usual. He chainsmokes and takes a few phone calls, but otherwise he's focused on other things. Later in the day, he gets called away to a meeting of liaison agents from multiple agencies. He returns in the afternoon and huddles with Mullen and me.

"Okay, we're about to hit the Libyans. The attack will take place tonight. We need to be prepared for any sort of retaliation. When the attack begins, I want you two to warn our troops. Send out word to every RSO. We're in for a long night."

In an effort to move into the modern age, we've now got a small TV in the office, tuned to CNN. The congressional leadership gets briefed as scheduled at 4:00 P.M. This is 11:00 P.M. Libyan time. Our air force planes are airborne, heading for their targets. The clock ticks by. The minutes drag. The wait slows time to a crawl.

Then Senator Robert Byrd and Senator Claiborne Pell show up on TV, telling the world that the president plans to address the nation at 9:00 P.M. eastern standard time. We shake our heads in frustration. This is another tip to the enemy. Will our planes be flying into a hornet's nest?

Somewhere over the Mediterranean, brave flight crews are getting ready to make their final runs into their target areas. This is our opportunity to hammer a foe who has caused the deaths of countless innocents. This is our chance to avenge not just La Belle, but every attack the Libyan diplomatic service has initiated against us these past years. La Belle just gave us the smoking gun that Reagan needed to pull the trigger.

At 12:30 A.M. local time, our carriers in the Med launch their strike packages. The pilots and crews are worried. The press has been reporting their every move. The element of surprise seems to be lost. Simultaneously, a wing of F-111 Aardvark fighter-bombers has flown from England, down the Bay of Biscay, around Spain and Portugal, and has entered the Med over the Strait of Gibraltar. The attack will be a one-two punch. The navy planes will suppress the Libyan air defenses, while the F-111s hit their targets.

At Foggy Bottom, we of the Counterterror office head over to FOGHORN to rally our troops. The moment the last bomb falls, our job begins in earnest. It'll be up to us to help deflect the counterattack Qaddafi's intel service is sure to launch.

eight

TWO HITS FOR EL DORADO CANYON

April 16, 1986

Thanks to modern media and communications, we have a real-time report of the attacks around Tripoli. *NBC Nightly News* has a man on the scene with Steve Delaney, who phones in a live report and even sticks his receiver out his hotel window so those of us at home can hear the roar of antiaircraft fire.

By dawn, Operation El Dorado Canyon is over. The eleven-minute attack transforms much of Qaddafi's compound at Al Azizyah into smoking rubble. So is the French Embassy in Tripoli, which we accidentally hit with a bomb.

One F-111 is missing. Everyone else is down safely, which is amazing given our press leaks and a subsequent report that shows the Italians and Maltese tipped off the Libyans after our carrier planes showed up on their radar systems. Nothing like having allies in this war against terror.

Now, we have to await a response. Much of the world is furious at our attack. The French, Italians, and most of the British see the operation as reckless military adventurism. In the Middle East and North Africa, there are protests in the streets of most major Arab cities. Our embassy in Khartoum just reported in, painting a picture of large-scale mobs chanting anti-American slogans. Several hundred tried to storm the embassy, and they would have succeeded had it not been for teargas-firing local Sudanese police. They drove off the attackers, but now everyone is worried about a repeat of the '79 embassy takeover in Tehran, or the attack on our embassy in Pakistan, where one of our marines was shot and killed.

A little after 3 P.M., a flash cable arrives from Khartoum. One of our embassy staff members has been shot. Gleason gives me the case.

There's not much to tell at first. William J. Calkins, a thirty-three-year-old former navy communications specialist, was on his way home for the night. He left the embassy just before 10 P.M. local time. Not far from his house, some locals found him unconscious and bleeding profusely, still strapped into his government vehicle. They rushed him to a nearby hospital, where he underwent emergency surgery. Someone, or some group of someones, had shot him in the head.

This is going to be a tough case. The Sudanese hate us, and Khartoum is a playground for terrorists. It is a city on the edge of anarchy, sort of a Beirut lite. All the chaos with a third fewer murders. The local police hardly function, and trying to get physical evidence from the scene to our FBI lab will be futile.

I begin working with the RSO at the embassy in Khartoum. Together, we manage to build a basic sketch of the attack. Bill Calkins worked erratic hours. He's the communication, or commo, guy there on the ground in Sudan, and this requires him to handle all the flash traffic, NIACT cables, and other messages that must be sent out. As a result, he tended to work until odd hours of the night.

He worked late on April 16. On his way home, somebody shot him. Now, he's clinging to life in a Sudanese hospital. If he survives, he'll be flown to Germany for further treatment.

Was this just a random act of violence in a Third World pit of mayhem? Or was this a deliberate hit? We're not sure.

A day later, our RSO in Khartoum reports back to us. He's found some witnesses. According to them, a small sedan with three males inside picked up Bill Calkins's vehicle and began to tail him. Somewhere along the road, the sedan swerved to the left and accelerated until it was even with Bill's car. Two men opened fire with pistols while the third drove. As Bill slumped over, bleeding from a bullet wound to the left side of his head, the hit team vanished into the night.

We have only one piece of forensic evidence to go on. The Sudanese police turned over a few shell casings. Our RSO in Khartoum promises to send those to us via overnight DHL right away.

This may just be the opening blow in Sudan. Another cable comes in from Khartoum with potentially dire news. The Sudanese prime minister declared he'd provide "material and human assistance" to combat "barbaric American aggression." Given this development, the earlier mob at the embassy gates, and the hit on Calkins, the decision is made to evacuate all nonessential embassy personnel from Khartoum. Altogether, with relief agency workers and regular staff, there are about five hundred Americans at the embassy. Plans are made to fly most of them out on a charter flight to Kenya.

As I work the Calkins case, more bad news flows in to FOGHORN. In Beirut, the bodies of three hostages, including our two academics, are found on April 17. This is clear retaliation for the bombing of Tripoli. A note with the bodies claimed as much. Later that afternoon, the British discover a plot to blow up an El Al jetliner departing from London.

The next day, a letter bomb arrives in the British House of Commons addressed to a member of Margaret Thatcher's cabinet. At the end of the week, a bomb squad in Istanbul defuses a device placed at the entrance of an American bank. The Turks also thwart another potential disaster when they catch two Libyans carrying a bag full of grenades, which they confessed they were going to throw into an American military wedding party.

Khartoum reports in at week's end. Most of the nonessential personnel are now in Kenya. Meanwhile, a few more details have emerged on the Calkins hit. First, he was shot in a residential neighborhood, not far from the Libyan People's Bureau. The two gunmen fired five times. Calkins will live, but right now he's blind, unable to speak, and partially paralyzed on his right side.

Were the Libyans involved? There's just not enough evidence to point one way or the other yet, although we did receive a report that Sa'id Rashid was seen in the city and left just after the attack. Rashid is a well-known Libyan intelligence operative and a member of the Revolutionary Committees Bureau, which is Qaddafi's elite terror and subversion organization. Rashid has been linked to numerous assassination attempts and an attempted bombing of a Pan Am airliner in December

1983, and he was last seen in Berlin around the time of the La Belle Discotheque operation. Is he orchestrating these attacks? It certainly couldn't be proven in a court of law, but right now it looks pretty suspicious. We must keep a closer eye on him. I send a message to our RSO in Khartoum, asking him to get the Sudanese to send us the passenger manifests for outbound flights to Tripoli in the days following the attack. The RSO is not optimistic he can get those, but he gives it a shot. The Sudanese turn him down cold. They aren't going to help us much beyond what they've already done.

Ten days after the Tripoli attack, we get hit again. This time, we receive a flash cable from our embassy in Sanaa, Yemen. It is another attempted hit on one of our diplomats. Gleason tells me to find out what happened.

I contact the RSO, who sends word that the victim is another communications officer, just like the hit in Khartoum. Arthur Pollick was on his way to the embassy when a car overtook his and shot him up. According to our agent on the scene, Art was shot in the leg, shoulder, and head. Somehow, he managed to stop his car and limp back to his house, where he called for help. He's going to live, but he's suffered serious wounds.

Fortunately, he'll be able to talk to me. Ten days after the Khartoum hit Bill Calkins is still unable to communicate. He's out of the woods, but he'll have permanent injuries, according to the doctors in Germany.

The two hits are extraordinarily similar. We need to get to the bottom of this quickly so we can prevent further attacks. In a few days, I'll be able to sit down with Art and debrief him. Hopefully, he'll give us something to go on. In the meantime, I send a cable to Sanaa, asking the RSO there to get to the crime scene and take some photographs.

Within twenty-four hours, some of the pieces start to fall into place. First, Art has identified his assailants' vehicle. It was a Toyota sedan, which the Yemeni police discover going into the Libyan Embassy later that day. The sedan also carries Libyan diplomatic plates. How careless is that? Of course, maybe they wanted us to know who pulled this off. Or maybe they just don't care. Either way, this is pretty brazen, even for the Libyans.

The Yemeni police also find spent shell casings by the side of the road. The gunmen fired multiple shots, and we've now got five more shells to run ballistic tests on when they arrive here in D.C.

Coordinating this investigation, getting our RSO to ask specific follow-up questions, and trying to work with the Yemeni police through our agents on the spot proves unwieldy and time-consuming. I shouldn't be shackled to this desk here in Foggy Bottom. I need to be out in the weeds, eyeballing this stuff for myself. I make a mental note to talk this over with Gleason. In the future, we need to send a team in to assist the agents on the spot. Between their normal security and protection duties and trying to ride herd on a multinational investigation, our RSOs are getting overwhelmed.

For now, I'll work from here, gathering the pieces so we can study the big picture.

By the end of the month, we've got more details from both attacks. In Khartoum, it looks like a Libyan surrogate terror group known as the Sudanese Revolutionary Guard pulled off the hit on Calkins. Our agent in Khartoum interviewed witnesses who saw the attack, and they gave a description of one of the gunmen that matched a known SRG operative.

The chance of catching these guys is remote. The Sudanese government has no interest in going after the SRG, especially on behalf of the United States. They're supporting the Libyans, and a few days ago recalled their ambassador from Washington.

In Yemen, we've got more details, thanks to the local police, who are British-trained. The real break comes, though, when I'm able to sit down with Art Pollick. Still bandaged up, he proves to be an outstanding witness to his own attack.

"Fred, I sensed something was wrong. There was this car behind me, and it seemed to be following too close," Art tells me. "It was a sedan with three people inside. Something just didn't seem right, you know?"

Art's memory of the incident is crystal clear. His balding head is still bandaged, but he's as sharp as they come. "I had this feeling. Not sure how to describe it, but it was unsettling. I glanced in my rearview mirror, but the car was gone," he continues. "So I looked over my left shoulder. As I did, the window shattered. Glass went everywhere. Two of the men were shooting at me with pistols."

Art's quick glance to the left probably saved his life. One of the first bullets hit him in the head just as he turned it. The bullet entered his forehead and followed the curve of his skull around until it exited near his left ear. That shot should have killed him. Instead, it blinded him in the left eye. He's a lucky, lucky man. I wish Bill Calkins had been as fortunate. Two weeks after his attack, he's only now starting to regain his speech, and most of his right side is still paralyzed.

"Did you notice anything unusual before the attack?" I ask Art.

He thinks about it for a minute, then replies, "You know, a few days before, I saw a car parked in our neighborhood. I'd never seen it before, and it stuck out in my mind. Do you think they were watching me?"

"Possibly." This is a critical piece of the puzzle. If this is connected, it means the terrorists have been watching our diplomats. Worse, they know where they live.

I arrange for Art to work with an Identi-Kit, which is sort of like a flat plastic Mr. Potato Head with which we can build a composite image of the suspects. It comes complete with hairstyles and colors, mustaches, facial shapes—everything an investigator needs to re-create a victim's memory of his assailant. When we're done, each of the three men in the car have olive complexions and black curly hair.

Next, I sit Art down with an FBI sketch artist. When the sketches are done, I take them and start comparing them to photographs of known Libyan diplomats and intelligence agents. We get a match. The Libyans had an agent from their embassy in the car when they hit Art Pollick.

In Sanaa, a Yemeni police captain has taken a personal interest in the attack. He's prosecuted his investigation with vigor, and he sends word back to us via our RSO at the embassy that he's come up with the names of the two other men in the vehicle. Both are local thugs, almost certainly recruited for a one-time job by the Libyan operative.

Not long after this revelation, the first batch of evidence arrives at Foggy Bottom. Crime-scene photos, photos of the two cars involved, mug shots of the local thugs, all have been neatly packaged for us, along with the shell casings. Not surprisingly, they're 9 mm pistol shells, just like the ones recovered in Khartoum. I first take them over to the FBI, as I want to have the lab there run a comparison on the casings. Could they have been fired from the same weapons? It would be a nice tie between the two hits. The FBI, however, decides it has better things to do with its time. These attacks happened overseas, and though I beg and plead for priority, the casings are dumped at the bottom of their to-do list. Frustrated, I take them to the ATF, hoping that they will prove more cooperative. They do, and I make a mental note to cultivate a tight relationship with the ATF folks. I know that connection will come in handy in the future.

A few more meetings with Art brings in a bit more granular detail. By early May, I've got a pretty good picture of the two attacks. First, they used the same modus operandi in both hits. It is simple and effective: Catch a lone diplomat between the embassy and his residence where he's most vulnerable. Then hit him with a drive-by shooting and leave him for dead.

The method is not tactically elegant by any stretch of the imagination. It is brutal and thuggish, which is how Libyan intelligence operates. It worked, too.

But there are some things about both cases that trouble me deeply. First, why did they hit two communications officers? Were they just in the wrong place at the wrong time? Did the Libyans plant their hit teams along known routes used by diplomatic personnel, then hit the first embassy staffer to come along? How would they identify them as American diplomats?

The license plates. I check. In both cases, Art and Bill were driving rigs with U.S. diplomatic plates. That's got to change. We can't have our people advertising who they are anymore, not with what's going on in the world these days. We've got to be more discreet.

There are no coincidences in the Dark World. And as I study the puzzle pieces, I'm convinced that the gunmen hit two communications officers for a reason. The one thing Bill and Art shared in common before the attack was the odd hours they kept. They moved between their homes and their embassies at night, in the early morning, and during the day. Their erratic movements must have been detected. And if I'm an agent watching these two guys come and go, what would I conclude?

I'd conclude they were agents. Most embassy staffers keep regular hours. The ones that work late or come in exceptionally early are usually intelligence types. CIA. Did the Libyans think they were striking at two CIA agents? That might be the commonality in both attacks. If so, they forgot about the commo guys and their need to deal with message traffic 24/7.

But there is a larger issue here. Peel back the onion a bit more and another question pops out. How did they know Art and Bill kept odd hours? They must have been watching the embassy, noting the comings and goings of each vehicle and each staffer. That requires patience and professionalism to pull off. What's worse, if Art's suspicions about the car in his neighborhood are true, the terrorists knew where he lived. They'd followed him home in the past. They'd observed his movements. They knew where to find him.

It is clear to us at Foggy Bottom that the Libyans pulled off both hits. These are acts of retaliation against us for the April 15 bombing of Tripoli. Yet all of this surveillance had obviously taken time to do. They had bided their time and gathered information about our embassy staff movements, their residences, and routes they drove between the two places. Then, when they were given the attack order from Tripoli, all the legwork had already been done. They knew where to go to lie in wait for their victims.

They've been watching us for a long time. And we never even knew it. We've been blind to just how closely our enemies observe us. If we don't open our eyes, we're going to lose more people. A lot more people.

Again we're playing catch-up here, always chasing the attackers. There's got to be a way to get out in front of them and stay out there. Right now, we're two steps behind and always reactive. Perhaps if we'd noticed the surveillance teams, we could have done something to prevent both hits. We need to change our thinking. We need to change our tactics. But in what ways?

nine

HUMAN POKER CHIPS

July 23, 1986
Foggy Bottom

My desk is stacked and double stacked with cables, documents, leads, my own notes, half-eaten doughnuts, and an empty can of Coke. Mullen's looks identical. Gleason's is its own unique disaster area, with top-secret-and-above documents scattered about. Gleason has anointed me our in-house specialist on the Beirut hostages. Number one priority, of course, is still William Buckley. Plus, I've spent weeks investigating the two post-Tripoli hits. I feel like I'm in a maze, running in circles. At the same time, we've had to cover a plethora of other threats that we received in response to our air strike on Qaddafi.

There's a knock on the big blue door. Mullen gets up and opens it, revealing a frail-looking man with a small briefcase in one hand. He announces that he's an auditor of some sort; I don't quite catch what he says. I'm just trying to keep my head down, working through my leads pile. Next to me is my own database of terror, the three-by-five card file box with all my notes from every case I've read or been involved in since February. I've almost filled the box already. Maybe I need a computer, but we don't have a single one in the office.

The auditor steps forward to stand near Gleason's desk. Cigarette stuck between tight lips, Gleason looks impatient. He stares at the uninvited guest with a *Get on with it, the world's on fire and we're up to our armpits in alligators* sort of expression.

The auditor begins with a bombshell. "This office is not in compliance with regulations regarding classified material."

What? Who is this guy? I turn away from my notes and surreptitiously watch what happens next.

Gleason's shocked into momentary silence. The auditor takes advantage of the lull and adds, "Your open storage of all these files is an issue...."

Before he can finish, Gleason points at me and says, "Fred, go close the door." I spring to my feet, brush past our guest, and close the door behind him. It slams shut with an echo not unlike a hatch cover might make on a submarine. We're sealed from the rest of the State Department now, down in our own little basement bathysphere. It instantly makes the auditor uncomfortable. I wonder if he's claustrophobic.

Gleason takes a long drag on his cigarette as he eyeballs the little man. This sort of silent scrutiny is not something the auditor's experienced, and I can tell by his body language he's well beyond his comfort level. His shoulders hunch up and his eyes wander away from Steve's.

Several seconds pass before Gleason plucks the cigarette from his lips, exhales angrily, and barks, "Look, I got no idea who the hell you are, but you're not even cleared to be in here, so get out now before I tell these two agents here to take you into custody."

Silence. Our visitor sags and takes a step backward. Fear registers on his face. He obviously realizes that Gleason is dead serious. If he's not out of here, I have no doubt the next order we get will be to take him down. Mr. Auditor knows it, too. Perhaps Gleason's reputation has preceded him. All over Foggy Bottom, people have learned not to mess with Steve Gleason. He plays hardball.

The auditor nods suddenly and bolts for the door.

Mullen laughs out loud at his hasty retreat. "I bet he just about crapped his pants!"

I can't help laughing either. It is a classic Steve Gleason moment. What's our fearless leader's reaction? Nothing. He's back to work, as if he'd never booted the geek out of our office.

A couple of minutes pass, and he tosses me a cable. "Incoming flamer from Beirut," he mutters. I study the cable. Marked "Eyes-Only for DSS/CT Gleason" it is actually a DSS channel message, not a cable, which means it is routed only through our office. Gleason stretches over and plants a yellow sticky note onto it. As he does, he orders, "We need to report this to the NSC. They need to factor it into the mix."

Whatever the mix is. I'm totally in the dark here, and obviously I don't have a need to know. One thing about Gleason, he does not have loose lips. A few weeks back, during a meeting with the DSS director, Clark Dittmer, Gleason stunned me speechless when Mr. Dittmer asked Gleason a specific question about one of our cases. "You don't need to know that, sir," he answered. Mr. Dittmer is a man I greatly respect, and he's given us much leeway to get our job done. When we need it, he also sticks up for us and backs us to the hilt. I wasn't sure how he'd take Gleason's comment. He didn't even look annoyed. He nodded and told us to carry on. It was an incredible sign of trust, and it went a long way toward cementing our loyalty to him.

So, on this Wednesday morning, I don't even bother to ask what the National Security Council is up to. I take the message as Gleason adds, "Go down to FOGHORN, Fred. Dial the number on the sticky note and read the message to the man who answers."

Who am I reading this to? Who is going to answer? How do I know the person who needs to hear this will be the same one to pick up the phone?

I've long since learned not to question an order from Steve Gleason. He once told me to go to the White House and deliver a briefing. I asked to whom, and his response was, "You don't need to know that. They'll be waiting." I did it and didn't have a clue whom I was talking to the entire time I was at 1600 Pennsylvania Avenue.

I get up from my desk and walk over to FOGHORN. FOGHORN lies on the far side of a nearby hallway, behind a heavy gray door. It is our operations and communications center. When I enter the place, I'm struck as to just how futuristic it looks. The room is dominated by a long, *Star Trek*–looking console, which is manned by three agents. They're busy answering phones, sorting through cable traffic, and monitoring various radio channels used by our DSS protective security details. From this console, the trio of agents can call in the cavalry if we ever get in trouble. And I mean cavalry. They have the ability to order fighter jets into the air, mobilize army resources in just about any location, and can get the White House on the horn in a matter of seconds. All of this, plus they can run ops, move assets around, and vouch for our undercover agents if they happen to get nabbed by local authorities. This is our service's nerve center, the Cheyenne Mountain of the spook world.

Of course, the place is as cluttered as our office. Dunkin Donuts boxes abound. Half-smoked cigars sit in overflowing ashtrays. Novels are stacked haphazardly about, and there are several new coffee stains in the carpet.

I greet the agents and tell them, "I need to use the Bat Phone." They nod and go back to whatever they were doing. I walk over to the far corner of the room where an old rotary phone hangs on the wall. It isn't just old; it's ancient. Scuffed green housing with white numbers and a black dial, this thing has probably been in service since the JFK hit—which I just read a bit about in the dead bodies cabinet last week. Whenever I get a free moment, I've come to enjoy launching little fishing expeditions to see where all the bodies are buried. I'll open a drawer at random and poke through the files until I find something interesting. Once, I even looked to see if we had a file on alien contact at Roswell, New Mexico. There wasn't anything on it. Given all the other stuff that's in those cabinets, I've concluded that if it is not in there, it didn't happen.

The Bat Phone is a secure line we can use to call any number of agencies and embassies. On it, we are allowed to discuss anything up to top secret. I look down at the number I'm supposed to dial. There's only five digits. Who am I about to call? I don't have a clue. And who in the world has a five-digit telephone number?

I spin the dial. The phone bleeps at me like British phones do. On ring six, a no-nonsense voice says, "Yes."

Not a question. Just "Yes."

What is going on?

"This is Agent Burton from CT," I offer. Silence. The line makes faint, funny electronic noises. "I have an incoming from Beirut that my boss wants me to pass along."

A heartbeat's hesitation follows. Then I hear the voice reply, "Okay. Go."

I read the message, slowly and clearly. When I finish, I say, "Over."

"Got it. Out." The line goes dead.

I look at the receiver for a minute, then sling it into its cradle. I could have been talking to the Wizard of Oz for all I know.

I beat feet back to the big blue door. When I reach my desk, Gleason gives me a sharp look and says, "Hey, Fred, did you pass that back channel to Ollie?"

Ollie?

"Just got done."

"Good. Thanks."

Ollie? There's only one person anyone calls Ollie in our line of work. He's part of the National Security Council.

I'd been talking to Lieutenant Colonel Oliver North, the gray ghost of the Dark World. I've heard rumors about him, but few people have ever seen him. He's a shadow whose comings and goings have led to many whispers within the spook community. Who knows if they are true or not? But I know one fact about him now. For whatever reason, Oliver North has an interest in our Beirut hostages.

William Buckley is one of them, but there are others. Father Martin Jenco, a Catholic priest, was grabbed off the streets about a year and a half ago. No word if he's still alive. Terry Anderson, an AP journalist, has been missing for months now after his abduction. Thomas Sutherland, the dean of the Agricultural School at Beirut University, has been in Hezbollah's hands since last June. His colleague David Jacobsen was snatched only a few weeks before that.

Five Americans. Each file I've created now has a photo of an abductee. They're hard to look at, as it brings home the human dimension of this crisis. More innocent victims caught up in the Dark World.

I pack things up just before six. I'd love to get home early and be with Sharon. I'd barely parked the Jetta in the garage when the phone rings. I look at the time: 6:30. With a sigh, I answer it.

"Fred?" It's Steve Gleason.

"Yes?"

"Be at Andrews at 2100 hours for a trip. Pack for a week, maybe two."

"Okay. Where am I going?"

"You don't need to know that yet."

Click.

So much for an evening with my wife. I've got two and half hours to get to Andrews Air Force Base. In the bedroom, I find my Hartmann suit bag and slide my gray Jos. A. Bank into it. Two button-down shirts and an extra pair of lace-up Johnston & Murphys soon follow. I zip it up, grab my carry-on bag, and stuff it full with my earpiece, protection pins, badge, creds, some gum, two newspapers, and a John le Carré novel. I'm reading *The Honourable Schoolboy* at the moment.

Sharon comes home, and I say a hasty good-bye to her. It must be tough on her, but she's stoic about this development, even though she won't have any idea where I will be for the next week.

I get to Andrews just before 9 P.M. The gate guard looks at my creds then gives me a smart salute and directs me to the special air-mission hangar.

An air force sedan rolls up a few minutes later, red light flashing on the roof. The driver waves me to follow him, and I throw the Jetta in gear. He leads me out to a remote hangar, where he points to a parking slot. I slip the Jetta into it, cut the engine, and pile out. The sedan disappears into the night, leaving me alone, bags in hand. This area of Andrews seems all but deserted. Not a soul is in sight. No airplanes are warming up or coming in. The silence is almost eerie. I turn to walk into the hangar, which is swathed in darkness. Only a few lights are on inside, creating little pools of brightness in the cavernous interior.

"Can I help you? Are you here for the flight?" a voice calls to me. I spin around, searching for its source. A second later, an air force master sergeant crosses into one of the puddles of illumination.

"I guess so," I reply. I don't know which flight he's referring to, and suddenly I get a stab of anxiety. What if I catch the wrong secret flight and end up in Togo when I'm supposed to be in Beirut or Cairo?

"My name is Agent Fred..."

With a wave of his hand, the master sergeant cuts me off. He's ten feet away now, regarding me severely. "No names, sir. We don't need your name. Just wait here."

He turns and vanishes into the darkness.

The roar of jet engines draws near, and down the taxiway I see a huge green air force transport jet cruising toward me. As it gets closer, I can see it is a Lockheed C-141 Starlifter.

Is that my ride? Sure enough, it turns toward the hangar, and I get a head-on view of its 160-foot-long wings. They droop slightly, giving the huge plane a beleaguered look, as if its four massive Pratt & Whitney turbofans are too much of a load for the wings to bear.

A moment later, the engines shut down and the crew emerges. One of the pilots, an air force officer about my age—twenty-eight—spots me and walks over to talk.

"Looking for a ride?" he asks.

"Yes, I guess so."

"Great. Where are we going?"

"You mean *you* don't know?"

The pilot shakes his head. "No idea." He seems matter-of-fact about this. It must be standard procedure.

We stand together in silence as I puzzle this through. Then Gleason bursts through the door with five or six other spooks in tow. He huddles with the pilots, then comes over and sits next to me. "Fred, we're heading to Rhein-Main Air Base in Germany. We'll stop there and drive to Wiesbaden. A hostage is coming out."

"Is it Buckley?" I ask hopefully.

"Don't know. We'll talk about it in the plane."

A half hour later, we climb aboard the Starlifter and spread out. Gleason finds a spot with an empty seat between us. After takeoff, he opens his briefcase and withdraws a pile of file folders. I notice that the stack includes my hostage profiles. Without comment, he hands me part of the stack. I start flipping through what he's given to me, and find that the top file is Jeremy Levin's debriefing report. Levin had been a CNN reporter held hostage by Hezbollah. He'd managed to escape on Valentine's Day 1985. The second one is a thick file full of debriefings related to the Tehran embassy crisis in 1979. As I leaf through it, I discover that our boss, Clark Dittmer, conducted them.

"Look those over," Gleason tells me. "Figure out what questions to ask, what we need to know."

"What are we looking for?" I ask.

"Everything. Find out how he was taken, who took him, where they took him. Get details of every place he was held. Pick up anything that might be useful to Delta Force and the special operations teams at Fort Bragg. Maybe if we can get enough, we can launch a rescue operation for the rest. Okay?"

"Roger. Am I doing this alone?"

"I'll be there for a while. There'll also be one agent from the FBI and one from the CIA asking questions with you. You'll be lead on these debriefs for us after this one."

I start plowing through the files. I scribble notes and use my own knowledge as a cop. If I were leading a rescue operation, what sort of intel would I want?

Guards: Number and armament? What sort of training? Professionals or thugs? How did they hold their weapons? That alone can telegraph how alert, disciplined, and prepared they are. When did they change guards? Were they on a regular schedule? How many were there? Are they paid lackeys or committed jihadists?

Location: Where do they lock the hostages up? Rural farms, urban basements? How many windows in the rooms or cells? How do the doors swing, into the room or out? Where are the hallways? Dimensions? Did they move the hostage around? If so, how did they transport him? Day or night?

How about sounds and smells? We must dig up anything and everything that might help our analysts find Hezbollah's makeshift prison cells holding our people.

Two hours into the flight and I'm shivering in my Barbour Beaufort. The freezing mid-Atlantic air is turning the passenger bay into a refrigerator. Leaning across the empty seat between us, Gleason says, "Look, Fred, we've got to confirm if Buckley is still alive or not. You know Islamic Jihad announced they executed him."

I nod. Last October they tipped the media and sent along a few fuzzy photos of a corpse to prove it. The jury is still out on his fate.

"He's one of us. He's a legend in the business. Company commander in Korea. Silver Star. Soldier's Medal. Two Purple Hearts. Military Assistance Command in Vietnam. He was William Casey's fair-haired boy. Had lots of latitude. Made some enemies. The Agency wants him back at all costs, okay?"

"And if he's dead?"

"Then we find out who did it, and who interrogated him."

I make a note to check with the hostage—provided he isn't Buckley—and find out if there were Caucasians working with the Hezbollah cell who kept him. If so, that means there's probably KGB involvement.

If the KGB got to Buckley, it would be a disaster far worse than if the Iranians had squeezed him. Buckley's been with the Agency since before Vietnam. He worked with the CIA's assassination program during the war, then later served in Cambodia, Egypt, and Pakistan. The stuff he knows could fill volumes.

"Look, Fred," Gleason's voice drops an octave and takes on a tenor I hadn't heard before. "I've been doing this for two and a half years without any help. I'm getting out soon. You and Mullen will be the institutional memory around here. I know I've left you in the dark a lot. I'm sorry for that, but there is a reason. I've been through a leak investigation. You don't want to go through that. The one thing that will help you survive is a reputation for tight lips, okay? Not everyone is with us."

His words flash me back a few weeks. We'd been trying to get some information out of a bureaucrat upstairs, but the guy had been stonewalling us. Gleason sent me up to tell him if he didn't shake loose the stuff we needed, Gleason would file charges against him for withholding evidence. These little moments made me realize the essential truth of Steve Gleason: He will get the job done at all costs. If somebody becomes an obstacle to his objective, he will go around him or through him. Or arrest him. Whatever it takes.

I've felt lost these past months, struggling to learn on the fly all the thousand things I need to know in order to do my job. In a way, my own game of catch-up mirrors our counterterror effort. Now, as I've progressed along the learning curve, Gleason's starting to put his trust in me. He's given me this assignment to get me ready. This is my step forward from rookie agent to veteran counterterror investigator. He'll hold my hand for part of the time, then he'll cut me loose to sink or swim in front of the FBI and Agency guys.

Gleason leans back in his seat, "It's been a long two years, Fred."

"I don't know how you did this by yourself."

He ignores my comment. "We're going to get more help before I leave. You and Mullen won't have to hold the fort down alone, okay?"

He stands and heads up the aisle to talk with one of the other spooks. I'm left alone, wondering if I'm ready to fly solo. This is what I wanted when I first decided to join the DSS. I wanted to do something more with my life than breaking up high school keggers and getting in the middle of domestic fights. I wanted a bigger role, and federal service seemed to offer it. This trip is my final exam as far as Steve's concerned. Pass it, and my apprenticeship will be over.

I bury myself in the files again. Hours pass, and my notes pile up.

Gleason returns, and says, "After the debrief, each agent will file a report. We'll send it flash precedence."

"Roger, sir."

"Bring your A-game, Fred. Your report will go directly to the NSC and to the White House. The president is very interested."

My report will be read by the president? Back when I was a cop, I was lucky if our watch commander read anything I wrote. I will be under a microscope, with all the pressure that entails.

"I'll oversee things and run air cover for you with D.C. and the DOD, okay? That way you guys can focus on your job."

"Thanks."

"How do you feel?"

"I'm ready."

"Good. Get some sleep. We'll be landing in a few hours."

Gleason slumps into his seat and I turn to the window. There's nothing but black beyond the glass. The Atlantic in the dead of night is the darkest place on the planet.

I find myself thinking about my father. He'd been in the army during World War II, serving as a military policeman in Western Europe. He saw the concentration camps, saw the worst of what humanity could do. He smelled the bodies, saw them stacked like cordwood. When the war ended, his MP unit guarded the Nazi leaders whom the Allies subsequently tried at Nuremberg. He stood in the courtroom, guarding the prisoners as the Allied prosecutors revealed all the barbarity and cruelty of Hitler's Germany. Day after day, the testimony revealed just how far the descent into madness had gone. The sallow-faced bureaucrats sitting in the dock were among history's greatest mass murderers. Nobody shed a tear when they were hung.

Years later, my dad's stories of his time in Germany filled me with indignation. His sense of right and wrong became my own. I learned through him that there is no space between black and white, there is only right and wrong. Take that first step down the wrong path, and it can lead only to evil. For me, my path through life has been a narrow one, defined by that sense of right and wrong. But in my world now, the justice my fa-

ther witnessed at Nuremberg seems such a distant hope. Today there are
only victims with faint hope of seeing justice served on their tormenters.
The two Libyan hits taught me that. Prevention is the best form of justice
in this line of work. But how do you prevent such random, brutal acts?

Maybe the Atlantic isn't the darkest place on earth after all. Maybe
that distinction goes to the human heart.

ten

ONE MORE GOLD STAR

July 27, 1986
Wiesbaden, Germany
U.S. Air Force Hospital

Staring out the hospital window at this ex-Luftwaffe base in Wiesbaden, our released hostage, Father Martin Jenco, answers our most pressing question.

"Buckley? William Buckley is dead."

I don't want to believe those words. From the look on the FBI and CIA agents' faces, neither do they. Father Jenco sees the shock register on all of us and offers, "He died of natural causes."

More surprises. "What?" all three of us ask.

Puzzled, he replies, "I assumed you knew."

Nobody answers. We just stare.

"I can't tell you much," Jenco explains. "It happened right after they moved me. I'd been chained to a radiator for six months by myself. For some reason, they decided to put me with the other Americans in early June of '85."

Father Jenco's voice is steady, but he looks weak from his ordeal. His eyes are ringed, his face is pallid, and his white, General Ambrose Burnside–style beard is bushy and untamed. He came out of Syria on July 26 and was flown straight to us in Wiesbaden. He hasn't even had a chance to see his family yet. I understand about a dozen of his relatives have just flown in from the States, eager to welcome him back to civilization.

"I heard him calling out. He was hallucinating, ordering breakfast from the bathroom. I think he said, 'I'll have blueberry pancakes.' He coughed all the time, and that got worse as he got weaker. David Jacobsen and I pleaded with the guards to get him medical assistance."

He pauses. His eyes are dry, but I can see he's in tremendous pain. He adjusts his wide, goggle-style glasses before continuing. "One night, they dragged him past me. They told me he was going to the hospital, but I knew he was dead."

And there it is.

"Father," I ask, "was he tortured?"

"Not to my knowledge. But I was only with him for a short time."

All I can think of are the stars on the wall at Langley. Buckley's will be another anonymous addition. The man was a hero, a patriot. He fought in two wars and countless skirmishes in the Dark World. He should not have died this way. *We* should not have let this happen.

We're only ten minutes into our debriefing with Father Jenco and already the pages of questions related to Buckley have been made irrelevant by the news. I set them aside and rethink how to proceed.

"After he died, they brought in a Jewish doctor to examine us. They later killed him." Father Jenco's voice trails off. The hospital room we're in is suddenly deathly silent.

The FBI agent asks, "On the videotape you brought out, Jacobsen says Buckley was executed."

I haven't seen it yet, but Hezbollah gave Father Jenco a seven-minute-long tape of Jacobsen. He apparently read from a script and asked President Reagan to do more for their release.

"I don't know about that," Jenco replies.

Nods all around. This wouldn't be the first time Hezbollah claimed to have executed somebody who died of natural causes in their hands. With Buckley, though, we need to learn more. What had happened to him?

"Do you know what they did with William Buckley's body?" the Agency man asks.

"No, I'm sorry. I don't know. I was almost always blindfolded. I was in chains. I never saw much."

We need to start at the beginning. I shuffle my notes. What do I need to learn from Father Jenco to help keep others alive? First off, we need to know how he was abducted. If we can dissect Hezbollah's snatch-and-grab tactics, maybe we can construct some counters to them that will dissuade further attempts on Americans in Beirut.

"Father Jenco, please . . . let's start from the point you were abducted. How did they do it?"

The priest takes a deep breath and begins the story of his ordeal. As his words tumble out, the angst on his face grows. He looks frail and even wearier than ever. It does not take long to understand why.

Five hundred and sixty-four days ago, Father Jenco climbed into his car and sped off to work. He served as the head of a Catholic relief operation in Beirut. Because he was well known around the city and because he helped everyone equally—Muslims, Christians, Jews—he did not fear abduction. What would they want with a priest, anyway?

Well, they wanted him. An eight-man team stopped his car not far from his office. The men, all armed with automatic weapons, dragged him out of the car, bundled him up, and threw him into the trunk of their getaway vehicle. At first, they kept asking him if he was Joseph Curtin and seemed confused that he was not. Curtin had been Father Jenco's predecessor at the Catholic Relief Service in Beirut. They had abducted the wrong priest.

But they held on to him anyway. In the first days of Father Jenco's ordeal, the Hezbollah guards wrapped him in packing tape until he resembled a mummy. Stuffing a rag into his mouth, they carried him to a truck and crammed him into the spare-tire well under the frame. They drove him into southern Beirut, leaving him limp from the exhaust fumes and claustrophobic conditions. This was the first of several times they moved him in this fashion.

The weeks that followed were a blur of degradation, humiliation, and torture. They kept him blindfolded and chained by the ankle. They threw his paltry meals on the floor, forcing him to eat with his hands. Cheese and water sufficed for breakfast. Sometimes they gave him rice and beans for lunch. Dinner was little more than bread and jam. The guards varied from polite and respectful to barbaric and sadistic. One thug stuck a pistol to Father Jenco's head and told him he was about to die. When he pulled the trigger, the hammer fell on an empty chamber.

Other times they beat him, stood on his head, kicked him, and punched him. One guard got a kick out of kneeling on Father Jenco and putting all his weight on the priest's pancreas.

And for what? Why had they taken this man of the cloth? Their stated demands have not varied. They wanted the Dawa 17 released. This was a group of terrorists who had bombed the U.S. and French embassies in Kuwait in 1983. They are murderers and fanatics whom the Kuwaitis will never let out of prison. They are far too dangerous. However, Hezbollah's éminence grise, Imad Mugniyah, has a personal stake in the fate of these terrorists. His brother-in-law and cousin, Mustafa Youssef Badreddin, is one of the Dawa 17. Mugniyah is a shadowy figure who is either Hezbollah's security chief or the operations specialist, we're not sure which. He's also the group's main link to Iran's Ministry of Intelligence and Security (MOIS). Mugniyah planned Beirut I and II, orchestrated the marine barracks bombing, and was the mastermind behind the hijacking of TWA Flight 847. No other terrorist leader has soaked his hands in so much American blood. Now, he uses our citizens as nothing more than bargaining chips.

Hezbollah—meaning Mugniyah—has never wavered in their demand for the release of the Dawa 17, which makes me wonder why Father Jenco was set free. Is there a deeper motive for these abductions?

For six months, Hezbollah kept Father Jenco locked up alone in a filthy cell somewhere in southern Beirut. In June 1985, they again mummified him in packing tape, threw him into the spare-tire well of another truck, and united him with the other American hostages.

"You mean you were all kept in the same location?" I ask him. The news surprises all of us. If they're in one place, we might be able to rescue them. If they were scattered all over the city and the Bekáa Valley, there's no way we'd be able to get them simultaneously. And any rescue attempt would surely bring severe repercussions to whomever we left behind.

Father Jenco confirms this. "Yes. We were kept together in stalls, makeshift cells. We were still chained and blindfolded. I developed an eye infection from the blindfolds."

We get Father Jenco a glass of water. He takes a sip and continues. "Several times they told me to dress in nice clothes they had given me. I was to be released. Then they'd laugh and say they were just kidding."

The torment continued. Once, when one of the guards suspected the priest had caught a glimpse of his face, he was pinned against a door and brutally beaten. Such treatment demoralized each hostage. They could hear it when their fellow Americans endured a beating. All they could do was wonder when it would be their turn again.

It wore away at their spirits. It wore away at their ability to hope. At Christmastime, Father Jenco tried to sing a Christmas carol. He managed only a few words before he broke down in tears.

Another time, in February 1986, his captors gave him a letter from home. It was the first time he'd received one, and he opened it eagerly. But as he read every precious word over and over, he heard Thomas Sutherland weeping in the cell next to his.

"Thomas had not been given any mail," Father Jenco explains. "It was so cruel to do that to him."

The other hostages angrily gave their letters back to the guards to protest what they had done to Sutherland. Later that day, their captors relented and gave each hostage three letters from home. This sort of minor victory gave them strength. It sustained them.

There were a few moments of humor. Once, when one of the guards asked if Father Jenco needed anything, the priest replied, "Yes, a taxicab." That elicited a few weary laughs. For the most part, each day became a struggle to survive, both psychologically and physically. For Father Jenco, his faith was his anchor in the storm. He fashioned a set of rosary beads from the loose strings of a potato sack. At times, he focused on Philippians 4:5–6 and said those words of comfort over and over to himself.

The Lord is near. Dismiss all anxiety from your mind.

The moves were the worst. Being bound up in packing tape and crammed into the spare-tire wells of those well-worn trucks left him in cold terror. His heart, already weak from cardiovascular disease, was strained to the limit by each of these ordeals. At first, he held fast to a button of Jesus Christ his captors let him keep. Unable to move inside the well, he prayed over the button as it lay in his tightly balled fist. It was his talisman and through the choking carbon monoxide fumes, he would recite prayers and try to block out what his tormentors were doing to him. Later, he threw the button away. He and God had a conversation, and Father Jenco realized he didn't need any physical proof of his faith. He'd already lost almost everything else, including a cross given to him on his twenty-fifth anniversary of joining the priesthood. In the end, he discovered none of those small artifacts mattered. All he needed was faith itself.

We turn the interview toward the guards. Father Jenco tells us that most of them were young Lebanese males, often barely out of their teens. All had been inundated with propaganda ever since they were kids.

"What sort of propaganda?" I ask.

"Messages of hate, Agent Burton. Messages of hate. I listened to some of it on a tape. It was terrible."

Some of the guards were hired help, unable to find jobs in the chaos of Beirut. One of them had been an air-conditioner repairman and just needed a way to pay the bills. He was one of the few kind ones and would occasionally bring Father Jenco things his wife had baked. Others seemed fanatical, or mentally ill. Maybe both. None of them had much formal education, which Father Jenco seized on. He told them he would like to bring them to America—not to punish them, but to educate them. He was not vindictive. He wanted these young men to do something meaningful and productive with their lives. They ignored him.

Once, the guards tied a bundle of plastic explosives to him. Father Jenco tried to find peace in what he thought would be the last minute of his life. When nothing happened, his captors said the bomb was a dud. Another time, a guard stuck his finger in Father Jenco's mouth. As he peered at the priest's teeth, he saw his fillings. He thought the fillings were transmitters and accused him of being a CIA agent.

It is clear that the hostages are not guarded by the first team. These guys are scrubs—nutcases and wannabes whom Hezbollah hires or trusts to do little but babysit their human booty. Delta would slaughter them. If only we could find out where they are.

That remains the problem. Fearing a rescue mission by the United States or Syria, the captors moved the hostages from location to location. Sometimes, they were moved from one place to another in southern Beirut. Sometimes they were taken elsewhere, probably the Bekáa Valley.

Several times, Father Jenco nearly lost all hope of freedom. At one point, the guards told him he would be free soon. He started to believe again. Then they replaced the door on his cell. After they left, he peeked at it from under his blindfold and saw it was a rugged, heavy door. Right then, he knew they were psychologically tormenting him again. A door like that could only mean he'd remain in his cell.

He broke down and began to cry.

Several nights ago, things changed. The guards came in and wrapped him up in packing tape again—a sure sign of another move. This time, though, they drove out into the Lebanese night, pulled him from the vehicle, and cut off all the packing tape. One of the guards stuffed some money in his hand. When Father Jenco asked what it was for, the guard replied, "A taxicab."

He wandered through the darkness until a Syrian army patrol discovered him. Within hours, he'd been whisked to Damascus and was put on a flight to Germany.

I glance at my watch. We've been debriefing Father Jenco for hours, and the poor man just needs to rest. Tomorrow, we'll start teasing through the details, gleaning those little nuggets that we can use to do our jobs. In the meantime, I have to ask this brave and decent man one final question for the day.

"Father, how did you endure? You must have felt like Paul."

Martin Jenco sadly shakes his head. In a self-effacing voice he says, "Paul survived so much more than I, Agent Burton. And I was weak at times. I learned hate, which I had to overcome with forgiveness."

The Agency man growls, "How can you forgive these men after what they did to you?"

"It is the only way. Violence achieves nothing. Rage, hate—they destroy the soul. What else is there but forgiveness?"

Silence greets his question. I know I am not that enlightened. I cannot forgive what my enemies have done to this kind and gentle human being. Perhaps a better man might, but not me, not now. Not after what I've heard.

Late that night as I lie awake, I make a promise to myself. I know I'm in this business for the long haul. This is where I belong, and while I've stumbled around these past months, I am learning. I will be the institutional voice for our department someday. I have no doubt of that—unless I get killed. Someday, I will be in a position to influence things. I'll have authority. And I will use it to do everything I can to track down these evil, vile human beings who do so much harm to those like Father Jenco who are only trying to do good.

I will make a list of those men. Men like Abu Nidal and Sa'id Rashid and whoever fired those shots at Art Pollick and Bill Calkins. There will be a reckoning. Father Jenco would not approve. Justice walks a fine line with vengeance, and that is an anathema to such a man, for there is no redemption in it. I am a cop to the core; he is a man of peace. We live in different worlds. Or maybe we live in the same world, we've just taken different paths to try to make it better. I want justice. And in this case, it starts with Imad Mugniyah.

eleven

THE GRAY HELL OF WAIT AND HOPE

In the weeks following Father Jenco's release, I swing back and forth between cautious optimism and puzzlement. By nature, I'm a glass-half-full person, and I'd like to believe that Jenco's newly recovered freedom is the first sign of better things to come in Beirut. Back at Foggy Bottom, all through August we heard nothing but positive rumors that more hostages would be set free. The tragedy of captivity, the horrors of deprivation and brutality, just might be over for those other Americans chained to radiators in dingy cells half a world away from home.

But then there's that little nagging doubt in the back of my mind that keeps stabbing away at my optimism. *Why all the optimistic rumors? For that matter, why was Father Jenco released?* Granted, Jenco was in ill health when he came back to us, but that didn't stop Hezbollah from letting Buckley die. What's the root of all this? Could it be Terry Waite?

Waite is the official envoy for the archbishop of Canterbury who has worked tirelessly around the Middle East to solve hostage crises peaceably. After a group of Westerners were taken hostage in Libya in the spring, he flew to Tripoli and successfully negotiated their release. He is universally respected, has a reputation for honor and honesty, and has done the Lord's work from Idi Amin's Uganda to the very lion's den it-self—Tehran. For months now, he's been quietly traveling to Beirut to find a solution to the hostage crisis there. Perhaps—just perhaps—this man of peace has found traction in the Shiite slums in the southern part of the city. Have they listened to him? Has his humanitarian approach succeeded? I'd like to think so.

But then, I know Mugniyah. This is not a man motivated by human-itarian principles. He's a stone-cold killer who has no problems sending his minions to certain death in suicide attacks. Tell me how a man such as he can find common ground with a man such as Waite?

I just can't see it.

Right after Father Jenco was released, a Hezbollah communiqué an-nounced that the United States should "proceed with current ap-proaches that could lead, if continued, to a solution of the hostage crisis." The American response was quick and vehement. The administration denied that any approaches were being used and castigated the Hezbol-lah statement.

I can't help but wonder. Wheels within wheels are always turning in the Dark World, and at the very least somebody in Washington had had advance notice that Jenco would be released. After all, we beat him to Wiesbaden. Is there some back-channel avenue open between Washing-ton and Hezbollah? I wish I knew, but if there is, it is way above my pay grade and need to know.

Back at Foggy Bottom, things in the CT office continue along at their usual frenetic pace. Our office's reputation is growing, and that has proven to be a double-edged sword. We're getting more cooperation throughout the Department of State, but at the same time our workload has grown. Agents overseas and the RSOs know that we'll help them out. We'll ride herd over their evidence that needs analyzing and we'll support investigations with additional resources whenever we can. It stretches us even thinner. At the same time, we are still required to perform protec-tive security duties whenever we've got important foreign dignitaries in town. An upcoming UN General Assembly session in New York, sched-uled for early next year, is not going to be fun. Already we've been told we're going to be up there indefinitely helping to protect a lot of foreign diplomats who have said plenty of things against our country.

The thought of living in a hotel for weeks on end protecting the likes of Yasir Arafat really isn't one I relish. American counterterrorism agents should not be used as human shields for the father of Palestinian terrorism.

In the meantime, I've managed to slip away a couple more times to see Fred Davis at the Brandt Place house. We've resolidified our friendship on those nights, sipping coffee on the porch and revisiting the good old days. Fred's starting flight school in a few months, which means he'll be in the Deep South for several weeks. I'll miss him, but when he comes home, I'll hold him to his promise to take me flying.

In the meantime, we work other cases, chase down more leads, and add whatever details we encounter to our hostage files. The job keeps us moving, but I can't help but feel caught in a gray zone I've never encountered before. On one hand, the hostage situation becomes a waiting game that runs relentlessly in the background of our day-to-day operations. It smolders and smokes, and several times a week leads or new developments force the issue back to the top of our in-boxes. At the same time, we have bombings, shootings, threats, and warnings aplenty that keep us bouncing from one crisis to the next. The hostage crisis is our bass line, the underlying beat of our CT office.

And as the summer starts to fade, bad things start happening in Beirut. On September 9, the embassy RSO sends us a flash cable that brings a grimace to Gleason's face. Hezbollah has abducted another American. This time, they snatched an elementary school principal named Frank Reed. His crime? Apparently little more than staying in the shattered city to run the Lebanon International School.

A group calling itself Islamic Dawn is claiming credit for the abduction. The name is a new one, and we don't have much information on them. But we send their statement to our analytical experts, who conclude it is very similar to the other ones released by Islamic Jihad and other supposed groups in Beirut.

Hezbollah prefers to operate in the shadows, using front groups for its public proclamations. I suppose they do it to try and keep us off-balance and guessing. It doesn't work. Evil is still evil no matter what words are used to cloak it.

Three days later, I get a call in the middle of the night again. FOGHORN reports another abduction in Beirut. By the time I get to the office, the RSO in Beirut has confirmed that Joseph Ciccipio, another academic with American University, has been snatched. This time, Hezbollah's operatives call themselves the Revolutionary Justice Organization. This particular front name has been used in the past. The RJO took credit for nabbing Aurel Cornea, a French television soundman assigned to Beirut with a news team.

Two abductions inside three days? What is the motive? Could Hezbollah be trying to increase the pressure on the United States? Are they trying to tighten the screws in hopes we will convince the Kuwatis to release the Dawa 17? Perhaps, but in neither case did the abductors issue any demands.

Could they be replacing the two hostages they've already released? Father Jenco was the second man of the cloth to be released by Hezbollah. Benjamin Weir, a Presbyterian minister who was kidnapped in 1984 while out on a walk with his wife, was released in late 1985 before I joined the CT office. Could these two latest abductions simply even the books from Hezbollah's perspective?

None of this makes any sense. The Dark World is full of murky issues, nonendings and huge questions. In that respect, the events in Beirut fit right in.

On September 26, a British reporter named David Hirst manages to escape from Hezbollah's clutches. We soon learn that he made his break while his captors were moving him from one slum prison cell to another in southern Beirut. He somehow was able to jump from the transport vehicle and reach safety.

Three days later, Hezbollah snatches a French TV reporter named Jean-Marc Sroussi. Was this in retaliation for Hirst's escape? Probably. Fortunately, a few days later Sroussi escapes from a shed that was serving as his holding cell.

By October, my summer optimism rapidly erodes. It is business as usual in Beirut, and that includes all the chaos and brutality of a civil war grafted onto a religious conflict. In the middle are our hostages, the human poker chips Mugniyah hopes to use to parlay the release of his brother-in-law's gang of murderers in Kuwait.

Ten days before Halloween, Hezbollah strikes again. This time, instead of trolling for academics around American University, they go for an easy target. Edward Tracy, a fifty-five-year-old wanderer and sometime writer, falls prey to Hezbollah gunmen while loose on the streets of

Beirut. The Revolutionary Justice Organization again takes credit for the abduction.

Why he's in Beirut becomes a minor mystery. His family has few answers for us. When we talk to his eighty-something mother, she tells us she hasn't seen her son in over two decades. What contact the rest of his family has is spotty at best. His letters from Beirut are peppered by odd comments and near-gibberish.

Buckley, I can understand. He had real value and his abduction served as a body blow to our intelligence efforts in the Middle East. Tracy just seems like a target of opportunity, guilty only of American citizenship and vagabondage in the midst of a war zone.

Then, just before Halloween, Gleason calls me at home again.

"Pack your bags. You're going to Wiesbaden."

The wait's over. Somebody else is coming out.

twelve

THE STENCH OF GOOD INTENTIONS

Saturday, November 1, 1986
Wiesbaden, Germany

Three were supposed to come out. That was the gist of my transatlantic brief this time as I tried my best to relax and enjoy another ten-hour C-141 Starlifter flight to the nation my dad helped subdue a generation ago. Now, we're back in Wiesbaden, playing the waiting game again.

I had hoped to see Sutherland, Jacobsen, and Anderson here at the hospital, ready to return home and be reunited with their families. So far, it hasn't happened. They were supposed to come out on Friday. Friday came and went with no word from Beirut. Today, the debriefing team has waited around all day for them to show up. We've cleared out the upper floor of the air force hospital on base. When and if our people get released, they'll each have a private room with a separate bath and lounge. Down the hall, we've set up a temporary communications room, complete with a STU-III secure phone. This is our portable version of the FOGHORN Bat Phone.

The wait gives me time to analyze the situation. Terry Waite's been very busy, traveling between the United Kingdom, Germany, and Beirut as he works his contacts on behalf of the archbishop of Canterbury. Has he scored a breakthrough with Hezbollah? If so, he transmitted his success and tipped us off so we could be here when the hostages arrive.

Nevertheless, the forewarning unsettles me. Granted, it could very well be that Waite's keeping us in the loop. On the other hand, I sense there's something else going on way above my pay grade. It doesn't seem right. This time, we received almost a week's notice of the impending release.

Fortunately, the press has not picked up a whiff of it. That in itself is unusual, given how leaky Washington is at the moment. Secrets are hard to keep in the current climate. Gleason's tight-lipped approach to everything is an anomaly. Usually some bureaucrat can't wait to spill the beans to his favorite pet reporter. Instead, things are very quiet. I've been on the job long enough to know that this in itself is a cause for concern. I just don't know what it means yet.

On Sunday, the STU-III rings in our makeshift commo room. The U.S. Embassy in Beirut passes us word that David Jacobsen is now in friendly hands. He was released earlier that day in the Christian-held sector of the city. He's at the embassy now, awaiting transport to Wiesbaden.

Only one of three. Jacobsen is the director of American University in Beirut. He was snatched off the street while taking a walk almost a year and a half ago. I wonder what sort of condition he'll be in when he gets here. Hopefully, he'll be in better shape than Father Jenco was.

The day passes quickly. The principals on the debriefing team sit down and gameboard our plan. This time, instead of asking questions on the fly, we've prepared a meticulous list of questions that should take two days to get through. This time, our team consists of representatives from the CIA, the FBI, the Defense Intelligence Agency (DIA), and the Joint Special Operations Command (JSOC). We each have areas we'll focus on in the course of the interrogation. Mine will be the mechanics of how Hezbollah kidnapped Jacobsen and how they moved him around the city. The mechanics of terror. If we break them down, we might be able to figure out how to stick a crowbar in their gears.

The next day, we gather at the airfield as Jacobsen arrives. The place is a mob scene. Once Jacobsen reached our embassy in Beirut, somebody notified the press. The media have flooded to Wiesbaden to capture his return to freedom. Flashbulbs fire so often I start to get dizzy. CNN covers the moment, and dozens of other TV crews jostle for position on the tarmac. When the plane from Cyprus finally arrives, the mob goes crazy. Jacobsen is given a rollicking welcome.

After he has a chance to see his family, we squirrel him away on the top floor of the hospital. The base is besieged with reporters, but air force security keeps them at bay.

Jacobsen appears haggard and world-weary when we sit down with him later Monday afternoon. Still, he looks better than the ashen-faced Father Jenco, and that is a relief. Perhaps they'd been treating the hostages better since July.

Wishful thinking.

Jacobsen's tale is one of horror upon horror. The torture, beatings, and brutality we heard from Father Jenco were compounded after the priest's release. It started with the videotape Father Jenco gave to us. In it, Jacobsen ad-libbed a couple of lines, which included a note of concern for William Buckley's wife and kids. Buckley didn't have children, and when the video reached the media, television newscasts focused on that segment and postulated that Jacobsen was trying to send a coded message to us.

Well, Hezbollah watches the news. The terrorists saw that speculation and it fed their inherent paranoia. They became convinced that Jacobsen had done something nefarious. The hostages lost all their few privileges. Books, radios, and pen and paper were taken away from them. Later, the guards stuffed them into trucks and moved them to a dank underground cell. From early August until yesterday, Jacobsen had languished in a vile hole.

Sitting on the edge of his hospital bed, Jacobsen begins, "September nineteenth ..." Then raw anguish swallows his long, gaunt face, and his words trail off. His head drops and he covers his eyes with both hands. For a moment, he tries to continue, but the emotions of whatever happened to him that day assail his self-control. He surrenders to it. His bones seem to sag under the weight of his experience. We stare on in sympathy. This poor man only wanted to educate, to help build Lebanon through higher learning. Instead, the ignorance he strove to erase rose up from the gutters and claimed him as a victim.

Finally, looking resolved, he turns his eyes on us. "They came to get me."

"Who?"

"Mokmoud, one of our guards. I knew it was going to be bad. As he pulled me to my feet, I heard him say, 'I'm sorry.' "

Mokmoud took Jacobsen into another room, where his other captors beat him senseless. They bound his feet and whipped him with a rubber hose. They punched him and kicked him, laughing all the while at the punishment they inflicted on this slender-faced academic. They laughed even as he screamed in agony. Somebody battered both his ears, leaving him in excruciating pain. Other blows fell upon his arms, legs, and genitals. At one point, they turned him upside down so his shoulders and head were on the ground and his legs were exposed in the air. Then they flogged the soles of his feet with the rubber hose.

He pleaded for them to stop. He begged them to just shoot him and get it over with. Instead, the rain of blows continued.

"When they finished," Jacobsen says, his voice choked with bitter tears, "one of the guards said, 'Relax. The boys were just having some fun.' "

This was punishment for the "coded message" he'd inserted into the July videotape. Thanks to the media's speculation, David Jacobsen had nearly been beaten to death.

As our debriefing evolves, it becomes clear to us once more that the guards are little more than armed thugs and that their own security is shockingly lax. Jacobsen tells us that not long after the September beating, the guards left a fully loaded AK-47 hanging on the wall next to his cell. After some serious introspection, he decided to try and snatch the weapon and shoot his way out of his cell. One night, he reached for it through the bars in his cell door. He pulled the rifle off the wall, but it was too big to fit through the bars. It took him the better part of an hour to get it hooked back onto the wall in its original position so the guards didn't know what he'd attempted. He was sure they would have killed him had they found out.

The JSOC rep asks Jacobsen how he was bound when transported. Jacobsen hops off the bed and tries to explain to us. Finally, when it's clear we're confused, he says, "Look, let me show you."

After scrambling for some props, we tie Jacobsen up on the bed. He guides us through the process, and while the FBI and CIA agents are busy binding him up, I frantically take notes. Suddenly, the door swings open and an air force psychiatrist walks in.

All of us freeze. I feel like my parents have just caught me drinking with my high school buddies in the basement. The air force shrink studies the scene, and as the absurdity of the moment sinks in, his jaw slowly unwinds.

Here we are with a hostage who has spent the last seventeen months in chains. What do we do to him on his first day of freedom? Tie him to a hospital bed.

The shrink doesn't say a word. He just shakes his head and closes the door. The tension breaks. Jacobsen starts to laugh, and pretty soon, we're all in stitches.

Later in the day, we throw a satellite map of Beirut down on a table in Jacobsen's lounge room. Together, the other agents and our freshly released hostage crawl across every feature of that map, searching for clues as to where the prison cells were hidden. Jacobsen's finger slides from one slum to another as he racks his memory for exterior details, but nothing comes.

His finger traces circles over a couple possible locations. We huddle closer, notebooks ready. If we can just get a location, Delta will be spun up and launched. We can get them out. I know we can. These guards are Mickey Mouse. They wouldn't last thirty seconds in a firefight with professionals.

"This looks familiar," Jacobsen says, squinting at the map. Our pens fly across our notebooks.

A knock at the door causes everyone to go silent. In walks an air force enlisted woman, who timidly approaches our group then withdraws something from her pocket. She stretches a hand out to Jacobsen and says, "Here are your glasses, Mr. Jacobsen."

"Thank you, miss," he replies. "I can't see a damn thing without these!"

All of us agents stare at one another with *What the hell?* looks on our faces. Then we burst out laughing again. We've just spent the better part of two hours looking at this map, which Jacobsen apparently couldn't see.

"Much better," he says with the glasses now perched on the bridge of his nose. "Now, where were we?"

We get back to work. But even with the glasses, Jacobsen cannot positively identify the current location of the hostages. It is not his fault. Though physical security is lax at times inside their makeshift prisons, Hezbollah has taken great care to ensure Jacobsen never saw anything outside that could tip us off.

We turn next to unfinished business. "Tell us about William Buckley."

"Buckley?" Jacobsen replies. "He died."

"Tell us how," I prompt.

Jacobsen takes a deep breath. Profound sadness creeps across his face as he launches into Buckley's story. "He was kept in solitary confinement. We rarely saw him. But we heard him. That was the hardest part. We could tell he was getting weaker."

Jacobsen goes into details. Buckley had been tortured repeatedly. He'd been interrogated thoroughly, probably by Imad Mugniyah himself. Jacobsen recognizes his mug shot when we flash it.

The Iranians surely had access to everything Mugniyah learned. This is as bad as we feared.

The beatings, torture, and interrogations, combined with the squalor of their captivity, demolished Buckley's immune system. At night, Jacobsen and the other hostages heard his phlegm-choked coughs. He began to hallucinate.

"We urged the guards to get him help," Jacobsen tells us. The guards seemed interested in getting him antibiotics, but they lacked a sense of urgency. One night in June 1985, Buckley's cries grew weaker and weaker, his coughing more labored and wet. Finally, he fell silent. The CIA's station chief succumbed to pneumonia, chained to a radiator in the slums of southern Beirut.

"I knew immediately he had died," Jacobsen continues. All eyes in the room are riveted on him. He sits on his hospital bed, and aside from his shaky voice, there's not another sound within earshot.

"An hour later, they came to get him. I heard feet shuffling and muffled voices. The guards were very upset."

Jacobsen's memory of that night hits him full force, and I watch as all the color drains from his face. "I can still hear it."

He stops, unable to finish. The FBI agent prompts him, "Hear what?"

Jacobsen's head falls forward. He studies the floor, his eyes shielded from ours. One hand goes to his face. He holds it over his eyes, then wipes away a tear. "Hear how they took him away."

He says those words so softly that we strain to catch them all.

"They dragged him past us. By his feet. Down the stairs. I heard his head thumping on every step." Jacobsen suddenly claps hard. "Thump." *Clap*. "Thump." *Clap*. "Thump." It is a slow and terrible cadence, and I wince every time his hands slap together. When he finishes, the silence leaves us shuddering. Buckley hadn't just died of neglect, he'd been defiled. Even in death, they had granted him no dignity.

I can't speak. Neither can the other agents. Nobody even tries. The minutes pass. Jacobsen stares at the floor, tears flowing freely now. The rest of us are so wrung out that I know we're done for the day. I stand up, put my hand on Jacobsen's shoulder, then leave the room. This will need to be reported back to Foggy Bottom, so I head for the temporary commo room. I turn left out of Jacobsen's room and walk to an intersection in the hallway. A quick jog to the right and through a door, and I'm in our communications hub—a hospital room with the beds removed.

Inside, I run into Robert Oakley, a career diplomat who is currently serving as the director of the State Department's Office of Terrorism. I'm surprised to see him here in Wiesbaden, but he greets me pleasantly enough.

I fill Oakley in on what we've just learned. He shakes his head angrily, then tells me to report back to D.C. Just as I reach for the STU-III, someone else walks into the room. I turn to see who it is and freeze, receiver in hand.

Standing in the doorway is Terry Waite.

What's he doing here? I thought he was in Beirut.

He takes a step into the room. He's a giant of a man, but his size is not imposing, thanks to his gentle demeanor. He greets us with an easy grace. Oakley and I nod and say hello. Waite walks up to me and hands me a slip of paper.

"I need to talk to Ollie. Can you dial this number for me?"

There's a connection between Oliver North and Terry Waite?

I look at the number. It is a direct White House line. I glance down at the STU-III and wonder what I should do next. Something doesn't smell right here. Why is Waite tied in with the NSC? Is Waite the administration's go-between with Hezbollah? I thought he was only working on behalf of the archbishop of Canterbury. I bring my eyes up and study Waite. He looks anxious and tense, like something's wrong. He's trying to cover that up with a low-key, matter-of-fact approach.

Wheels within wheels, that's how the Dark World works.

I dial the White House number. It rings twice before an NSC official answers it with a hurried "Hello."

I begin slowly. "Yes, this is Agent Burton in Wiesbaden."

He waits a beat before responding. "Go ahead, Burton."

"I have Terry Waite here with me, and he wants to talk to Ollie."

Another pause. The phone makes all those odd background electronic noises. Finally, I hear the NSC official say, "Ollie's en route from Beirut, but let me talk to Waite."

I hand the STU-III to Terry Waite. Oakley and I start to leave to give Waite some privacy, but he waves to us to stay. "What's going on?" he asks into the phone. Standing next to Waite, I can hear the man's voice on the other end but I can't hear what he's saying. Waite goes green. By the time he finishes the conversation, he looks like he's seasick. He thanks us and hurries from the room.

Oakley and I exchange *What just happened?* glances.

I pick up the STU-III's receiver. I still have to call the office and report what we know about Buckley's death. Gleason answers my call and listens silently as I relate Jacobsen's story. When I finish, my boss says, "Okay, Fred. Keep your head down. Bad things are happening."

"Okay. I will."

"When you get back, the FBI wants to talk to you."

The line goes dead, but Gleason's final words linger. Am I in some sort of trouble?

I return to Jacobsen's hospital room. The mood is somber, and everyone is fatigued. After a spell, it is clear that Jacobsen and the other agents are done in and we'll need to pick it up in the morning. A little small talk ensues before the group disperses for the evening. As we leave, one of the other agents takes me aside in the hall and asks, "Have you heard?"

"Have I heard what?"

"A paper in Beirut ran a story about an arms deal."

"Arms deal? Between who?"

"Us and Iran."

"What?"

"Yeah. We gave them antitank weapons. They gave us hostages."

"That can't be true."

The agent shakes his head. "The press is going crazy. I just heard that Ollie North and Robert McFarlane were in Iran in May."

Oh my God.

thirteen

By the time I return to Andrews Air Force Base, a media tempest has engulfed Washington. Every hour, more details of the secret negotiations between the United States and Iran are revealed on the news. The sordid mess grows steadily worse. The Iranians confirm the negotiations publicly. Locked in a bloody World War I–style conflict with Iraq, the Iranians are desperate for modern weapons that can break the frontline stalemate. They don't seem to realize how devastating these revelations are in the West.

We made a deal with the devil. Terry Waite was just the cover for the real negotiations, ones that treated each hostage as capital that the Iranians and Hezbollah could use to buy TOW missiles. No wonder Hezbollah grabbed three more Americans in September and October. They weren't bargaining chips at all. They were currency.

My stomach is twisted in knots. I haven't slept. We bargained with the enemy. There are few countries the American people despise more than Iran. The embassy hostage crisis six years ago filled our nation with a collective hate for Iran that was only inflamed by Beirut I and II and the barracks bombing. Dead marines, stolen honor, our prestige in tatters. That's what Iran has done to us. And now we've been caught selling them missiles that will help sustain their war effort. There's talk of a congressional investigation. Already, the FBI has unleashed its hounds. Everyone's scrambling to save their own skins. I wonder if my career will end before it really begins. Six months on the job, and I'm already on the edge of the storm. Was it worth it to get the hostages out? Do the ends justify the means here? I don't know. I struggle with this all afternoon as I review the paperwork that had piled up while I was gone.

Neither Father Jenco nor David Jacobsen had any idea why they were released until the story broke on the major networks. I can't even imagine Father Jenco's reaction. He must be horrified that his life was traded for weapons that surely will kill countless Iraqi soldiers.

Ignorance of the drama playing out over my head may save me. I don't know anything. I'll have nothing to offer when I'm interviewed. All I can do is tell them what I know. And what I know is nothing—nothing beyond Terry Waite's suspicious phone call from the commo room in Wiesbaden.

Waite must be reeling as well. He's been negotiating with his contacts in good faith. Now it turns out that Ollie was using him as nothing but legitimate cover. He's been used, and his reputation has taken a huge hit. Before I left Wiesbaden, I heard he was going to return to Beirut and try to repair the damage to his reputation. I hope he doesn't do that. Hezbollah shows little mercy.

I get home well after midnight. I come through the door of our townhouse feeling dispirited and exhausted. Sharon wakes up and greets me. "I know you were in Germany," she tells me. "I saw you on CNN when that hostage was released."

I wish I could tell her everything. I can tell her nothing. Instead, I must keep my silence and face the FBI in the morning.

Sharon soon falls back asleep. I lay in bed, my mind running through all the things that have happened. Periodically, it flits back to the hospital room, and I see Jacobsen, head down, clapping his hands as he described Buckley's head smacking on the steps outside their apartment prison.

"Thump." *Clap.* "Thump." *Clap.* "Thump." It was a fate no patriot like Buckley should have faced. If only we'd been able to get to them. If only we'd been able to find where Hezbollah had them stashed. *If only . . .*

And what of Hezbollah? What sort of game is Mugniyah playing? All along, his public demands have focused on the Dawa 17. Hezbollah's hostages would be freed when the Kuwaitis released Mugniyah's terrorist brother-in-law and his cell. Was that just a cover, too? Was it always about weapons?

Nothing is ever as it appears. Washington is seething right now, and it is axiomatic that D.C. will eat its own in the flame-fest that is sure to follow in the weeks to come.

I just hope I don't end up as collateral damage.

Morning comes. Tyler Beauregard and I go for our predawn run. It is cold and dark on the street, and my beautiful dog senses my foul mood. She stays close and casts anxious looks my way. She knows something is dreadfully wrong. She doesn't know what to do but reveals her loyalty to me by refusing to budge from my side. That makes me wonder if true loyalty can really exist outside a man's relationship with his dog.

A quick shower back at our townhouse and I'm ready to face whatever is to come. I strap my Smith & Wesson into its shoulder holster, throw my coat over one shoulder, and head for my Jetta.

I reach the office before six. Three hours later, the FBI comes calling. I head for a conference room, where an agent greets me with a perfunctory "Hello." And then the grilling begins. It is obvious from the outset that I don't know anything about the negotiations. The agent is still thorough. He goes through a list of questions, almost none of which I can answer. I was never in the loop. This time, it looks like my ignorance will save me.

The interview reveals the depth of the machinations at work. A witch hunt is afoot. People will go to jail for this. The search for scape-goats has begun.

By lunchtime, I'm back behind the big blue door. Gleason looks burnt out. Mullen is nowhere to be seen. He's probably on assignment somewhere. I'm shaky after the grilling. I try to get back to work, but my mind refuses to focus.

The whole deal has the smell of good intentions gone awry. I heard a rumor on the flight home that President Reagan met with Father Jenco's brother shortly after Hezbollah grabbed the priest. Jenco's sibling demanded to know what the president was doing to get his brother out of captivity. Reagan tried to assure him that the government was doing everything possible. Jenco's brother refused to relent; he was like a terrier and he shattered Reagan's placid façade. When the meeting ended, Reagan told his staff to do whatever it took to get the hostages out.

That is a dangerously broad license for a president to issue, no matter how good his intentions. Now we've been embarrassed, and all the globe has born witness to our humiliation. Year after year, we have piously proclaimed that we will not negotiate with terrorists. We've totally undermined our international position on that front, and no doubt it will take years to rebuild our credibility.

Still, Ben Weir, Father Jenco, and David Jacobsen are free men because we funneled arms to a rogue nation.

I am a man who lives by a strict code. Life until now has been black and white, right and wrong. There's no wiggle room. You're either acting honorably or you're not. Where does swapping arms for hostages fit into this equation?

I don't know. Or maybe I do know, but don't want to face it. My country has made a dreadful mistake. The consequences are sure to be sharp and painful.

As November continues, the crisis spirals into a full-blown scandal. President Reagan addresses the nation and admits we did try to improve relations with Iran by selling them weapons. He denies we got Weir, Jenco, and Jacobsen in return. The press continues digging. More revelations emerge. The Israelis transferred the initial shipments. More than just TOW missiles went to Iran; we also sent them Hawk antiaircraft systems and were negotiating about spare parts for their F-14A Tomcat fleet. They purchased those F-14s in the seventies just before the shah fell.

There is a deeper, darker side to Irangate, as the media is now calling it. The Iranians not only paid for their weapons with our three American citizens, they also forked over millions of dollars in cash. Where did that money go? Some media outlets reported that thirty million dollars is missing, and Oliver North's fingers are all over the disappearance.

Just before Thanksgiving, Oliver North and his secretary, a blonde named Fawn Hall, get caught shredding documents. Four days later, Attorney General Edwin Meese releases the truth: The money the Iranians paid us was funneled to the Nicaraguan contras. Oliver North was in charge of that operation. Later that day, he is fired from the NSC. His boss, Admiral John Poindexter, resigns. It looks like both will face criminal charges for what they have done. The disaster is complete: arms for hostages for cash funneled to the contras via the NSC. It is a media feeding frenzy extraordinaire.

Late that afternoon, I close the open files on my desk and stuff them into my safe. I'm done for the day. I've got to get away from this craziness before it eats me alive. A half hour later, I'm on the Brandt Place porch, drinking coffee with Fred Davis. I can't tell him what's going on, but I suspect he knows.

"I saw you on CNN the other night," he tells me.

"Yeah, so did my wife." I take a sip from my cup of joe and start thinking of ways to change the subject.

"Didn't know you were in Germany."

I nod my head. "Neither did I until I got off the plane."

We both laugh. I steer the conversation in a different direction. "I heard there was another Bradford Bishop sighting in Europe."

Interest flares in Fred's eyes. "Really?"

"Yeah. Unconfirmed though."

"He gets around."

"That he does." I finish my coffee, place the cup on the table between us, and lean back in my chair.

"What do you think? Is he still alive?"

Fred's mutt comes over and sits next to his legs, waiting for some attention. Absently, he reaches over and strokes the dog's head and ears. "I don't know. I always kind of thought he committed suicide in that national park."

Growing up in Bethesda, Bradford Bishop was the Lizzie Borden of our generation. While we were still kids, Bishop moved into our neighborhood with his wife, mother, and three boys. The oldest was our age. Bishop worked for the State Department as an assistant director in the special activities and commercial treaties office. He was a quiet man, one who by all reports was thoroughly henpecked by his wife and mother. For years, they had ganged up on him, deriding his achievements and telling him what a failure he was as a human being.

One day in 1976, after getting passed over for a promotion, he came home and murdered his entire family with a ball-peen hammer. He killed his wife first, then his mother when she came back into the house after walking the family dog. Then he killed his boys, one at a time, while they slept in their beds.

That night, he gathered the bodies in the family station wagon and took off. He drove to North Carolina and burned them in the woods. It was three weeks before anyone discovered the family was gone.

The Bethesda–Chevy Chase Rescue Squad responded to the house once a neighbor and police officer discovered blood on the front steps. Inside the house, blood was everywhere—in the living room, on the walls, the bedrooms, and the beds. Sitting around the station house on the weekends, the old-timers would tell us stories of that crime scene. It was a chamber of horrors. One of the boys' bedrooms was drenched in blood from floor to ceiling.

By the time the bodies in North Carolina were linked to the crime scene in our neighborhood, Bishop was long gone. The station wagon later turned up at a Great Smoky Mountains National Park campground, but there was no sign of Bishop. The station wagon was covered in dried blood. Some of it had pooled and congealed in the spare-tire well.

For years, on slow nights at the station house, we would speculate on what had become of Bradford Bishop, the henpecked bureaucrat turned mass murderer. It led to endless discussions on his whereabouts.

I reach forward and scratch the mutt's ears. He growls happily and tilts his head my way. I'm glad for this diversion. I'm glad to be thinking about anything other than the hostages and North, and the unfolding national embarrassment that has exposed so much of the Dark World to media scrutiny.

"Well, they never found any evidence that he committed suicide," I offer. We've been over this ground many times before. It is comfortable and it sets me at ease, even if the subject is a gruesome one.

"True, but none of the sightings have ever really been confirmed."

Being a diplomat, Bishop knew how to travel incognito. I think he's stayed off the grid all these years by moving frequently and using false identities.

"Well, remember a friend of his spotted him in Sweden back in '78."

Fred shakes his head and says, "Tentative at best, just like the one in Italy when that other DOS guy said he saw him in a bathroom."

We discuss the other possibilities. Some say he defected to the Soviet Union. There's no evidence of that, and he's never surfaced in Russia. I don't buy it. More than likely, he's living the life of a fugitive, staying one step ahead of the authorities with frequent moves and ID changes.

"Well, someday I'll look into that case, if I ever get any authority," I tell Fred.

He looks at me for a moment and says, "Yeah. That one and that other one. You know? Where that Israeli was whacked right in his front yard. What was his name again?"

"Alon. Yosef Alon."

"That's right. Alon. Man, Fred, you have a memory for these things."

I guffaw. "Yeah, but is it a blessing or a curse?"

"Maybe just your purpose."

The sudden sincerity leaves me silent. I'm not sure how to answer that.

"The old crew responded to Alon's murder, too."

"That's right." The rescue squad was right on the scene. Alon had been killed only a few blocks from the house I grew up in. He'd been coming home from work that night—he'd been assigned to the Israeli Embassy as an air and naval attaché—when a car rolled up behind him. As he stood in his front yard, gunmen in the car opened fire on him. Five shots hit him. By the time the rescue squad's old rig arrived on the scene, it was too late. He died in our neighborhood, victim of a professional hit. Media speculation hinted that he'd been assassinated in retaliation for the death of an Arab militant in Paris.

None of us believed that, especially after the killing was so quickly swept under the rug. It has always bothered me, and someday I want to reopen that old case.

Fred Davis gets to his feet and gives me a smile. "When you do get to the bottom of that one, please let me know, okay?"

"You know I will."

We wrap things up for the night. I want to tell Fred how grateful I am for this diversion. I just don't know how. Instead, all I manage to do is say good-bye.

Thanksgiving comes and goes. Christmas approaches. The country has been rocked to the core by the Iran-contra revelation. President Reagan's popularity is plummeting. A congressional commission, led by John Tower, is picking through the wreckage, trying to figure out who knew what and when. The special prosecutors are lining up. This one is sure to get ugly.

And the main problem remains. Hezbollah still holds five Americans hostage. We must find a way to get them out—that is, if Mugniyah doesn't decide to quit the game entirely and summarily execute his captives. Given what's happening, I wouldn't put it past him.

January proves me wrong.

fourteen

February 1987
Wiesbaden, Germany

Terry Waite has vanished. Against all advice, he returned to Beirut last month to try and salvage something of his honor—and to assure his own network in the city that he had nothing to do with the hostage-for-arms dealings. Last seen on January 20, Waite was en route to a meeting with his Hezbollah contacts.

I shudder to think what's happened to him. Either he's dead and buried in a shallow grave in the Bekáa Valley, or his good intentions earned him a shackle and a slumside prison cell.

I'd like to be surprised by this development, but I can't be, not after what's happened in the past year. I feel myself growing cynical, a state of mind that is required if you intend to survive long in the Dark World. And I intend to survive. I intend to thrive. I have things to do. Wrongs to right. Mass murderers to catch.

Terry Waite is only one new disappearance in Beirut. All month long, Hezbollah has declared open season on Westerners in the city. The situation is so out of hand that the American government issued a flat ultimatum to its own citizens: Get out of Lebanon, we can't protect you. And, if you get kidnapped, you're on your own. After Iran-contra, there's no way the Reagan administration can negotiate with terrorists now. Exactly why Hezbollah's gone on an abduction spree is anyone's guess, but from the American perspective it doesn't make much sense. The time when our citizens were used as currency and bargaining chips is over. The Tower Commission and the special prosecutors have seen to that.

The universities and their apparently oblivious staff of ivory tower types are the easiest hunting ground for Hezbollah snatch squads. In one haul on January 24, they grabbed three professors from American University in Beirut. That operation also netted Hezbollah an Indian academic. He must be lonely among all the Westerners.

Another Frenchman has been taken as well. He disappeared on January 13, just before things got ugly with the West Germans. That's one reason why I'm here, back in Wiesbaden. The Germans are now caught up in the hostage crisis, too.

Last month, the West Germans arrested Muhammad Ali Hamadi, a Shiite leader and terrorist who worked with Imad Mugniyah to plan the TWA Flight 847 hijacking. In apparent retaliation for his arrest, the so-called Strugglers for Freedom bagged two West Germans in Beirut. Rudoph Cordes and Alfred Schmidt are now prisoners of Hezbollah. The Strugglers for Freedom is just another front name for Iran's puppet terror organization in Lebanon.

Which brings me to this snowy German night in February. I'm alone on a street within the U.S. Air Force base at Wiesbaden. The weather has driven most folks indoors. I pad along atop the freshly fallen snow, pulling my Barbour Beaufort's collar tight to my neck to ward off the cold. The snow is quite lovely tonight. It is still pure white, untrampled by passing cars and people.

The air force base is one of those places that has come to symbolize the enduring American occupation of West Germany. Thousands of U.S. airmen and aviators are stationed here at this ex-Luftwaffe airfield, and on weekends they flood into town to fill the beer halls with American voices. The locals have come to accept, if not enjoy, the company of their conquerors turned allies.

Tonight, I have a meeting in one of the local beer halls. It is a small place and poorly lit, but the food is supposed to be excellent and the beer plentiful and cheap. That makes it a perfect spot for two spooks to talk.

I make my way to the beer hall, walking past an enormous Luftwaffe eagle painted on the side of a building. Why nobody has bothered to paint over that symbol of Germany's darkest age is puzzling. The paint is flecked in places, but from a distance, it still looks almost fresh, as if this is 1943 and the local *Nachtjäger Geschwader* was just waiting to scramble off the runway and intercept an incoming British bombing raid. A different age, a different war. Who knew that the victory in 1945 would lay the foundations for the chaos we face today: a cold war between superpowers overlayed atop a growing struggle between the Christian world and radical Islam?

I reach the beer hall's door and plunge inside. The place is noisy, with lots of small groups of airmen clustered around tables. Toward the back, in a shadowy corner, I see my contact. He's about my age, twenty-eight, and looks totally out of place among the buzz-cut military types taking up the other tables. His blond hair is long and bushy. He sports a droopy, poorly groomed mustache. He wears a brown corduroy jacket with a paisley tie that does not match his shirt. He looks like a cross between Frank Serpico and Sergeant Schultz.

I slip into the chair across from him and say, "Good evening."

"Good evening," comes the reply. His voice is gravelly, but his English is so good I can hardly detect an accent.

I notice he has a leather-bound folder sitting on the table in front of him. I wonder what's inside. He notices me looking at it. Unconsciously, he puts one arm protectively across the folder.

"Thank you for meeting with me, Agent Burton."

"We face the same enemy. We're allies. It is the least I can do."

"Allies, yes," the German says, "unlike the French." He leans back in his chair and awaits my reaction. He is searching for some common ground here.

I can't help but agree with him. "They chart their own course."

"And it has bitten them in their arrogant ass. Again."

That's true. In September, a radical group called the Lebanese Armed Revolutionary Faction launched a series of five bombings in Paris that killed or wounded almost two hundred people. Instead of retaliating, we think the French government negotiated some sort of truce with LARF.

"Do you think they will find the courage to convict Abdallah?" the German asks me.

"I hope so. He killed two diplomats." Georges Abdallah is the heart and soul of LARF. He was caught and sentenced by a French court to four years in prison for weapons and explosives charges. In just a few days, the French will put him on trial for the murder of Lieutenant Colonel Charles Ray, the American military attaché in Paris, and an Israeli diplomat. Both were gunned down in 1982 by Abdallah and his men. The bombings in Paris coincided with the news that Abdallah would stand trial for murder.

"I will tell you something about that," the German begins. He leans forward across the table and starts to say something in a very low voice.

"Hamadi has been talking," he says. The news is tantalizing. I find myself on the edge of my chair.

"He and his brothers all have senior positions in Hezbollah. His brother Abdul Hadi is the chief of security."

"Are you sure?"

"Yes. He's also told us that Hezbollah's behind the Paris bombings. Their agents cooperated with some Iranians working out of the embassy in Paris."

This will be news to Foggy Bottom. The German has given me a nugget. Two months after the bombings, the French released three hundred million dollars of a billion-dollar loan to Iran that had been frozen. Shortly after that, three French hostages were released in Beirut. The French have their own contacts with Hezbollah. But they overpaid for their people, at least if our own thirty-million-dollar deal is any indication.

Every nation says they don't negotiate with terrorists. That's just a farce.

I think this news over. "We have all been affected by Hezbollah."

"That is true. It is too bad that your country failed to kill Fadlallah."

I'm caught off guard by that comment. He's referring to the 1985 bombing of Sheikh Fadlallah's motorcade in Beirut. The blast killed about eighty civilians but failed to take out the spiritual head and founder of Hezbollah. He survived, and accusations that the CIA was behind the attempted hit have floated around the Dark World ever since.

I make no reply. We sit in awkward silence for a minute until the waitress shows up with our food and drink. The German clutches the pitcher of beer and pours me a frothy glass. Then he fills his own glass and offers a perfunctory toast. We clink glasses and set to work on our schnitzel.

Through a full mouth, the German changes the subject. "We want our people in Beirut back. But we are constrained by our own laws."

I want to say, "So are we." But after Iran-contra, such a comment has no credibility. Instead, I stick another forkful of schnitzel in my mouth and avert my eyes.

"Sometimes I wish we could handle this like the Soviets did."

I swallow and smile ruefully. "If only."

In 1985, four Soviet diplomats were kidnapped in Lebanon. Dark World gossip held that the Soviets responded by tracking down the families of the abductors and kidnapping them in retaliation. Then they started sending Hezbollah body parts—fingers mainly. Whether this was true or not, I don't know. The fact is one of the diplomats turned up dead, but the rest were released in a matter of weeks. It certainly didn't hurt the KGB's hard-core reputation for playing dirty.

I take a long pull from the glass he's poured for me. The beer is a delicious and rare indulgence for me. Since seeing how the pressure-cooker atmosphere affects my fellow agents at the DSS, I've been very careful. The fact is, we are agents first, family men second. The DSS demands that; it is a sacrifice too many fail to understand until they're already caught up in the Dark World. By then, it is too late.

I ask, "Anything new on the La Belle bombing?"

The German polishes off his mug of beer and reaches for the pitcher. "No. Nothing except that we think the Stasi was involved."

This is news to me. "How?"

"They supplied intelligence to the Libyans. They might have had a hand in the preoperational target surveillance, too. Maybe even in the target selection."

The East German secret police helped kill American servicemen. The revelation drives home a key point about the Dark World: Justice is ever elusive. The East German agents involved in La Belle will get away, just like the Libyan hit teams that tried to kill Calkins and Pollick. After almost a year in this business, it is hard not to feel resigned about this. It's just the way things work.

Finally, just as I feel my belt constricting my stomach, we scour the last morsels off our plates and sit back, stuffed and satisfied by the wonderful meal. The German hands me the leather-bound folder.

"These are the men we want. Some we have names for, others we don't. Would you show them to the hostages who have come out? Perhaps they might recognize some of them."

I open the book and see a page full of mug shots. The very first one is Imad Mugniyah.

I look the spook right in the eye. "Of course I will."

Noticing my reaction, he asks, "You know that man?"

"Yes. Mugniyah." I spit his name like a curse.

"He is top on our list."

"On ours, too," I say.

"Why do you think the French let him go last year?" the German asks me. This is true. The French actually caught Mugniyah, but after we requested that they hold him, they let him go. They set free the mastermind behind the deaths of 241 marines. That same operation killed 58 French paratroopers. Mugniyah walked and justice was betrayed. Those in power deemed politics more prudent.

What about his victims? Who will speak for them?

The Italians did the same thing with Abu Nidal in 1985. A U.S. Air Force officer actually chased Nidal's flight halfway across the Med, trying to get permission to divert it to an American base. He never got it, and Nidal escaped—again. If the West could ever get serious about Islamic terrorism, we'd be able to stop it. Right now, we all have divergent interests in the Middle East.

"They play their own game."

"Yes. Yes, they do," the German says as he slaps a few marks onto the table to cover the meal. "I hope you get him."

"I hope we get him, too."

Twenty minutes and a walk through the snow later, I'm back in my hotel room. I start to pack my things, as I have another C-141 to catch later tonight. I reach for my briefcase and pop it open, intending to put a few things into it.

The small black Italian moleskin journal I recently purchased sits inside. It catches my eye, and I stare at it for a long moment as an idea hits me. I reach down and withdraw the journal. It feels smooth and cold to my touch.

This will be my legacy. I got into this business because I wanted to make a difference in the world. I wanted to help make it a safer place for Americans. For anyone, really, who respects the rule of law. Someday, if Sharon and I ever have children, I will be able to open this journal and show them what I have accomplished for them. The world they will inherit will be minus these blights. At least, that is my goal.

And blight number one is Imad Mugniyah.

I move to the small, hotel-room desk and sit down. I open the journal and stare at its empty pages. Right now, it is a blank slate, just like my career. From my shirt pocket, I produce my black Parker rollerball pen. The tip hovers over the virgin paper. It is time to commit.

With great care, I begin to write.

1. The Fox.

Mugniyah, Imad Fayez.

Imad Mugniyah is believed to have been born in Lebanon in 1962 to a prominent Shiite cleric. A member of Hezbollah, Mugniyah has been linked to nearly every major terrorist operation the group has executed; however, his exact role within the group is unclear. Mugniyah has variously been reported to be Hezbollah's chief of operations, security chief, director of intelligence, chief of international operations, and the overall commander of Hezbollah's armed wing. He also allegedly possesses close links with the Iranian Revolutionary Guard Corps and Iranian intelligence, as he appears to act as a bridge between Hezbollah and the Iranian government.

He has proven extremely elusive because of his sound operational security and reliance on individuals he explicitly trusts. Mugniyah's whereabouts are unknown.

Mugniyah is the first. There will be others. Before I leave the Dark World, I will do whatever I can to see each name crossed off this list. Justice will be served and the victims will have peace.

PART II: THE VETERAN

fifteen

Not long after my return to Foggy Bottom, Mr. Dittmer calls up the CT office as reinforcements for the protective security details in New York. As if chasing terrorists and trying to find hostages isn't enough for us, now we've got to pull dignitary duty as well.

Actually, it turns out to be kind of fun. We set up shop in a midtown hotel and take turns racing around Manhattan in our Ford Crown Victorias and Jeep Wagoneers, covering convoys of foreign diplomats who've come for the UN General Assembly meetings. We carry Uzis, get to use our earpieces, and hassle irritable New Yorkers as we weave around traffic jams. In the past few days, I can't even tell you how many times we've received the finger from some expletive-spewing Manhattan driver.

When we protect motorcades, we run with a lead car and a trail car, five agents to a Jeep, four to a Crown Vic. The agent riding in the front passenger seat of the lead car scans the road ahead. Both he and his driver carry Smith & Wesson Model 19 revolvers, tucked away in shoulder holsters for easy access. We've learned not to wear hip holsters when pulling this sort of duty. Between the confined spaces and the seat belt, it takes too long to draw our hand cannons that way.

In the backseats, two agents cover the sides with Uzis and shotguns. They keep their windows rolled down and their weapons hidden by their doors so average citizens cannot see them. That way, if a gunfight erupts, they'll be ready to engage in a split second.

The Jeeps also have a tail stinger. Where most Americans would put groceries in their Wagoneers, we have an extra jump seat. The fifth agent is stationed there, Uzi at the ready, covering the rear.

The lead car, usually a Crown Vic, is the motorcade equivalent of a fullback. It runs interference for the rest of the formation, its driver prepared to swing out left or right and block any incoming vehicular threat. The follow car, usually one of the Jeeps, needs to be heavy and powerful. It is our blunt defensive instrument in case the motorcade comes under serious attack. The driver's job is to deflect any incoming threats, ramming them if necessary.

Foggy Bottom assigns me to protect Giulio Andreotti, Italy's foreign minister. We worked up a profile on him prior to his arrival and discovered some disconcerting facts about the guy. Andreotti is one of the doyens of the post–World War II Italian democracy, which means he's been a power broker and cabinet member in some capacity in dozens of governments since the 1950s. In his thirty-plus-year career, he's made plenty of enemies and seems to have had the temerity to off a few.

For the past year, there has been increasing speculation that Andreotti had a hand in murdering Michele "the Shark" Sindona, an Italian banker and heroin trafficker. Somebody poisoned Sindona's coffee while he was serving a life term in prison for murdering a lawyer.

Giulio Andreotti apparently doesn't like journalists any more than Mob bankers. In 1979, a reporter named Carmine "Mino" Pecorelli started investigating Andreotti's Mafia connections. For his efforts, he was assassinated by a hit team in Rome. Exactly who was responsible has never been made clear, but there seems to have been some involvement from a criminal right-wing syndicate known as the Branda della Magliana.

What does this all mean—besides the fact that Italian politics are obviously a lot more interesting than ours? Well, for those who have to guard him, it means potential trouble. Andreotti is a big target, and lots of irate Italians want him gone. He apparently doesn't mind playing hardball in return, which only made his enemies list grow. Guarding this guy could be the most dangerous thing I do as a DSS agent.

I spend a sleepless night in my midtown hotel room, reading and rereading the file my fellow agents have worked up on Andreotti. He's a powerful man with a long reach, and many, many friends in the United States—not to mention a few enemies here. We'll have to take special precautions wherever we go with him. Before dawn, I write down a laundry list of extra security procedures we'll need. Some will require the help of the New York Police Department.

The next day, I begin my shift with the Italian foreign minister. He's in town for the UN General Assembly meeting, but he also has some associates he needs to meet. He tells us he wants to dine at a swanky restaurant in Little Italy. Fine. We send over an advance agent to conduct a site recon and check the place out.

The advance agent reaches the restaurant, only to find it closed. The entire street is deserted and no cars are parked anywhere on the block around the eatery. Something does not seem right.

I decide we need to do an EOD sweep. These are the NYPD bomb squad guys—EOD stands for Explosive Ordnance Disposal. I've had them on call all day for just such a scenario. We launch them, but while they're en route, the advance agent makes contact with the restaurant's owner. He's an Italian American with a thick accent and a bad disposition. He tells our agent on the scene that there's nothing to worry about, he has ensured that his restaurant is secure. He tells our agent that everything's already been taken care of in preparation for the foreign minister's arrival.

We can't trust that.

We send in the EOD team as soon as they arrive. As they check for bombs, we scour the place for weapons. Nothing. The place is clean.

Meanwhile, I climb behind the wheel of one of our black Crown Victorias. I'll have the lead car for this motorcade. Ahead of my ride is an unmarked NYPD intel car with four plainclothes detectives inside. Their job is to scout the road ahead, finding the best route to our destination.

We hit Little Italy right on schedule. As soon as we reach the restaurant's general neighborhood, we encounter hardly a single moving vehicle. All the shops are closed. Nobody is on the sidewalks. Only a few parked cars line the streets.

We press on as my eyes roam from the street ahead to the buildings on either side of the road. I scan the doorways, windows, and balconies, praying I won't see an assassin or a sniper team. Every nerve is jangling. I feel raw and adrenaline-rushed. The Smith & Wesson's weight against my side feels reassuring. Of course, if I end up having to use it, it'll mean we're in last-stand mode. The driver's job is to drive, not shoot. He only pulls his piece as a last resort.

I wonder if this is how Custer felt riding into that box canyon in Montana. Instead of Sioux warriors, we're driving headlong into a man-made canyon of shops and apartments, surrounded by Italians. Though I can't see anyone, I sense we're being watched. There are eyes out there in the night, tracking our every move.

I key my radio and call our advance agent. "Five minutes out."

The agent replies, "Roger. Site clear. We'll meet you curbside."

We make a final turn and reach our destination. Limousines are parallel parked all up and down the avenue. I notice some of the limos have New Jersey plates. It looks like we're going to a millionaires' club meeting.

Andreotti's limo finds a parking space and slips into it. We burst out of our rigs and quickly prepare for the foreign minister's arrival. Near the entrance to the restaurant, I spot several oversized men. Hired muscle. They all look like Luca Brasi on steroids.

Andreotti slips from the rear of the limo and hits the curb. We escort him into the restaurant. The place is empty, save for a single rectangular table in the back occupied by a dozen or so men. Baskets of bread sit on the starched white linen tablecloth between bottles of Chianti. At the head of the table sits an elderly gentleman in dapper attire, whom the others treat with deference. He smiles. They smile. He frowns. They frown. They're speaking Italian, which I can't understand. I take a long look at the old man, trying not to be too obvious about it. I recognize him from somewhere, but I can't place his name.

As the foreign minister steps to the table, the men welcome him with obvious affection and friendship. He sits down with them and is soon immersed in the flow of the conversation. I stand nearby, keeping my head on a swivel until a waiter comes over and asks me to follow him. He leads me to a table prepared for us out in front of the restaurant. We'll be dining outside while business is conducted within. He gestures for me to have a seat.

I take it. I'm sitting only a few feet from the limo, an interesting place to have dinner. Glancing up the street, I see a van parked at the end of the next block. There's no mistaking it: It's an FBI vehicle. I've seen them in the Bureau's motorpools in New York and in D.C.

I wonder how many FBI special surveillance groups (SSGs) are out there in the evening, watching every move we're making. I'm probably being filmed right now by one, quite possibly from that van. The FBI's just doing their job—keeping an eye on the Mafia. But I'm doing mine—guarding a Mob don. Feds spying on feds. What would the taxpayers say?

This would be a perfect setting for a hit. There are some very powerful people in the room tonight who have made their share of enemies over the years, just like Andreotti. The threats are out there. And with all these figures in one place, under one roof, it would be an assassin's dream. They could scrub out some key members of New York's underworld in one job and nail the foreign minister as extra credit.

If I have to die in the line of duty, so be it. But I'd just as soon not die protecting La Cosa Nostra.

From my vantage point up front, I keep tabs on everything out on the street. For whatever reason, hardly a soul appears on either sidewalk. The place is like a ghost town. Well, that just gives the FBI cameras an unobstructed view of us DSS agents. What a goat rope. Visiting dignitaries and diplomats require protection. That's the DSS's job. What I didn't count on was this: What if we are hosting a criminal in a suit? We guard them anyway, just like tonight. Their diplomatic status gives them that right, just like if Fidel Castro came to town—or Mikhail Gorbachev. We guard our enemies as zealously as our friends to ensure they do not suffer harm while visiting our nation.

I feel slightly sick inside. When the moment of truth came, would I throw myself in front of the foreign minister to save him from an assassin's bullet? That is my duty. I would have no other choice.

I wouldn't do it for Andreotti. No, from what I've seen here tonight, the Mob ties are real. But I would do it for the service—for the DSS. Failing to do our duty would dishonor our badge and forever smear our hard-won stellar reputation. If it came to that, it would be black and white after all. I'd do whatever I had to in order to protect the integrity of my fellow agents. That would be worth the bullet.

Before long, the waiter brings us food—lots and lots of food.

The meal is an extended affair with plenty of courses. We dig in.

Soon we're all stuffed. The entire scene could have been lifted straight from a Mario Puzo novel.

I turn to one of the NYPD detectives, who is sitting next to me. "This could be an outtake from *The Godfather*."

The detective grunts, "Let's hope not. We're in for a shit storm if that's the case."

True. These sorts of meetings never end well in Mob films. Somebody always ends up feeding the fishes.

Finally, the meeting breaks up. I really wish I spoke Italian. I'm sure I would have heard plenty of things that could be used to indict everyone in the room. Or maybe not. They're probably not that careless; after all, feds are feds, even when they're watching one another.

Atlantic City is next on the agenda. The foreign minister is scheduled to fly over to the Trump Castle Casino. Andreotti climbs back into his limo. We scramble for our faux-wood-sided Wagoneer and jet-black Crown Vic. As we speed out of the neighborhood, I glance in the rearview mirror. Only blocks behind us, the scene takes on an altogether different character. Cars fill the street again. People suddenly appear on the sidewalk. Lights go on and businesses are opened. Life in Little Italy returns to normal.

How does an entire community get word to lie low? That's one dialed-in neighborhood.

We stop at a midtown helicopter port. Waiting for us is Donald Trump's personal Sikorsky Sea King. One of the other agents on this detail leans into me and whispers, "It used to serve as Marine One. That helicopter flew presidents around."

I climb aboard, along with Andreotti's personal bodyguard. With a pilot and copilot, there will only be five of us on this flight. I move to the back of the helicopter and marvel at its luxuries. The seats are leather, and each one has a telephone. A wet bar dominates one corner. I'm suddenly in a toy right out of *Lifestyles of the Rich and Famous*. I feel underdressed. I should have brought a larger gun.

With Andreotti aboard, the helicopter lifts off into the New York evening. The pilots take us on a skyscraper-hopping tour of downtown Manhattan. The skyline's beauty leaves me breathless as we weave in and out of the city's major landmarks. We make a complete 360 around the World Trade Center from about fiftieth-floor level. I have to strain to look up and see the top of those awesome silver monoliths. There is nothing more impressive than the Twin Towers on a clear night. They become bright beacons of power, symbols of American economic might. It is hard not to feel a swell of pride as the pilots give our Italian guest an aerial tour of the greatest city on the planet.

When we turn for the Jersey shore, I use that newest of modern conveniences—a cellular phone—to call our detail in Atlantic City. They're ready and waiting for the foreign minister's arrival.

We touch down at Trump Castle's helipad. Our agents pick up Andreotti as soon as he descends from the Sikorsky. He leads them down to the casino floor, where he spends the rest of the night gambling.

I spend the rest of my night in the casino's ultramodern security center. Trump's chief of security is a knowledgeable and intelligent man, and he walks me through all the safeguards within the facility. It is the most sophisticated setup I've ever seen. There are an impressive number of cameras, and the display terminals make the security center look like a miniature version of NORAD's headquarters in Cheyenne Mountain. Everyone and everything is under constant surveillance. If you are inside Trump's casino, Big Brother is always watching.

"How much cash do you move out of here?" I ask the security chief.

"You mean a night? 'Bout a million."

I do the math. No wonder Trump can afford to buy Marine One.

"Ever seen that old Sinatra film, what was it…?"

"*Ocean's Eleven?*"

"Yeah, that's the one."

"Never happen here."

"How can you be sure?"

The security chief waves a hand at all the techno-gadgets in the room. "They didn't have all this in 1960."

Point taken.

Long after midnight, Andreotti decides it is time to get some sleep. I've been too busy to see how he made out, but he seems in perky spirits when we meet him back at the Sikorsky on the rooftop helipad. We climb aboard and fly back to midtown Manhattan.

The next morning, we set up the motorcade out in front of his hotel and await his arrival. He comes down, looking fresh in a new suit and coiffed hair. We speed off out of the city, the NYPD intel car on point again. This time, we spend the day at Belmont Park, watching the races. The foreign minister meets a few friends, and they pass the day betting on the ponies and drinking Belmont Breezes.

On the way home, my cellular phone rings.

"Burton."

"Fred, we need you back at Foggy Bottom," says Steve Gleason.

"Okay, but at the moment I'm on my way back to Manhattan with the foreign minister," I report.

"Get back to D.C. tonight. Ahmed's coming in."

Finally. A well-laid trap we've been preparing for months is about to be sprung. I hit the gas pedal and the Crown Vic surges forward. I'm anxious to get back to midtown so I can catch a bird out of the Big Apple. I've got a date with a terrorist.

sixteen

MICE

Back at Foggy Bottom I sign for a black Ford sedan and head for the parking garage where our department vehicles are kept. Today I have an interpreter named Ibrahim and a new CT agent in tow. Over the past few months, Gleason's been good to his word, and we have received some help. We've got three new agents working for us, though it looks like Mullen will be leaving soon.

The interpreter climbs into the back of an '86 Crown Vic. I drive. The other CT agent, "David," rides shotgun. We're going to have to take some serious precautions on this drive. Hezbollah has a long reach, and we don't want to lead anyone back to our catch. Today we're going to pay a visit to Ahmed.

We burst out of the parking garage at a good clip. I make a hard turn and swing onto the streets of D.C. The sun is shining and the shadows are long, giving the capital a high-contrast sort of look. Lots of light and lots of shadows, very appropriate given today's mission. Brownish-black snow lies in slushy piles along either side of the road. The asphalt itself is icy and wet. Not a good day to drive evasively, but you take what you're given in this business.

I goose the accelerator and the Ford speeds to fifty. Like all our sedans, this one is totally clean and comes equipped with buried plates. Officially, the car does not exist.

Inside our stealth Ford, we're all in street clothes, but we've got blue raid jackets that say FEDERAL AGENT in big yellow letters on their backs tucked away in the trunk should we need them. They're stashed right next to the Remington shotgun and the extra shells loaded with number 4 buck.

We come to a four-way intersection whose light is already green. At the last possible second, I brake hard and spin the steering wheel. The sedan skids into a tight right turn and we flare around the corner. As soon as we're at the apex of the turn, I'm on the gas again. We shoot out of the intersection doing sixty. Meanwhile, David and I are scanning the side and rearview mirrors, checking every vehicle behind us in case we've got a tail.

I hit another intersection. A quick right turn at the last second and then I'm powering out of it, running up the street for the next intersection. We reach it, and I cut across incoming traffic in a surprise left turn.

This is called a surveillance detection route, or SDR. Basically, the driver stair-steps through a city grid, making frequent turns while still trending toward his eventual destination. The chance that any random civilian car would follow the driver through these gyrations is astronomically low. Thus, if you come out of a stair-step maneuver and see the same green van behind you that was there when you started, well, you've got a tail. And a problem.

I make another sudden right turn and stair-step up a few blocks before careening across the oncoming traffic lane again to dodge into a side street. I check the rearview mirror. No familiar vehicles. In fact, nobody followed us in that turn at all.

In the mirror, I catch sight of our interpreter in the backseat. Under his saucer-sized eyes, the rest of his face has turned a nice shade of green.

We come to a 7-Eleven convenience store, and it is time to use another SDR tactic we call a timing stop. Without warning, I wrench the steering wheel and the sedan's back end skids sideways for a second before the back wheels find purchase and propel us forward into the 7-Eleven's parking lot. We find an empty space and park, motor running, eyes on the street. We watch the traffic trickle by, David and I carefully noting every vehicle's color and make. We're trained observers, and we soon have a mental list of sedans, vans, and trucks that have cruised past us. We'll watch for any of them to appear again once we continue our journey.

Ten minutes later, we back out of the parking space and drift to the driveway. A quick look left. A quick look right. All clear. I stomp the gas pedal and the sedan lunges onto the street, bouncing on its shocks as we hit the asphalt again. Behind me, the wild maneuver throws our terp into one of the back doors. I hear him grunt.

He hasn't seen anything yet.

Two blocks from the 7-Eleven, the oncoming traffic lane is empty. I spin the steering wheel left, the car heels around, slipping on the ice. We start to spin, and I fight to keep the back end from fishtailing. And then, we're 180 degrees from where we started and it is time to drop the hammer again. The engine roars and we tear back up the street past the 7-Eleven again. Any civilian watching us would think we're idiots. In the Dark World, such tactics keep people alive, and we're exceptionally well trained at this game.

"Helluva U-turn, Fred," David says to me through a big grin.

I don't respond. I'm too focused. I take this seriously; if we don't do it right, we could get our asset killed.

We roll through one intersection and go up a few more blocks. Just as we reach another one, I swing the sedan into a violent right turn. Behind me, the interpreter blurts, "Oh, God!"

I hear him thump into the door again.

"Tighten your seat belt," David tells him.

He frantically does as he's told.

Twenty minutes later, we've stair-stepped all over Rosslyn. Both David and I are confident that we don't have a tail. If we had one, we lost him. If they had multiple vehicles set up to follow us, we would have noticed that, too. Plus, our random movements would have made intercepting us almost impossible. We break out of the SDR and roll south for Arlington. Before we reach our destination, we execute another series of stair-steps, just to be sure nobody's picked us up. When we're convinced we're clean, we make the final turn to the safe house. Actually, it is a safe apartment.

I guide the sedan into a parking lot not far from the safe house. The terp bails out of the back and mutters something about feeling like a human pinball. These types don't like to hang with us on these sorts of missions. I wonder why.

The safe house is located inside a swanky high-rise apartment building right here in D.C. Forget how the spy novelists portray safe houses as creepy places way out in the woods. That's the worst place to hide an asset. If you want to hide a needle, where's the best place? In a stack of identical needles. That's the philosophy we use with our safe houses. We hide in plain sight. It works, thanks in part to the many adulterers in the D.C. area.

All over the capital, it is easy to find high-rise apartments or condos that are leased to innocuous-sounding corporations like "Global Research, LLC." In reality, these are love nests for the rich and powerful. Call them their crash pads, the place where they can bring their trophy girlfriends without fear of spousal intrusions. People like that tend to keep to themselves. They don't ask questions. They aren't nosy neighbors. In that sort of environment, we can come and go as we please, with whomever we want, and not raise any neighborly eyebrows, even when we bring handcuffed men into the building. That just looks kinky to them.

And what if we do run into a Betty Busybody who spends her retirement keeping tabs on which blonde emerges from which apartment night after night? Well, we put her on the payroll and she goes from gossip magnet to quiet lookout. Problem solved, and we've got another asset covering our safe house.

This apartment complex looks like any other one in this area of Arlington. Only a studious observer would notice the extra security cameras secreted around the exterior. We walk to the front entryway, where there is no doorman waiting for us. We never pick a building with a doorman. They're too indiscreet.

We ride the elevator to the fifth floor. When the doors open, David asks, "How do you want this to go down?"

"Let me do the talking. We'll see if he's fluent in English."

I turn to the terp. "Don't let on you speak Arabic until I give you the signal, okay?"

After the ride down here, Ibrahim is not in the mood to question any orders. He nods weakly and tries to smile. It comes across more like a scowl. He still looks carsick.

Room 511 awaits. Watercolers and landscape oil paintings hang on the walls. Oak and cherry furniture give the place a down-home sort of look, but the prisoner in a chair in one corner adds sort of a Mansonesque twist to the Martha Stewart décor.

I step into the living room. It is bright and sunny, and the apartment is extremely warm. I notice there's a sliding door leading to a balcony. The drapes are open, and the view to the north is spectacular. The Washington Monument stands out above the rest of the D.C. skyline. No wonder CEOs bring their bimbos to places like this one. High rent. Good view. All-around cozy love nest.

The man does not look very chipper. I ignore him for a minute and check out the kitchen. There's a flock of Chinese takeout containers sitting on the counter, along with a stack of empty Stouffer's TV-dinner trays. Bottled water sits next to the sink.

I walk to the back bedrooms. The door to one is open. The bed is unmade, but aside from a couple of lamps, there's nothing on the nightstands or the chest of drawers. The next door is closed. I knock, and it swings open. This is normally the spare bedroom, but for our purposes it is Big Brother Central. Sequestered within are a couple of beefy agents looking tired and unkempt. They are the watchers. They've been here since we bagged Ahmed at the airport last night.

The room is full of electronics gear. Several TV monitors occupy one wall. There are cameras hidden everywhere in the living room, bedroom, bathroom, and kitchen. The monitors show various angles of the apartment, plus the hallway outside the door, the entry lobby, the parking lot, and the building's perimeter. We have more cameras than a television studio.

Audio and video recorders, radios, and other stuff sit on folding tables. The entire place is bugged; microphones have been placed in every lamp, in the walls and vents and other nooks and crannies throughout the apartment. Not a word will be spoken that doesn't get recorded.

More cartons of Chinese takeout litter the scene. One of the agents is busily pecking away at some crispy beef with a set of chopsticks.

"Damn, I hate these things," he complains as he fumbles a slice of beef. It falls back into the carton, and he digs after it.

A TV in the back of the room is tuned to CNN, the ubiquitous station of our Dark World lives. Next to the TV sit a couple of Uzi subma-chine guns and a quartet of gas masks.

"Gentlemen, we're going to get started."

"Roger that, sir."

I close the door and head back into the living room. The man cuffed to the chair glances at me with fearful eyes. He's trapped. There is no es-cape, and he knows it. He's a man who holds no cards in this game.

"Ahmed," I ask, "do you speak English?"

His dark eyes focus on mine. Through bad teeth he answers, "A lit-tle."

"Good."

I grab another chair and place it right in front of his. When I sit down, my knees are almost touching his. He recoils from the invasion of his personal space and pushes his chair back into the corner as far as it will go. I don't let him off the hook. I sit up and scoot my chair forward until I'm right in his face again. He looks utterly miserable. I'd feel sorry for him if he wasn't a treacherous, murdering scumbag.

We've been laying this trap for months, ever since we got word from one of our informants that Ahmed was a relative of his. We persuaded him to write Ahmed and invite him to the United States. He could leave Lebanon and start a new life here in America. Our informant did just that, and Ahmed took the bait. We fast-tracked his visa application and his green card, and sure enough, Ahmed decided to immigrate to the Land of Opportunity.

Funny thing. The last time I'd seen him, he was wearing an AK-47 and chanting, "Death to America" on *World News Tonight*. That was after he and his confederates had taken an unarmed U.S. Navy diver and shot him in the right temple. His body fell out of the TWA airliner Ahmed's fellow terrorists had hijacked. It landed with a sickening thud on the tar-mac at Beirut International Airport.

Ahmed was part of the terrorist cell responsible for TWA Flight 847 and its hostage-crisis aftermath. Last night, he got off his plane and strolled into a Dulles terminal as if he were just another weary immi-grant coming to make a new life.

Of course, he never got out of the terminal, not as a free man. Our DSS and FBI agents descended on him like hawks on a prairie dog. He had nowhere to hide and knew it. He offered no resistance as he was stuffed into a government rig and whisked away to the safe house.

"Ahmed," I begin.

His eyes stray from mine. I notice he's fixated on the balcony, and I wonder if he's heard the same stories I have about one notorious terrorist's interrogation experience. The CIA caught that particular bad guy in New York a few months back. When he wouldn't talk, the spooks hung him out over the balcony, apparently so he could get a good look at the street, some thirty stories below. He sang like Michael Jackson on speed after that.

We do things differently here, but I won't tell Ahmed. Not yet, anyway.

"It could be worse, Ahmed," I tell him. He looks surprised, like I've gotten into his head. Perhaps he was thinking about the Syrians and how they interrogate their Lebanese prisoners. Generally, the Syrians start by stripping the detainee naked, strapping him to a chair, and then stuffing a running garden hose down his throat. It gets less pleasant from there. Think electricity.

"Let me advise you on your rights."

Ahmed's eyes grow wide. I'm not sure if he's surprised or uncomprehending.

"You have the right to remain silent. Anything you say will be used against you. You have the right to an attorney. Do you understand?"

I firmly believe in our system of laws. I believe in justice. Reading Ahmed his Miranda rights makes my stomach do slow rolls.

Our prisoner looks over at Ibrahim, then back to me. "I understand."

"Good. Tell me. What do you know about the Americans held hostage in Lebanon?" There's nothing like getting to the point.

Ahmed starts sweating in his black turtleneck. He doesn't answer me at first, preferring instead to steal surreptitious glances at the balcony again.

"Ahmed. What do you know about the American hostages?" I get right in his face now. My nose is inches from his. Our knees are touching. We're trained to do this, as it makes the detainee uncomfortable.

He averts his eyes. "Which ones?"

Good answer. This means he knows something.

"Which ones?" I say. "The ones you know about."

He doesn't reply. He's shaking now. He looks pathetic and lost. It is funny how mean he looked in his photos we've got on file when he hefted an AK across his chest. Now, with his curly black hair parted down the middle, his skinny body and starched jeans, he looks lost and helpless. I don't want to feel sorry for him, not after what he's done, but a part of me can't feel anything else. A small part.

"I know of hostages," he says softly. I study him hard and wonder if he's near tears.

"Which ones, Ahmed?" I ask. I'm close enough to him to smell him. Dial soap can only do so much. I try not to breathe.

"The ones off the plane," he confesses.

When TWA Flight 847 was hijacked, it was on a scheduled run from Athens to Rome. The terrorists, who called themselves the Organization for the Oppressed on Earth (a rather laughable front name for Hezbollah), ordered the pilot to go to Beirut. After landing at Beirut International, about twenty passengers were released in exchange for fuel. The plane then flew to Algiers, where another twenty passengers were let go. After a short stay, the plane flew back to Beirut where they executed the navy Seabee diver, a Maryland kid named Robert Stethem, and dumped him on the runway.

Beirut International Airport sits in the middle of a Shiite neighborhood and lacks even basic security amenities, such as an outer perimeter fence. Anyone could come and go onto the tarmac, which proved a major advantage to the terrorists. They began pulling passengers off the plane and stashing them around Beirut. Seven Americans, all with Jewish-sounding names, were the first ones to disappear into the Shiite slums. Then the hijackers forced the pilots to fly the plane back to Algiers. All this ping-ponging back and forth between Lebanon and Algeria served to whip the media up into a feeding frenzy. It turned into a full-scale international news drama played out on scores of networks 24/7. Hezbollah loved it. They're media whores.

Finally, the plane returned to Beirut. The terrorists removed the remaining passengers and locked them up in various parts of the city. Altogether, by this point in the drama, they still held forty hostages from the flight. Nabih Berri, a local warlord who controlled the Amal militia, ended up with the passengers, and it was his men who guarded them in safe houses scattered around Beirut. At the time, Berri also served as Lebanon's minister for justice.

Why did Hezbollah hijack Flight 847? Retaliation and leverage were their two main motivations. In their list of demands, the terrorists insisted that the international community condemn the March 8, 1985, attempted assassination of Sheikh Fadlallah. The hijacking was Hezbollah's immediate response to it. At the same time, the terrorists demanded that Israel release seven hundred Shiite prisoners taken in southern Lebanon.

For most of June, the hostage drama continued. In the end, the Israelis released their prisoners. In return, Hezbollah trucked the Flight 847 passengers north and turned them over to the Syrians. Mission accomplished.

The axiom that we do not negotiate with terrorists is a huge myth. Every nation has made its own deals with these devils. All too often, terror is a blunt but effective political weapon. As long as it works, terrorism will never be stamped out.

I look at Ahmed, one of Barri's foot soldiers in this game. Is he Hezbollah, too? We'll need to find out.

"You saw the passengers off Flight 847 then, right?"

"Yes."

"Did you see any other hostages besides them?" What if this wretched man was one of the thugs who tortured Father Jenco and David Jacobsen? Reap the coming whirlwind, my friend. There will be no mercy for you.

"No, nobody else." Ahmed maintains eye contact with me as he says this. He doesn't squirm or fidget. He looks like he's telling the truth. I feel a little let down.

I change the subject. "Okay. What about threats against the U.S. Embassy in Beirut?"

"What?"

"Are you aware of any plans to hit the embassy?"

"No. None."

"What about attacks against Americans in Beirut?"

"I hear nothing."

Time to change course again. "Do you know anyone in Hezbollah?"

He laughs bitterly. "Of course I know Hezbollah. They are all over the place."

"Do you know the Fox? Imad Mugniyah?"

Silence. He won't look me in the eye now. The question makes him fearful.

"Do you know Hasan Izz-Al-Din?"

His eyes drop to the floor. He won't answer.

"You know Hasan Izz-Al-Din?"

More silence. He looks terrified now, but not of me. Of them. Hasan is Mugniyah's right-hand man. He helped plan and execute the Flight 847 operation. He and Mugniyah are Hezbollah's most dangerous men. Ahmed clearly knows that. He's probably been warned that talking about either man will get his family killed.

I try a few more approaches, but he won't talk about Mugniyah, though it is obvious he's tied into both Hezbollah and the Amal militia.

MICE: money, ideology, compromise, ego. Our interrogation classes taught us that everyone has a motivation. Everyone has a price. It is our job to discover those two things.

Ahmed is a poor Lebanese male. He was born into nothing and has accomplished nothing with his short life. He came to the United States hoping for a fresh start. That tells me something about his commitment to Amal and Hezbollah's ideology. It also gives me insight into his motivation. He came here to make money.

Okay, let's stroke that. "You say you know Hezbollah."

"Yes. Anyone who lives in Lebanon knows Hezbollah."

"We could use somebody like you to talk to Hezbollah for us. To find out things."

He guffaws and looks away.

"You could get paid."

His eyes lock on mine. I see a flare of hope in them, along with a touch of eagerness. He knows I'm offering him a way out.

"How much?"

I ignore the question and add, "If you get in trouble, we'll pull you out."

"How much?"

We have him.

The rest of the day we negotiate a deal. Ahmed will become an informant for us. He'll go back to Lebanon and burrow deep into Hezbollah. Will we trust what he sends back to us? Of course not. No informant, especially one motivated by money, can be considered trustworthy at first. We'll spend months cross-checking and vetting the information he provides before we decide what sort of value he has as a mole. But he'll know that if he wants to get paid, he's got to bring us useful nuggets. We'll dole the cash out like heroin to an addict. If he stops delivering the goods, his cash flow gets choked off.

We need human assets on the ground. We're desperately short of that in the Middle East. Nothing beats a reliable set of eyes and ears in important places. We have precious little inside information on Hezbollah, and Ahmed will be the first step toward building a network that can give us advance warning on what Mugniyah is planning next. We may even get intel on his location, or Hasan Izz-Al-Din's. This is our first step in turning the tables on our enemies and fighting back.

By day's end, Ahmed is ready to betray his fellow terrorists. We own him, but it is far less satisfying than I thought. We've trapped Ahmed, and now we're using him. True, he's allowing us to use him thanks to his inherent greed. If he didn't take this deal, he'd spend the rest of his life in a federal prison. Or worse. We could send him back to Lebanon and tell the locals that a suspected terrorist is on board. The Lebanese authorities would not interrogate him gently.

He knows this. This was not a choice. This was a form of coercion designed to get him to sell out his own people. And he'll do it because we control the game. This is a dirty business. It is also necessary.

A week later, we launch our freshly minted double agent back at Hezbollah. The game has entered a new phase.

seventeen

THREAT MATRIX

Summer 1987
Foggy Bottom

HUMINT is a precious asset, the gold nuggets of our profession. We're finally making progress in the Middle East, but we need more assets, more penetration into the inner workings of our enemies. This is why we cannot help but be delighted when a Libyan diplomat walks into one of our overseas embassies and asks for political asylum.

What a break. Libyan defectors are few and far between. After the initial vetting, he doesn't appear to be a double agent or a throwaway. He seems to be one of the rarest of the rare: a legitimate defector motivated by ideology. He came to us wanting a new life. America's global moral authority pays off again. It will take months of checking and rechecking to confirm this, but right now, it looks like a promising source just fell into our laps.

I want to talk to him. I have a lot of questions that can be answered only by an insider within the Qaddafi regime. We'll start with who pulled off the Calkins and Pollick hits and move on to La Belle. Maybe this guy even has knowledge of future attacks, and his intel will finally help us get in front of the terrorists. If he's carrying that sort of information, I hope

WITSEC—the Witness Security program—sets him up with a mansion in Beverly Hills. He'll have saved lives.

Not surprisingly, we soon get word from our Dark World sources that the Libyan intelligence service is doing their best to find our defector and kill him. Once we get him to the United States, we move him from safe house to safe house every few days. Those transitions are the most dangerous times—a good hit team will be hard-pressed to penetrate a safe house, but on the street moving from one location to another our defector is a much easier target. We take extra precautions. He rides in one of our new black 1987 Chevy Suburbans. With its smoke-out windows and huge size, the Chevy looks like the mutant offspring of a farm pickup truck and a family station wagon. It is beefy and powerful and can hold six Uzi- and shotgun-armed agents and the protectee. The Suburban will make a hard target for any hit squad.

We hopscotch the Libyan around D.C., a coterie of DSS and FBI agents protecting him. Every agency wants to debrief him, yet we're not sure how much he knows. We have confirmed that he was part of the Libyan diplomatic corps. Given how much the Libyan embassies support terror operations, I can't wait to talk to this guy and see what he can tell us.

After several days in D.C., we convoy our defector to a small motel room in Winchester, Virginia. He looks jumpy and ill at ease. I would be, too, given what he's going through.

This isn't an interrogation, so I don't sit knee to knee with our defector. Instead, I take a seat across the table from him as he half-rises to shake my hand. After a brief introduction, I waste no time getting down to business.

"Last spring, we have reason to believe your country's intelligence service tried to kill two of our diplomats. One in Sudan, one in Yemen. What can you tell me about those two operations?"

He thinks for a minute before answering in almost flawless English, "I have not heard anything about that."

He looks earnest, like he wants to help.

"What about the nightclub bombing in West Berlin in April? Can you tell me who orchestrated the attack?"

"No. I do not know." He pauses again for a minute then adds, "You have to understand, I was not involved in intelligence operations. Haiat amn al Jamahiriya is very secretive. Our offices don't talk to each other."

"Do you mean compartmentalized?"

"Yes. I believe you refer to Jamhirya as the ESO, right?"

"Correct." The External Security Organization is Libyan intelligence.

"It has two branches. Internal Security and Foreign Security. The foreign liaison office conducts operations and works with other organizations."

He's obviously very intelligent and well educated. I think he's telling the truth. "What sort of organizations?"

"You would call them terrorists. Abu Nidal's group. The PLO. Italy's Red Brigade."

"Hezbollah?"

He stares at me. "I don't know."

I change course. "Are you aware of any plans against U.S. targets?"

He shakes his head. "No. There have been many, especially after your country almost started a war between Libya and Egypt four years ago."

That's something that I had just learned about during a fishing expedition in the dead bodies cabinets. In February 1983, Egypt was poised to strike at Libya after it looked like Qaddafi would invade Sudan. The Reagan administration promised air support for the Egyptians if war came. We redeployed several aerial refueling tankers and AWACS early warning radar planes in anticipation of the fighting. Nothing ever came of the situation, and the administration later announced that the deployment of air and naval assets thwarted the Libyan attack. The American planes were withdrawn a month later.

"What can you tell us about Qaddafi?"

"It is a regime run by fear. What else can I say?"

The conversation continues for an hour. An insider's view of the Libyan regime provides an interesting perspective. There is no initiative; everything originates from the top down. Libyan operations are highly compartmentalized and secrecy is taken very seriously. It isn't surprising that we've never penetrated the ESO. They're vigilant, ruthless, and paranoid.

Interesting perspectives on the regime aside, our defector has little valuable information for me and the cases I'm working. I leave Winchester disappointed and frustrated. I had hoped we'd have a real catch with this guy. No joy. He was another dry hole. We still have almost no HUMINT on what the Libyans are working on these days.

God, I wish there was some way to close these gaps. In 1984, the Act to Combat International Terrorism included a provision that established the Rewards for Justice program. Basically, it is a global tip operation where we pay handsomely for information leading to the capture of key terrorists. Millions of dollars are sitting in the program's fund, and we've advertised it all over the world. The DSS manages the program, but for the past year and a half I've been around, we seem to spend more time in meetings trying to fend off the FBI than anything else. The Bureau wants the program badly, but we're not going to give it up.

Rewards for Justice has brought many tips to our ears. We get phone calls and walk-ins every day. Most of the time, the tips come from individuals looking for a quick buck, and their intel is suspect. However, the program has yielded some valuable pieces of information.

A few days after the fruitless meeting with the Libyan defector, I get a call from the security desk upstairs. A guard there tells me an Iranian-American just came in through the front door. He says he's got crucial information for us. I grab my notebook and head upstairs.

We get two or three walk-ins a week, and they usually are serious time wasters. Some of them are wannabes looking for attention. Others are delusional or mentally imbalanced. Most just want a chunk of change but have nothing of value to offer in return. Some of these folks have become regulars. They show up at different agencies and different locations, always looking for money. Fortunately, we now document every walk-in and get a full workup on their backgrounds. We share that information with the FBI and CIA; that way we expose the charlatans and nut jobs. When we identify one of these types, we send a burn notice out to all agencies, warning them that this person is only going to waste their time.

But every now and then a nugget walks through the door. This is why we suffer the other fools. It is the 1 percent rule. We have to cut through the other 99 percent to find the one with a key bit of intelligence that will help save lives.

I reach the front security desk and find a sharply dressed Iranian waiting for me. He shakes my hand, and I lead him down a hallway to a secure debriefing room. When we sit down, I offer him a drink of water.

"No, thank you," he says in broken English. He's got just a hint of a southern accent. It sounds strange, sort of like Ayatollah Khomeini channeling Rhett Butler.

"What would you like to talk about?" I ask.

"I have information that can save President Reagan's life."

He has my attention now. "Is somebody going to kill him?"

"Yes. There is a plot to assassinate the president."

"How do you know about it?"

"I have friends," he tells me cryptically.

"When is this going to happen?"

He ignores the question. "Iranian agents are assisting."

"You mean Iran is helping plan an assassination attempt on the president of the United States?"

"Yes, exactly."

"Tell me about the plan."

"I have heard about your Rewards for Justice program," the Iranian says as he fidgets with his tie.

Here it comes. "Yes," I say in a noncommittal tone.

"How much would you pay for this sort of information?"

He wants money. Still, we must vet the threat. Perhaps he's in the 1 percent. I pull out my pen and start a full workup of my new Iranian friend. It turns out he's a businessman from Florida with contacts all over the Iranian-American immigrant community. At first glance, his vitals look good. He may be telling the truth. If he is, he may end up with a payday after all.

Over the next few weeks, Gleason has me run down what little the Iranian has given us. We check our own sources. I meet with the FBI and CIA. He's not one of the repeat nuts or wannabes. FOGHORN unearths no criminal history. I bring the Secret Service into the loop. They start their own investigation and want to meet with our Iranian informant. He refuses. He says he trusts only me.

I finally convince him to meet with myself and a Secret Service agent, whom I introduce as a fellow DSS investigator. Throughout the meeting, the Iranian seems sincere and the threat sounds plausible. He drops a hint that there's a connection between the plotters and Iranian intelligence in Vienna.

The Secret Service puts the Iranian under surveillance. At the same time, we vet his information and check out his Vienna lead. We come up dry. Is he on the level? I can't tell, but we have to take the threat seriously, no matter how much time this sucks out of our schedules.

I meet with the Iranian two more times. Each time, he drops another hint, another tidbit for me to follow up. When I ask him to take a polygraph, he initially balks at the idea. Later, he changes his mind. He comes in, we hook him up, and then we fire questions at him.

The results are inconclusive. In the Dark World, everything exists in shades of ambiguity, especially the information that goes into our threat matrix. We ignore these tips at our peril.

We take other precautions, and security around the president is tightened. Nevertheless, after several weeks of dancing with our Iranian informant, the Secret Service comes back with sensitive information. The threat is not credible. I look over what they uncovered and am forced to agree. Iranian intelligence is not trying to kill President Reagan. At least, not yet.

Such cases come and go. We vet so many that they blur together in my mind after a while. I hear everything from the bizarre to the outlandish. Aliens are controlling the secretary of defense. The Russians want to steal the Statue of Liberty. Qaddafi is secretly plotting to take over the United Nations. There's an unending chorus of delusional baloney flowing from the streets to our front desk. All of it must be listened to because of that 1 percent. We cannot miss that one valid warning that could save lives and prevent catastrophe.

Toward fall, a call comes in at the end of another long day. It is a tipster, warning us that the U.S. ambassador to Colombia is about to be hit. The drug cartel has it in for him. The cocaine lords play a particularly ruthless game, so we take the threat seriously. I miss Mullen's expertise on the subject. He's gone now, and I'm helping to cover South America until we can develop one of our new agents into the regional expert.

During our vetting process, our informant mentions that a Colombian enforcer named Victor may have additional details for us. I run down this lead and discover Victor is now in federal custody. The U.S. Marshals Service has him stashed away in WITSEC.

I contact an acquaintance in the U.S. Marshals office and ask if I can meet with Victor. I might have well asked for a face-to-face with Pope John Paul. The Marshals Service takes witness protection extremely seriously, and they trust no one until proven otherwise. In my case, I'd already worked with several U.S. Marshals during the UN General Assembly meeting back at the beginning of the year. The DSS generally has a good relationship with the Marshals Service, and we worked well together in New York. Nevertheless, before they will let me sit down with Victor, they will thoroughly check my own background.

When it comes to the cartels, you never know who is on the payroll.

Just before 8 A.M. a few days later, the phone rings at my desk.

"Agent Burton," I say into my receiver.

"Agent Burton, this is Bob."

A pause. I try to think of the Bobs I know, but I don't recognize the voice.

"What can I do for you, Bob?"

"I understand you want to meet with Victor."

I try to conceal my excitement. "Yes."

"Okay, ten hundred this morning." Bob gives me a D.C. address, then issues gives me final instructions. "Come alone. Go to the fourth floor and wait. No backup surveillance. No partner. Just you. Clear?"

"Very. See you at ten hundred." But I'm talking to a dead line. Bob's already hung up.

An hour after the call, after briefing Gleason, I leave the office and head for the street, where I catch a cab. I give the cabbie an address several blocks from the rendezvous point. He drops me off and I begin to stair-step toward my final destination. Running an SDR is not limited to vehicles. You can do it on foot as well. At each intersection, I make sure to take a casual glance over my shoulder, the one I've practiced so many times while running with Tyler Beauregard. A few times, I stop and watch the foot traffic pass my location. I double back twice, then find another observation point and people-watch again.

Just before 10 A.M., I reach the address Bob has given me. It turns out to be a construction site, surrounded by a chain-link fence. I walk the fence line until I find a gap that I can squeeze through. It is a tight fit, but

I manage. I step into the ground floor of what appears to be a future office building. It is hardly more than a steel girder skeleton right now. The floors are unfinished. There are no exterior or interior walls. As I climb a set of stairs built into one corner, I'm greeted by dozens of pigeons that have taken roost here.

I reach the fourth floor and my hand unconsciously reaches for my Model 19, snug in its shoulder holster. Gripping the handle, I move off the stairwell into a maze of wires and cables, stacks of cinder blocks, plywood, and tools. Up ahead, there's a room already framed and drywalled. It is the only one finished in the entire building. I approach silently, moving with short, smooth strides until I reach the doorway. Peering inside, I see only two chairs. The room is unfinished; the exterior wall has yet to be built. Somebody could be thrown right off the building from that side of the room.

I check my watch. Ten A.M. Showtime. I move to one of the chairs and position it so my back is to the outside opening. I cover the doorway. A flock of pigeons soon fly in to settle down along the exterior I-beam. A few wander deeper into the room. They don't even appear to notice me. If they do, they don't seem to care.

Footsteps in the stairwell focus my attention. I hear a soft shuffle outside the room. Every nerve is alert. My hand is poised to skin my S&W at a split-second's notice. A tool clatters, followed by a soft muttered curse. A moment later, a shaggy-looking transient steps into the doorway. He's dressed in an old army fatigue jacket that has long since seen better days. It is threadbare and covered in stains. His jeans and boots aren't much better.

"Burton?" the bum asks.

I nod.

"I'm Bob." He grins at my surprise. I stand up and shake his hand. He's unshaven and smells like soap is but a distant memory for him. It is an excellent cover. He's obviously a pro.

I sit back down. He slides away from the door and asks, "Do you have a gun?"

"Of course. Two."

"No problems. You're okay."

"Yeah, I'm one of the guys in a white hat." We both chuckle, then he adds, "I checked you out myself."

"Trust, but verify," I reply. That's one of the cornerstones of our profession.

He looks at his watch. "They'll be here in two minutes."

Like clockwork, 120 seconds later Victor walks through the doorway, trailed by three other U.S. Marshals, all of whom look like refugees from Woodstock.

Who's next? Jimi Hendrix?

Victor takes a seat, and I'm instantly repelled by the man. His wardrobe looks like a cross between *Miami Vice* and *Saturday Night Fever*. It's a pseudo-macho, bottom-feeder-meets-fortyish-disco-junkie sort of look. He's sporting a white leisure-suit coat over a button-down shirt that Victor apparently forgot to button. This oversight reveals a tangled, hairy chest and a thick gold chain draped around his neck. I wonder if he's bought this stuff off the rack. Where does one go for such attire? Drug Scum Emporium?

He has long black hair, which he's pulled into a ragged ponytail. It dangles below his collar like a coonskin hat gone bad. It serves to highlight a diamond earring dangling out of his left lobe. His black eyes settle on me. It gives me the creeps watching as he checks me over. This dude has a bad vibe. A very bad vibe.

He crosses his legs, and I see he's sporting a pair of off-white sharkskin dress shoes. Slip-ons, no laces. Obviously, he doesn't plan to kick anyone.

The marshals form a perimeter around us. One of them takes up a position behind and off to one side of Victor's chair. He crosses his arms and scowls. He looks like a hippie bouncer.

Victor reaches into his shirt pocket. The move makes everyone tense. He pulls out a cigarette case and extracts a smoke.

"What do you want?" he asks. His voice is low, accented, and hostile.

"I need some information about some associates of yours."

Victor scoffs. "Associates." He finds a lighter in his jacket pocket and spins the flint until he gets a flame. He lights his smoke and watches me.

"Associates," I agree with him, "in Colombia."

A fleeting expression of fear scrabbles across his face. He quickly stamps it out. His face hardens, and by the time he answers me, he looks utterly ferocious. I find myself missing Ahmed. At least he looked harmless—without his assault rifle, anyway.

"Who?" he growls.

I give him the names.

"Bad men. Very bad. You'd do wise to stay away from them."

"What are their roles in the cartel?"

He shakes his head, blows a lungful of smoke at me, and says, "They are killers."

"Assassins?"

"Whatever they need to be."

I think about this for a minute. This is bad. I may be dealing with the 1 percent here.

"Tell me more about them."

Victor flashes me a grin that could send children fleeing in terror. "Bombs. They like bombs."

"What sort? Letter bombs? Grenades?"

Victor shakes his head. "No, no, no. Their specialty is the car bomb. They're very good and very thorough. They kill their targets."

This is a key piece of information. We will take precautions with the ambassador to minimize this threat.

I ask some follow-up questions and probe for details. Victor answers with short, blunt replies. After forty-five minutes, I'm done. Without another word, Victor stands up and storms out of the room. The three hippie-marshals follow right behind him. I'm left alone with Bob.

"Get what you needed?" he asks.

"Yeah. Not good news, though."

"Sorry to hear that."

"I appreciate the help," I tell Bob.

He shrugs. "No problem. You took care of my guys in New York."

"I was impressed with them. Very good men."

"They said the same of you."

I nod at the professional compliment.

"So, what's with Victor?" I ask.

Bob steps forward and puts a hand on the back of the empty chair in front of me. "What do you mean?"

"He's pretty creepy." I don't really expect an answer, but I felt compelled to mention it. The whole meeting has left me feeling sullied and unclean.

Bob leans toward me. He lowers his voice and says, "Victor gave up three Colombian cartel members."

That's why he's in WITSEC. That's why all the secrecy and the crazy rendezvous point.

Bob leans even closer. He's only a few feet from me now. "The cartel has a million-dollar bounty on his head."

"They must want him bad." Victor obviously burned some powerful people back in Colombia.

"No doubt. He's also a killer."

I'm not surprised. Bob rakes one hand across his neck as he continues, "He cut an informant's throat with a four-inch buck knife. Watched him bleed out. Like a kid stepping on a bug."

"Nice guy."

Bob shakes his head, stands upright, and walks back toward the door. "You have no idea," he says over his shoulder.

"What do you mean?"

He turns and leans against the doorway. "If he thought you were dirty, he would have tried to kill you, too. Even with us here."

I go stone cold inside. I have no doubt Bob is right. Victor was like a coiled snake.

"Don't worry, we had your back the entire time." Bob gives me a sardonic grin.

My mind flashes to the hippie-agent who stood behind Victor, arms folded. He had a shoulder holster under that Berkeley love-in costume he was wearing. He spent the entire meeting with one hand on his piece. That's how much they trusted their WITSEC protectee.

Bob sees the recognition in my face. "Yeah. He's that dangerous. Glad you got what you needed."

He heads through the door. "See you around, Agent Burton."

And then I'm alone with the pigeons, mind swirling with a dozen thoughts at once. My body uncorks one long shudder. That's part of the post-adrenaline-rush letdown. I've never come face-to-face with pure evil until now. And here he is, under the protection of the federal government. He's a killer who not only got away with his crime but will live on the taxpayers' dime for decades to come. Why? He gave up three higher-ups for his own miserable skin. Somebody made the call to trade up and go for the bigger catch.

Justice became just another bargaining chip.

This is the way the world works. We've got to make these deals if we're ever going to bring the cartels down and take out their leadership. Still, the idea that U.S. Marshals have to guard a man like Victor makes my skin crawl. Though logically I recognize that the Dark World is morally ambiguous, I cling to my black-and-white view of things. Right and wrong, they are the pillars of what I stand for and believe in. But the big gray gap between them just got a little bigger today.

I sit and consider that as the pigeons peck around my feet. I've got to be careful in this business. If I let it own me, I'll lose my moral compass like so many others have in the past. You grow so obsessed with catching the bad guys that you'll do anything to get them. Ultimately, it is all too easy to go too far. That's when congressional hearings get held, careers are flushed, and once-good men get sent to prison.

The pursuit to protect can distort all logic, can justify any means. Take that first step, and it will be a long slide down. I don't want to become what I revile—a man corrupted by his own good intentions.

I don't want to make deals with the Victors of this world. There has to be a way to do this job and not lose the sense of right and wrong that's motivated me all my life, thanks to my father. That was his gift to me, part of his legacy and an enduring wellspring of pride for both of us. Now I am my own man, and it defines who I am.

The pigeons grow curious. They approach me and wait, hoping for some bread crumbs. I scuff one shoe across the concrete floor. One of the birds flaps its wings and backs off. The others follow suit. For a long moment, they stay at arm's length, studying me, assessing me as a threat. Funny, that's what I came here to do, too.

Now I just hope the Dark World doesn't take my soul.

eighteen

November 1, 1987
Bethesda

This is one of those days I've needed for a long time. Day after day of craziness, threats, terror, bombings, death, and hijackings will drive any man over the edge sooner or later, unless he can take a sanity break. Today, Fred Davis and I finally got a chance to go fishing again. We left early and spent the day casting fruitlessly into the Potomac River, jawing about old times. He starts flight school in a few weeks, so it was good to see him before he heads down to Alabama.

After I got home, my wife and I actually got to spend some time together. It is a rare Sunday when we're both free from work commitments, and by dinnertime, I almost felt happy. Now, with the clock just about to strike nine-thirty, I'm more relaxed than I've been since joining the DSS. Shoes off, Tyler Beauregard asleep on the floor next to me, we're kicked back on the couch watching Chris Berman recap all the NFL action of the day. The 'Skins beat the Bills 27-7. Thank God the strike is over and the real players are back on the field. Of course, football hasn't been the same since Joe Namath retired. Then the Colts broke everyone's hearts when they stole out of town in the middle of night a few years back.

The phone rings.

Oh, God.

Part of me doesn't want to answer it. Today was too perfect. It rings again. I hesitate. Duty compels me to pick it up, but is it too much to ask for one night to myself?

It rings again. I know it's just in my head, but with each ring the tone sounds more insistent, like it is trying to warn me of a brewing crisis. By ring four, I'm off the couch. Sitting on a nearby table is my new STU-III secure phone. It takes up most of a small briefcase, and every night when I come home, I plug it in. It has replaced the old code cards, which were such a pain to use. Now, from the comfort of my own townhouse, we can scramble all calls from FOGHORN and talk up to top secret. It is a great invention, but right now, I hate it.

"Burton."

It's FOGHORN. I listen to the agent on the other end of the line. Then I say, "Okay, going secure."

I push a button on the STU-III. After a pause, it switches into scramble mode. We can talk freely now.

"Okay, go," I say.

His first sentence knocks the relaxation clean out of me. His second has me reaching for the car keys. When we end the call, I make a beeline for the garage. I hardly have time to say good night to Sharon, who looks on at my departure with saddened eyes.

Fifteen minutes later, I reach the office and dash down the hallway to FOGHORN.

The agents on duty watch expectantly as I burst inside our communication center's inner sanctum. My mind is racing. We've got to act fast.

"Okay guys, let's crank up NLETS. Eastern seaboard. Send out descriptions of the suspect and his car. He's heavily armed and dangerous. We've got to find him." NLETS is the National Law Enforcement Telecommunications System. It allows us to mobilize police agencies all over the country.

The duty agents get busy. I get over to another secure phone and call the regional DSS office in Boston. "This is Agent Fred Burton. I need to talk with Special Agent Neeley."

I'm patched through to his line. Neeley is the Boston ASAIC—assistant special agent in charge. He was the one who called out the hounds on this one, and now I need more information.

Neeley tells me everything he knows. By the time I get off the phone, I have no doubt that we've got a serious situation on our hands. A lone nut is on his way to kill the secretary of state and the president.

Rose Gallo had called Neeley at 9 P.M. She told him that her son, Edward Louis Gallo, had been acting stranger and stranger throughout the weekend. On Sunday morning, he watched the TV news programs and suddenly erupted in anger. He paced around the house, screaming obscenities and threats. On one program, he saw both President Reagan and Secretary of State Shultz. That pushed him over the edge. He blew a gasket, shouting, "Kill! Kill Reagan! Shultz, you're *dead*."

It was in that state that he went for his guns. He'd recently purchased two shotguns and a civilian version of the M16. He wrapped them up in an old army fatigue jacket, dropped them in the trunk of his 1986 Buick sedan, and bugged out of his Worcester, Massachusetts, neighborhood, leaving his mother in a state of near panic.

She hadn't seen him since. So, at nine o'clock this evening, she made the hardest phone call of her life.

All night long we wait for word from the street. The local D.C. cops are supposed to be checking motel parking lots for the Buick. Others are on patrol, hoping to intercept Gallo before he reaches the capital. Meanwhile, we alert the Secret Service to the threat and give our own agents guarding the secretary of state a thorough briefing. Everyone mans their battle stations. We hunker down and wait.

A deranged man is coming to kill two key American leaders. Our protective security teams are the last line of defense. We've got to trust the local beat cops to do their jobs. They are the front line of this battle.

Dawn comes. No word. Rose has yet to hear from her son. She grows so concerned that she reports him missing later in the morning, despite the fact that every law-enforcement agency between Boston and D.C. is already out looking for him. This is understandable; she's being a mom.

Monday night, and nothing. The evening drags on without a single clue. Gallo's Buick has simply vanished into the vast American landscape. Finally, I have to get some sleep. Before midnight, I head home and fall asleep in my suit.

FOGHORN's phone call shakes me out of exhausted slumber. I grab the STU-III and even before I go secure, the agent tells me, "The car's been located, sir."

"On my way."

God bless the D.C. police. An alert Metropolitan Police Department beat cop spotted Gallo's black '86 Buick in the parking lot of the Regency Congress Inn. I know the place. It is a fleabag motel in a very poor, mostly African American district in north D.C. It sits on New York Avenue, one of the major thoroughfares into the capital from the northern suburbs.

Time to call in the cavalry. The MPD are already bringing in reinforcements, and we do the same. At Foggy Bottom, I grab a G-ride (a government car), another Crown Vic, and speed to the scene with lights flashing. Scott Tripp, the ASAIC from Secretary of State Shultz's security detail, meets me at the motel. He's the number-two man in what we call "the Detail." For us, guarding SECSTATE is like guarding the president is for the Secret Service. There's no higher duty within the DSS.

By the time we get to the scene, the MPD have already brought in a SWAT team. The area's cordoned off. Gallo is an out-of-work chemist, and there is concern that he's got explosives with him. The police stop traffic and clear the block. Very quietly, the MPD evacuates everyone from the motel. We confirm Gallo is in there.

Scott and I huddle up with the MPD leadership and discuss our options. We don't want this to turn into a siege. We decide waiting him out is a poor option. He could be heavily armed in there. Once he wakes up and sees us out here, he could start shooting. Better to surprise him. We decide to send in the SWAT team.

The entry squad lines up near Gallo's motel room door. Scott and I are not far away, watching the scene from behind a parked car. Our weapons are drawn. We'll be the SWAT team's backup should things go wrong.

The entry team moves to the door. Using a heavy battering ram, they smash the door in just as they start yelling, "Police! Police!" Within seconds, the cheap door crumples inward. Now comes the most vulnerable moment: getting through the doorway. If Gallo's in there waiting, he can kill the entire team should it get hung up in the entrance. That's why doorways are called fatal funnels.

The SWAT guys pour inside the room. We hear shouting and the sounds of a scuffle. Then a gunshot rings out. Scott and I look at each other, and without a word, we charge across the parking lot, weapons in hand. We reach the doorway, pause on the outside, then together swing through it.

We are too late. Edward Louis Gallo is lying handcuffed, facedown on the bed. He doesn't appear to be hurt, just pissed off. He's swearing at us. I look over at Mike Brooks, one of the SWAT team members, and ask, "What happened?"

Mike shakes his head and replies, "Accidental discharge. One of our guys tripped. Had his finger on his Uzi's trigger."

"Damn near blew my head off!" screams Gallo from the bed.

Thank God nobody was injured. What would we have told Rose Gallo if we'd accidentally killed her son?

A D.C. cop walks through the door and announces, "Press is here. The traffic situation must've gotten their attention."

I look at my watch. It is after eight. The morning commute has started, and we've got New York Avenue sealed off. It must be a total goat rope out there, especially with the press on the scene now.

We get Gallo on his feet and call for a cage car. He looks disheveled in a pair of trousers and a white T-shirt. We stuff him in the back of the car, which will take him to MPD headquarters. We'll follow in a few minutes. Both Scott and I are eager to talk to Gallo and find out what he'd been planning.

Before we leave, a bomb squad gingerly opens up Gallo's Buick. There'd been some fear that he'd wired it with explosives, but that turned out not to be the case. However, the trunk contains a mini arsenal. We find the AR-15, the civilian version of the M16. Nestled next to it is a Remington Model 820 Wingmaster 12-gauge shotgun. Gallo had sawed off the barrel and had removed the stock. He'd built himself a nice, compact street sweeper with it. He also had a Mossberg pump shotgun with him. Altogether, we gather up 110 shotgun shells and nine magazines for the AR-15—that's over 200 rounds of .223 ammunition. Edward Louis Gallo wanted a fight.

An hour later, Scott and I reach MPD headquarters. Traffic had been utter gridlock, and local news radio station WTOP covered the scene live. The press is all over this one, and reporters are hanging around the headquarters, trying to get some information out of the police. Fortunately, they ignore us as we head inside to meet with our would-be assassin. We link up with a Secret Service agent and an MPD detective. To-gether, we'll do the first interview.

The D.C. cops give us an interrogation room and bring Gallo to us still in handcuffs. When he sits down across from us, I see that his eyes have a hollowed-out look. It is eerie. Gallo isn't all here. He starts mum-bling to himself. Scott and I exchange quick glances. We may not even be able to interview him. He's clearly not well.

"Mr. Gallo," I ask, "what are you doing here in D.C.?"

Without looking at me, he shouts, "I'm a tourist! I'm an American tourist!"

"What did you come down to see?"

"I'm a hunter! I was going hunting."

"Hunting for what?" I ask. "What do you hunt with an AR-15?"

He doesn't respond at first. Then he mutters something under his breath. He becomes incoherent again, but suddenly through the non-sense, he recites Secretary of State Shultz's private address.

"How did you know that?" I ask, stunned by this revelation.

Gallo mumbles incoherently. In mid-babble, I hear him say some-thing about his television controlling his mind.

Thirty minutes later, we end the interview. "The guy's a whack job," the Secret Service agent says as we part ways.

"Maybe. But how did he know the SECSTATE's home address?"

The Secret Service agent shrugs and heads out. The MPD detective turns to me and says, "We'll probably transfer him to St. Elizabeths Hos-pital. Your fed buddy's right. Gallo's a nutcase."

I return to Foggy Bottom unsettled by the entire episode. Something is not right here. Gallo should not have known where George Shultz lives. That is closely guarded information. We need to do a full workup on Gallo.

In the days that follow, Gallo is held without bail on multiple weapons charges. The MPD does transfer him to St. Elizabeths Hospital, where he receives psychiatric care. In the meantime, the pieces of his past start to come into focus.

Edward Louis Gallo was once a brilliant chemist with great poten-tial. He worked for ten years as a manager at the Upper Blackstone Water Pollution Abatement District in Millbury, Massachusetts. His coworkers had nothing but praise for his intelligence and analytical abilities. He was well liked and affable enough, though he wasn't close to anyone in his office. His neighbors said the same thing. Nice guy. Very smart. Kept to himself.

Then his dad died in 1982. His grandfather passed away not long afterward. Gallo was devastated by their deaths, and he never really recovered. He began hearing voices. He flew into fits of rage without any provocation. Sometimes the neighbors would see him standing in his front yard, screaming and cursing at invisible people. At work, his performance deteriorated. He got into verbal altercations with his coworkers. He developed an explosive temper and sometimes threw books around when upset. A couple of times, his peers found him walking in frantic circles around a bench outside their office.

In 1986, Gallo lost his job. He spent the next fourteen months watching television and living with his mom. He grew angrier, and his rage gradually focused on two individuals: President Reagan and Secretary of State Shultz. He would curse them every time they came on his television. He would shout their names and scream that he would kill them. When he finally left the house on Sunday, November 1, he'd been fixated on the two men for months.

Edward Louis Gallo may be a mentally ill chemist, but he is also a combat veteran. After graduating from college in 1968, he joined the army and served as a young lieutenant in Vietnam. He was a ninety-day wonder, and he served with great distinction. His unit saw heavy combat around Saigon, and before he came home in the fall of 1970, Gallo had been awarded the Bronze Star for valor. Bronze Stars for meritorious service are a dime a dozen from Vietnam, but Gallo's is for bravery on the battlefield. He's a war hero.

His military records also show that he is an expert marksman.

Gallo is not your off-the-rack, loser, lone-gunman type. He doesn't fit the profile. I need to talk to him at length. In mid-November, I make arrangements with St. Elizabeths to sit down with Gallo for a series of interviews. When I arrive at the hospital, I'm shocked at Gallo's transformation. They have him medicated, and instead of a delusional, muttering lunatic, I'm met by a calm and highly intelligent human being. Whatever had gone wrong inside Edward Louis Gallo could obviously be controlled.

"Mr. Gallo, how did you know Secretary of State Shultz's address?"

He answers matter-of-factly, "I followed his motorcade."

What? How did our agents not detect him?

"How did you do that?"

Gallo shrugs and replies, "I sat on a bench outside the Truman Building. Watched the motorcades come and go. After a while, I figured out which limousine was the secretary of state's. It wasn't that hard."

He goes on to recite a typical day for George Shultz. He's spot-on, and his description is chillingly detailed.

He concludes by off-handedly mentioning, "One day, I parked near the VIP entrance and just followed him home."

Unbelievable. I'm reeling at this.

"What did you do once you followed Shultz to his house?"

"Watched things. That guard in the front yard with the Uzi made it tougher, but I still was able to do it."

He starts recounting our security arrangements. He has an amazing memory and an eye for detail. He figured out how many agents protect SECSTATE, where they are posted, when shift changes take place. He found the gaps in the security screen and developed contingency plans to penetrate them.

He also spent hours watching the Truman Building from different positions on the street. He took note of our security arrangements for motorcades and knew where each agent was placed. He noted their fields of fire and areas of responsibility.

Gallo deciphered and compromised everything. Worst of all, we never even noticed him. Had it not been for his mother, I have no doubt he would have been able to execute an attack on the secretary of state. Gallo in his nonmedicated, delusional condition could have delivered a devastating blow to the United States.

I spend hours debriefing Edward Louis Gallo. When I come away from our meetings, I can't help but feel sorry for the man. He had built a successful life for himself, only to see it ruined by family tragedy and mental illness. Once treated, he seemed utterly normal. But by then, it was too late. His career had been derailed, his relationships had frayed, and his delusions drove him to attempt assassinations. Now he's a brilliant but ruined man who will spend years behind bars.

At the same time, he has highlighted profound weaknesses in our security operations. How was he able to conduct such extensive surveillance without attracting our attention? How was he able to follow the Detail around, snoop out our tactical deployments at Shultz's house, and figure out the best places to launch an attack? Clearly, we need to do something different.

We never saw him coming. That fact haunts me. It underscores our vulnerability and makes it blindingly obvious that we need to totally revise how we do business on protective security details. If we don't, somebody in our charge is going to die.

nineteen

PAK-1 DOWN

August 17, 1988
Bethesda

Flash Precedence

We have been informed by the Pakistani foreign minister that the presidential aircraft, PAK-1, crashed near Bahawalpur. There were no survivors. President Zia-ul-Haq, Ambassador Raphel, and U.S. Army BG Wassom plus the Pakistani joint chiefs of staff were killed in the crash. Pakistani military units are en route to the scene and martial law has been declared.

Post requests further guidance by flash precedence.

From my desk behind the big blue door, I reread the cable with a sinking feeling. Pakistan's senior governmental and military leaders are all dead. Zia barely held the country together with terror and an iron rule when he was alive. With him dead, Pakistan could dissolve into total chaos—with nukes. And all of this is going down at ground zero for the biggest Cold War conflict since Vietnam.

Zia was our closest ally in south Asia. He spearheaded our covert war against the Soviets in Afghanistan. It is through Pakistan that all our weapons, money, and ammunition flow to the mujahideen. Now, just as the Soviets have cried "uncle" and started pulling out of Afghanistan, the key architect of our victory has been burned to ashes.

I wish Steve Gleason was here; he always handled these crises with a cool hand. Unfortunately, he left the office a few months back to take an RSO slot overseas.

I huddle with our new chief, who is a good man, to gameboard how we'll handle the news. We decide to send an immediate intelligence tasker (IT) to every embassy and RSO across the globe. An IT is an urgent message designed to marshal all our assets, sources, and contacts to focus on one series of specific questions. It is our way of broadcasting a need for detailed information, and fast.

We don't know if PAK-1's destruction was a result of an accident or assassination. We've got to find out if there were any threats leveled at Zia or the ambassador prior to the flight. That's question number one for our tasker. Question number two assumes the worst. If it was a hit, is anyone taking credit for it? Is anyone boasting about it? Are there any clues out there?

The taskers are sent out with flash precedence. All over the world, our intelligence operatives scramble. They work their own sources and meet with security and intel agencies from Germany to Canada, Saudi Arabia to the Philippines.

The Dark World is totally silent today. No threats are reported. No bragging or credit taking is heard. This has never happened before, at least not since I joined the DSS. After huge geopolitical events, the Dark World's communication sinews always sing with rumor and innuendo. Then the walk-ins start trickling into our embassies and office here at Foggy Bottom. And of course, we get the crazies, too.

With this crisis, there's nothing. Not even the whack jobs come out of the woodwork this time. What's it mean?

In Washington, the CIA, FBI, NSA, DIA, NSC, and the State Department all frantically review their files, looking for anything that we collectively might have missed. Was there some warning that got overlooked? Other than the typical saber rattling between Pakistan and India, and the Soviet Union's hostility toward Pakistan over their defeat in Afghanistan, there's nothing specific to indicate a plot against President Zia.

Maybe the crash was an accident—an accident that happened to wipe out the better part of an ally's leadership.

There are no coincidences in the Dark World. This smells like a hit. If it was, it'll rank as one of the most successful in history. The assassins essentially decapitated Pakistan's command-and-control leadership with one event.

Within a couple of hours of the crash, the situation in south Asia has deteriorated even further. The Pakistani army and air force are at each other's throats, tossing accusations and recriminations back and forth. The surviving members of the government are paranoid that a coup is under way. Simultaneously, India has increased its military's alert status. Some Pakistanis suspect the Indians have assassinated their president. The tension between the two nuclear-armed nations is growing by the hour. Troops are massing along both sides of the border, and their nuclear readiness has been increased. In the middle of it all, we still have the CIA running a covert war out of Pakistan against the Soviets in Afghanistan.

My phone rings. Mr. Dittmer and our new CT chief want to see me ASAP. Apparently, I'm going to Islamabad.

twenty

The air force executive jet speeds us over the Atlantic. This time, I cross the pond in comfort. The seats are plush, the heater works so I don't need the extra-thick coat I brought along, and the coffee is first-rate. I sit in shirtsleeves next to Brad Bryson, both of us sipping our java as we talk about the mission ahead. Brad's working for me on this mission, though we were in the same training class back in 1985. He joined the CT office only a few months ago, and now he's getting the same hard-core introduction to the Dark World that I did. He's not much older than twenty-four.

Time to brief Brad.

"Okay, here's the situation. Pakistan is coming unglued. They had a weak central government to begin with. But now with Zia and most of the rest of the leadership dead, the country could very well fall into civil war. At the same time, we've picked up some intelligence suggesting that India is considering a preemptive strike against Pakistan. They're afraid the Pakistanis will blame them for Zia's death and launch their nukes. A first strike takes care of that fear."

The color drains out of Brad's face. "Jesus Christ," he whispers.

"Yeah. It's bad."

Brad says, "And we're flying into the middle of it?"

"Yes. To defuse it."

"By finding out who really killed Zia?"

"Not exactly," I reply. "Look, the National Security Council and the boys on the seventh floor at Foggy Bottom talked this over. What the world needs right now is a cooling-off period. A crash investigation will buy time for everyone. It forces the Pakistanis to wait for our conclusions before they respond to anything. Plus, if we discover it was an accident, the international implications evaporate. The Pakistanis will still have internal issues to deal with, but at least they won't be tossing nukes at the Indians."

Brad asks, "But what if we conclude the Indians assassinated Zia?"

"Well, let's hope they're not that stupid."

Brad doesn't respond. He looks as tense as I feel. I didn't even get a chance to say good-bye to Sharon. If I end up as collateral damage in a Pakistan-Indian nuclear war, she'll never even know how I died.

"Okay, the NSC decided to send me as the lead investigator for the State Department. You and I will be working with an air force crash investigation team that we'll link up with in Germany. We'll fly out to Islamabad together."

Brad starts taking notes. As he writes, he asks, "Why isn't the NTSB doing this?"

The National Transportation Safety Board has the best crash analysis and investigation unit in the world. Brad's question is a logical one. I'm not surprised he thought of this. He's an exceptionally sharp agent and possesses not just a keen intellect, but common sense as well. He had no prior law-enforcement experience before coming to the DSS. This is a rare thing for our service, but the powers that be saw a young college grad with tremendous potential.

"NSC decision. The NTSB team includes an FBI agent. Mr. Dittmer told me that the NSC concluded that his presence would actually ratchet up the tension, not relieve it. It would send a signal to the Pakistanis— and everyone else—that the United States believes the crash site is actually a crime scene."

"It could be."

"Yes, but we don't want to telegraph that. The world's in a precarious

position right now. Perception is everything. An air force crash team
sends a better message. Zia's plane was an old C-130 Hercules built during the Vietnam era. The air force team wants to find out what went
wrong mechanically. See the difference in perception? Besides, right now
if we sent the FBI in, the Pakistanis would take it as an insult. Like they
can't investigate their own president's death. Their pride is at stake."

"Okay, but the FBI must be pretty pissed to be shut out."

"That's their problem. We've got plenty of others. Besides, the NSC
will run interference for us. Colin Powell, Dick Armitage, and Robert
Oakley made a point of taking care of us and have already paved the way
for our arrival with the Pakistani authorities. They've been assured we'll
get complete cooperation once we get there."

Brad thinks this over for a minute, then asks, "Why won't our presence get the same reaction the FBI's would?"

"Good question. We're there because of Ambassador Raphel's death.
Don't forget that it is the DSS's job to investigate any diplomat's death
overseas. We'd be there no matter what the situation, so our presence is
just standard operating procedure."

"Right. Okay. What do you need from me?"

I've never been the lead investigator on a case like this. With all the
international entanglements and tension, it could get ugly, and the truth
could get lost. I'm going to need his eyes, ears, and analytical skills on this
mission. Brad worked in the DSS's Washington Field Office fresh out of
agent training. I wanted his mind in the CT office, and the first chance I
got, I convinced Gleason to snag him away from the WFO.

"Observe everything. The little details, the subtle vocal inflections
of a witness, the body language of our hosts—watch for these things. Figure everywhere we go, we'll be under surveillance, so be careful what you
say to me, okay? Our rooms are bound to be bugged. So be discreet."

Brad's face pales. Beneath the color drain, though, I see resolve. The
kid's okay. He's got mettle. He just needs experience.

I finish off my coffee and stare into the bottom of the cup for a couple of heartbeats. "The most important thing is the truth, okay?"

"Okay."

"There's going to be a lot of pressure on us. No doubt there will be
conclusions that the Pakistanis want, conclusions that our government
will want, conclusions that others want—the CIA, Pakistan's Inter-

Services Intelligence. Who knows. Ignore all that. Keep your mind open and don't let any of the politics influence you."

As the senior man, I can't show the stark terror that's boiling beneath my professional façade. The truth is, I'm not sure I'm ready for what's ahead.

"One more thing," I add. "We may be targets ourselves. If this is an inside job, whoever did it will not want to get caught. Right now, everyone's a suspect."

"I've got your back, Fred. Don't worry about that."

Brad's a straight arrow whose character is rooted in his middle-American upbringing in South Dakota. He's a good man to have at my side on this mission. We're going to have to walk a tightrope. If we screw up, we could very well precipitate a war. That was made clear to me before we left Foggy Bottom.

"Pakistan has always been a dicey post. Don't forget what happened in '79. They came over the embassy walls in Islamabad and a marine got killed. It looked like it was going to be a repeat of Tehran. Not much has changed. If anything, there are more radicals on the street, and there could be some in the ISI and their air force. Keep your head on a swivel."

We both fall silent. The executive jet speeds us to our rendezvous with the air force crash team. I spend the rest of the flight staring out my window, lost in thought. Outside, all I see is impenetrable darkness. I wonder if I will ever see my wife again.

twenty-one

In Germany, we bid adieu to our executive jet and climb aboard a cavernous monster of an aircraft. The air force calls it a C-5A Galaxy, but I think that name is an understatement. The thing can hold a battalion of troops, or a pair of tanks, or even a couple of helicopters. Looking around in the cargo bay is like standing in the hold of a supertanker. It makes the C-141 look like an anorexic teenager.

Along with the crash team, we're this beast's only cargo. We'll leave from Rhein-Main and fly nonstop straight to Islamabad. Besides being the largest plane in America's inventory, it also has a true global reach. Galaxy pilots think nothing of flying to destinations half a world away. They do it all the time. It's going to be a very long flight.

We stow our gear aboard and find seats.

We've still got about an hour before departure. The crew is busy with all their preflight duties, and we're pretty much on our own until it is time to go. Brad and I decide to take this time to go meet the air force guys.

I find the crash team's commanding officer, Colonel Dan Sowada, standing near the C-5's back ramp. Brad and I go over and introduce ourselves.

"What do you make of the reports so far?" I ask Colonel Sowada.

"Well, we're gathering as much information as we can right now on prior C-130 crashes. But I will say this: C-130s are used all over the world. They fly hundreds of thousands of hours a year. They don't just fall out of the sky."

"That's for sure," his team's engineer confirms as he walks up to introduce himself. "The Herk is one of the most reliable planes we've got. That's why so many countries use them."

"Most of the ones produced are still flying, even the ones built in the fifties."

I ask, "When was Zia's plane built?"

The engineer responds, "In 1962. Came off the line in Marietta, Georgia. It was a C-130B-LM. The B models had better engines than the earlier variant, the A."

"Still, the plane was twenty-five years old," Brad says.

"True, but most of the C-130 fleet is that old anyway."

Sowada says, "Let's not jump to conclusions. We've got to do this one right and be thorough."

"Agreed," I say.

One of the C-5 crew members walks over to our little group. "Gentlemen, we're ready to go. Time to load up."

We turn and walk inside the Galaxy. As we find our seats, Brad's earlier comment hits me right between the eyes.

What if we find out the Indians did it?

God, I hope this was just a tragic accident. But that would just be too tidy, too coincidental, especially give the fact that there were thirty-one high-value targets on board. Deep down, I know this one's bound to get ugly.

The C-5 lifts off and wings eastward. The flight is long and cold, and I'm glad I have my Barbour Beaufort handy. I hunker down in it and try to get some sleep. When we get in country, sleep will be a luxury.

Almost half a day later, we make our final approach into Islamabad's Chaklala Air Base. We arrive in the middle of the night and the C-5 rolls to a stop in a remote corner of the airport. The Galaxy is quickly surrounded by a mixed group of Pakistani special forces soldiers and U.S. Air Force security troops. When we deplane, we find the CIA waiting for us with blacked-out vans.

The vans race us into the city, where Pakistani soldiers armed with assault rifles stand guard on every street corner. The capital is basically in lockdown mode.

The vans take us to the Holiday Inn. Here we are in a city on the brink of war, and we'll be staying at a vacation destination. I can't help but laugh at the irony.

Fifteen minutes later, the embassy RSO shows up in an armored vehicle and picks us up. I've met Mel Harrison before in Washington, D.C. He's a good man, a straight shooter who has had a very unusual career. He served as an economics officer in London during one tour. On another, he spent six months at the NATO war college studying military history and tactics. He's tall and lanky with a studious persona and a broad mind, thanks in part to his atypical career path.

Tonight, he's extremely quiet. He says little until we get to his house, where dinner is waiting for us. While we eat, he drops a bombshell.

"Fred, I was supposed to be on that plane." He can't even look at us as he says those words. Instead, he stares out a window. Arnold Raphel was his friend. Right then, the human cost finally becomes real to me. Up until now, I've been approaching this from the geopolitical perspective, with all its implications. Seeing Mel's grief drives home the painful truth of this tragedy. Thirty-one families are without loved ones tonight. Two of our own men are dead. On top of his case of survivor's guilt, Mel is grieving for his lost friend.

"I was supposed to be on that flight," Mel says again, almost under his breath.

"What happened?" I ask.

"Ambassador Raphel decided at the last minute that he wanted to go. He figured it would give him an opportunity to talk to President Zia about an attack on an American nun. He wanted some assurances that those responsible would be punished."

This is news to both Brad and me. "Wait, you're saying Ambassador Raphel was not scheduled to be on that plane?"

"Right. He bumped me at the last minute."

Brad says, "Well we can discount the chance that this was a hit on the ambassador then." Mel agrees.

I breathe a sigh of relief. That was one of the first things we were told to investigate. We can put that one to rest.

"Mel, tell us what you know about the crash," I say.

The RSO launches into the complete story. President Zia, the joint chiefs of staff, the head of the ISI, and other VIPs took the trip from Islamabad to Bahawalpur to attend an M1 Abrams tank demonstration. The U.S. government had just sealed a deal with Zia to sell Pakistan a bunch of these formidable machines, and the VIPs wanted to get a first-hand look at them.

The demonstration had been planned weeks in advance.

President Zia's C-130 lifted off from Chaklala on the morning of August 17. It flew down to Bahawalpur without incident. The VIPs watched the tank demonstration and returned to the airport that after-noon. The C-130 taxied out to the runway and took off after the crew went through the normal preflight checklist. Five minutes after takeoff, the plane went down. Nobody survived. It was a catastrophic impact. Only pieces remain of the aircraft.

"Tomorrow morning, you'll get an introduction and full briefing by the Pakistani Air Force. After that, they will fly you down to the crash site," Mel says.

I have many questions, but Mel looks weary. He probably hasn't slept since the crash.

"Were there any prior threats against President Zia?" I ask.

"None that we picked up."

"Any warning indicators at all that an operation was under way?"

"No. We never saw this coming. If it was sabotage, it was done very quietly."

"What about the ISI?" Brad asks.

Mel shakes his head. "They had no threats on the board either." He hesitates for a second, then changes his statement. "Let's put it this way. If they had any information on an imminent threat, the ISI did not share it with us."

"Would that be unusual?" I ask.

"No. I wouldn't put it past the ISI to hide something from us. But if they had a warning, they've shredded all evidence of it by now. And Zia did have a long enemies list."

"If that's the case, we'll never learn the truth," Brad says.

"Maybe. But look, given all the things we know so far, I'm inclined to believe the plane crashed because of mechanical failure. The weather was clear, so that couldn't have caused the crash. If somebody was planning to hit Zia, we probably would have had something come in, some sort of a threat. There's been nothing. It is hard to keep an operation of this magnitude totally blacked out."

That's true. "Well," he says while staring out the window again, "I hope it was mechanical failure. The implications are too grim if it wasn't. If it was a foreign-backed plot or a coup attempt, this could get out of control very quickly."

Brad and I finish our meals. The table is cleared. We're exhausted from the flight, and I suppose we look as weary as Mel does. He decides to take us back to the Holiday Inn, but before we leave, he gives us a word of caution. "Look, tread lightly on this one, Fred. I know your reputation. Be careful, okay?"

When it comes to the truth, I'm not really sure how to tread lightly. But I try to reassure him. "That's why we're here, Mel. The NSC didn't want to send the wrong signal with an NTSB team or the FBI."

"Good. One other thing."

"What's that?"

"Your hotel . . ." Mel falters for a minute. He seems to be trying to phrase something in his head and is having a hard time finding the right words. "Look, there's a lot of anti-American sentiment on the street here. Plenty of people hate us. Your hotel is where most Americans stay when they come to the city."

"We'll be careful, Mel," I assure him.

"Good, because the hotel's been bombed several times already."

Brad and I exchange looks. I doubt either of us will sleep tonight.

twenty-two

Back at the Holiday Inn, I lie awake in a strange bed in a stranger city awash in tension. I sense that the days ahead will be some of the defining ones of my life. If we help to avert a war and save lives, it will more than validate my decision to turn fed and leave my old neighborhood and precinct behind. If we blow it and fall off the tightrope... well, I don't want to think about that.

We left the United States in darkness, departed from Germany at night, and got to Pakistan after sunset. I've lost all concept of time, and my body doesn't know if it should rest or be up and moving.

In the darkness of the night, the Muslim call to prayer blares from speakers all over the city. I get up and peer out the window, listening to this half song, half chant that is such an embedded part of Islamic culture. For the life of me, I can't help but think it sounds sinister.

When the baying of the muezzin ends, I slide back under the covers and return to the mystery at hand. What do we know? Not much so far, though two things stand out in my mind. First, the weather was good on the day of the flight. That rules out a lightning strike or turbulence as an accident cause. Second, and much more worrisome from a security and counterterrorism perspective, is the event President Zia and his entourage attended. The tank trials had been scheduled far in advance. If the time and date had been leaked to the wrong people, an orchestrated assassination could have been arranged.

In the Dark World, assassinations are driven by opportunity. You must have the killer or killing device in the right place at the right time. To do it right, the assassin needs foreknowledge. Where is the target going to be on a particular day?

With JFK, it was Dallas. Since the route was public knowledge, Oswald knew where he needed to be to get the best shot on the motorcade. With Archduke Ferdinand, it was Sarajevo in June 1914. His arrival in the city was known long in advance, giving his enemies a chance to station assassins all along his motorcade's route.

Take away that foreknowledge, and the assassin is left without a way to get to his target. This is why the schedules of heads of state are usually closely guarded secrets. Was Zia's compromised? Did the tank trials make him vulnerable?

Yes, they did. Now we need to find out if somebody or some organization took advantage of it.

The next morning, we're stuffed into the blacked-out Agency vans again and rushed through the city toward the airport. Again, soldiers stand on every street corner, assault rifles at the ready. At one point, we stop at an intersection, and I look out my window to see one particularly crusty-looking Pakistani noncommissioned officer. I'm just a few feet away from him, separated only by a tinted window and a few inches of aluminum. He fingers his assault rifle's trigger and stares at our van. How easy would it be for him to kill us all right now? Our security is zero. We're in the middle of a city full of hostility toward Americans. If something went down, we would not stand a chance.

My pucker meter is pegged. But all I can do is hang on to my seat rest and keep my head on a swivel. If they come after us, at the very least they'll have a fight on their hands. I have fifteen rounds, and I will make every one count.

Very few people are out and about, which I take as a good sign. If there were mass protests and riots going on, the surviving members of the government might overreact. They're already paranoid that somebody's orchestrating a coup. Put crowds on the street and soldiers with guns on every corner and nothing good can come of that. Just ask the British after the Boston Massacre.

We reach Chaklala Air Base and go through security again. We're taken to Pakistani Air Force headquarters and ushered into a conference room full of officers and Pakistani ISI-types. One intel officer wearing a general's uniform glowers at us from a back corner of the room. Spooks can almost always pick up other spooks in this sort of situation. This guy's eyes say to me, "We see everything and we are watching you."

Point taken. We may have some trust issues here.

Brad and I are introduced to everyone in the room. Most of the left-over senior military leadership has come to greet us and listen in on this first briefing. The air force colonels and generals standing nearby appear nervous and downcast. I'm not surprised. PAK-1 was their most important bird. Now that it has crashed, their necks are on the chopping block—literally. Pakistanis do not suffer failure well.

A round-faced, slightly bug-eyed Pakistani colonel introduces himself and shakes my hand. With his big, bushy mustache, he reminds me of Cheech Marin from the early eighties Cheech and Chong movies.

"Welcome to Pakistan, and thank you for coming," he says. From his eyes and body language, I don't think he's happy we're here. He turns to Colonel Sowada and continues, "Anything you need, please tell me. I am here to make sure your team has full cooperation."

"Thank you, Colonel, we appreciate that," Sowada replies diplomatically.

"Gentlemen, please find a seat. We will give you a full briefing."

Cheech steps to a podium at the front of the room and surprises us with his first words. "We have already solved the mystery. We know how PAK-1 went down."

He has a flare for drama, I'll give him that. A brief caesura follows his opening statement. It gives me time to think. It took us twenty-four hours to get from the United States to Pakistan. Did something break in the interim? If so, why didn't Mel know about it last night?

Cheech reaches down behind the podium and produces a ragged chunk of metal. He holds it up and announces, "This is a piece of PAK-1's fuselage. Notice the hole in it?" He points to it and pauses again. "This proves a missile struck the C-130. This is the entry hole."

Silence. Is anyone buying this? I steal a glance around the room. The

Pakistanis look grim and serious. The ISI spook in the back spears me with his eyes. That is one hostile dude. I wonder what his beef is with Americans.

Cheech continues to hold up the fuselage piece for everyone to see. The exterior side still has some of PAK-1's paint on it. "It was a surface-to-air missile, probably shoulder-fired. This happened once before, seven years ago, and almost brought down PAK-1 then. Fortunately, that missile missed."

Colonel Sowada doesn't look impressed. He and Brad watch me, expecting me to respond. I need to be a leader here, and I need to remember all the warnings we've had. Tread lightly. This is a precarious situation. Diplomacy is paramount.

"So, we've solved the mystery," Cheech repeats. Between the lines I read *Which is why you Americans don't need to be here. Thanks for coming. Bye-bye, then.*

I can't help myself. This is nonsense. I stand up and say, "There's no way that hole was made by a missile."

Cheech coldly responds, "Oh? What makes you think so?"

It is so obvious that I'm not sure how to be polite about it. "Well," I begin, "if you look at the way the hole is torn in that piece from the fuselage, you'll see whatever went through it went from inside to outside. That hole was made by something exiting the aircraft, not penetrating it."

"How do you know this?" Cheech's face reddens. Is he angry or embarrassed? I'm not sure, and at this point it doesn't matter.

I pick up my pencil and tear a sheet of paper out of my notebook. I hold them both up and push the pencil through the paper. "See how the paper's torn edges push outward from the hole I've just made? They follow the path of the pencil. Take a look at that piece of metal. See all the jagged pieces flowering out of the hole? They are bent the wrong way for a missile hit. Something came *out* of the C-130 through that hole."

There's no way to dispute that. With a roomful of generals and colonels staring at him, Cheech looks utterly humiliated. Obviously, he'd staked his credibility on his theory, and I've just yanked his pants down in front of his superiors.

Off in the corner, the ISI spook starts taking notes. That can't be good for Cheech. Or me, for that matter. This was my first diplomatic test, and I blew it. Still, there's something to be said for the tone I just set. We'll let the facts speak for themselves, and the Pakistanis now know that. Hopefully, they'll respect our approach. We won't be bullied into any conclusions.

Cheech stands in silence. The room waits expectantly, and as the awkward moment continues, I realize I may have really done some damage here. Time to get things moving again.

"Colonel, could you give us some background on the flight?"

Cheech recovers. "Certainly, Agent Burton." His tone is frosty. He flashes me a look like he wants to skin me alive.

"At 3:46 in the afternoon of August 17, PAK-1 took off with thirty-one men aboard. Before takeoff, a Cessna security plane swept the area and saw nothing. Five minutes after takeoff, the C-130 crashed in the desert several kilometers from the airport at Bahawalpur. Everyone was killed on impact."

Colonel Sowada asks, "Did you recover the cockpit voice recorder?"

"The plane was not equipped with one." The news surprises all of us in the American team. No voice recorder? That could have been a major help to our investigation.

Colonel Sowada probes that issue. "If there is no voice recorder, did the tower at Bahawalpur hear the pilots say anything out of the ordinary? Did the tower hear a distress call?"

"All communication with the tower was routine. The pilots did not issue a Mayday."

This is an important piece of the puzzle. No Mayday. We'll need to figure out how long the aircraft was in trouble before it crashed. If it exploded in midair, the absence of a distress signal would be understandable. But what if they had time to call for help and didn't? What does that mean?

Cheech continues, "The Cessna security plane did hear a brief transmission shortly before PAK-1 crashed."

"What?" Colonel Sowada asks. This is a revelation to all of us.

"They heard somebody inside the aircraft shouting 'Mash'hood! Mash'hood!' The command pilot's name was Wing Commander Mash'hood Hussan."

I ask, "Any idea who was shouting?"

Cheech shakes his head. "No. We do not know. We do know that it was not the copilot. The voice probably came from the VIP capsule located inside the cargo bay."

"What about the pilots? Were they reliable?" I ask.

"They were handpicked by President Zia himself based on their experience and loyalty. They were absolutely reliable. They were our best."

That's good to know.

Colonel Sowada changes the subject. "Colonel, can you tell me about PAK-1's maintenance cycle?"

"It went through a major overhaul less than a month ago. The C-130 had been flown less than fifty hours since."

"Was the hydraulic fluid changed during that overhaul?"

Where's Colonel Sowada going with that question?

Cheech looks as puzzled as I am. "I do not know, but I will find out the answer for you."

"Thank you. How about the fuel used in PAK-1? Could it have been tainted or tampered with?"

He is ready for that one. "PAK-1 was fueled here at Chaklala before the flight down to Bahawalpur. It was not refueled before takeoff for its return flight. We have tested the fuel used here and found no contaminants whatsoever. We have ruled that out as a cause of the crash."

What about a bomb on the aircraft? I probe that carefully. "Colonel, what sort of screening procedures do you use on packages and items coming aboard PAK-1? And was there anything brought aboard in Bahawalpur?"

Cheech grabs the sides of the podium with both hands. He locks his elbows and looks angry and embarrassed. "I do not know the answer to either question, but I will find out for you."

The meeting breaks up a few minutes later. Cheech makes a point of avoiding me. Dealing with him from now on will be like waltzing with a porcupine. As we leave the room to convoy back into the city, I notice the ISI spook's eyes never leave us. He's setting the tone, too. Big Brother, Islamabad-style, is watching.

We stop at the embassy, where we meet with Mel Harrison and the deputy chief of mission, Beth Jones. Beth underscores the need for us to be diplomatic. I don't have the heart to tell her I already blew my chance to learn the Pakistani two-step. The truth doesn't dance.

We brief them both about what we've learned. In return, they tell us that things are reaching a boiling point with India. Publicly, the Indians have declared three days of mourning for President Zia, which is clearly a gesture designed to defuse the growing tension. Behind the scenes, though, both the Pakistanis and Indians have escalated their readiness. Their fingers are on hair triggers. One twitch and a lot of people are going to die. It makes me think of that scene on Lexington Green two hundred years ago when the British Army confronted Captain Parker and his Minutemen. Both sides were cocked, locked, and ready. Who fired "the shot heard round the world"? Nobody will ever know. If it happens here, will it matter who launched first?

As we leave, Mel walks us to our spook convoy. He tells us, "You'll be flying to the crash scene in the morning. Do what you can, and do it quick. This thing is getting out of hand. The last time the world was this close to a nuclear exchange was 1962. Cuban Missile Crisis."

"Well, the sooner we get to Bahawalpur, the better."

Brad nods in agreement.

"Before we leave, can we have a sit-down with the station chief?" I ask.

Mel stops walking with us. We come up short, turn, and watch him. "Funny thing about that, Fred. The station chief left for Washington a few hours after the crash. While you were flying here, he was flying back to D.C."

"Really?" In the middle of a crisis like this one, the CIA's top officer in country has gone home? That is very odd.

"Yeah. Strange, isn't it? You can talk with his deputy after you examine the crash site."

"Okay, that sounds good. We'll do everything we can to get answers in Bahawalpur."

"Good. I just hope we're still here when you get back."

twenty-three

"You've got to be kidding me," Brad Bryson says to me. We're standing side by side, looking at our ride to Bahawalpur. It is an ancient-looking C-130 Hercules. Just like President Zia's.

"Remind me to cuss out the CIA for not giving the Pakistanis newer planes."

"Amen to that," Brad says.

We're dressed in jeans, boots, and khaki button-down shirts covered by tan vests. Brad and I look ready to go on safari. All we need are pith helmets.

The absurdity of the moment is just too much. We're going to go check out a smoking crater that once was a C-130—and we're flying to it in a near-identical aircraft.

"Don't they say these things happen in threes?" Brad asks.

"Yeah. I hope we're not number two."

Cheech comes over to us and must sense our trepidation. "Agent Burton, we have assigned two of our best pilots for your flight."

That's a comfort, seeing as number one and number two are in pieces somewhere in the Punjab desert. Should I say that? No, Beth Jones wouldn't consider that being diplomatic. I bite my tongue.

"I have answers for you to your questions from this morning." He seems to be genuinely trying to be nice. Maybe I didn't get him in trouble after all. "Okay, there were some items brought aboard PAK-1 at Bahawalpur. Two crates of mangoes and a couple of model aircraft."

I think this over for a moment. "Were they screened for explosives?"

"Yes. They were visually inspected."

Okay, that's something. "What about bomb dogs?"

"Dogs?" Cheech asks, puzzled. I sense a hint of disgust in his voice.

"Bomb-sniffing dogs. Were any used to check out the things that came aboard?"

"Agent Burton, dogs are filthy creatures. We would never have them anywhere near the presidential aircraft."

I'm not sure how to respond. He went from cordial to borderline hostile again. As he walks away, he tosses another bone our way. "I checked with the maintenance officer. The hydraulic fluid was replaced last month during the routine overhaul. Please convey that to Colonel Sowada."

Once he's out of earshot, Brad notes, "Muslim culture believes dogs are vile animals."

I'd forgotten that. I'm now two for two with Cheech. I've insulted him and humiliated him. So much for that relationship.

A few minutes later, we pile aboard the C-130 through the back cargo ramp. The seats are all positioned sideways in the bay, which means we'll be looking at one another from opposite rows on either side of the fuselage for the entire flight. I guess it might be better that way. If we crash, at least we won't have to see the ground spinning our way.

Colonel Sowada's team feels right at home. I'm sure they've traveled by C-130 before, as they strap themselves in without a hint of concern. Brad and I fumble with our seat straps until we finally figure them out. Just as we get settled, a Pakistani airman walks through the cargo bay to hand each one of us a set of earplugs. I take mine, tear open the package, and say, "Guess we won't be talking much on this flight."

The pilots arrive and move to the flight deck. They go through their checklist, flipping switches and turning knobs. They finish, and the engines fire up.

Holy cow. The earplugs do no good. There are four gigantic turbo-prop engines over our heads turning sixteen massive propeller blades. The din is staggering. The entire plane vibrates and shakes, and the roaring sound of the engines burrows straight into my head. It engulfs us, and within seconds my senses are overloaded. God, we're not even off the ground yet.

The pilots go through another checklist. When complete, the Hercules starts to move. We taxi toward the runway, and the pilots stop for one more preflight check. The engines are run up, and the cacophony grows to the point where it feels like my skull will split open. I'm vibrated so badly that I wonder if my fillings will break loose.

Brad shouts something in my ear. I have no idea what he's trying to say. Across from us, Colonel Sowada and his team appear placid and at ease. I hope that's just for show, otherwise I would have to throttle them all.

The Hercules lurches forward as the pilots get off the taxiway and position the big bird for takeoff on the main runway. Once again, they open the engines up and we thunder along, gaining speed. The cargo hold is racked with noise. We're being rattled to death. How does the infantry suffer through this when the Herk becomes their taxi into combat?

And then we claw our way into the sky. A whining sound and a sudden clunk indicate the wheels are up and retracted. We're airborne, and I breathe a long sigh of relief. That was the hairiest takeoff I've ever experienced.

We level out under ten thousand feet. No oxygen necessary, and the C-130's cargo area doesn't appear to be pressurized. We shake, rattle, and roll our way south, we DSS spy-types looking suitably terrified while the air force guys kick back and either nap or read.

As we jolt and bounce along, my eyes notice the flight-deck door. It is open. Is that standard procedure for the Pakistanis? Is this how PAK-1 was operated? If so, everyone aboard had unrestricted access to the pilots. It's a terrorist's best-case scenario.

Looking at the door, I realize this flight may not be just an exercise intended to cause premature aging in us nonaviators. It also is an opportunity to see how a Pakistani flight crew operates an identical aircraft to the one we will soon study. The in-flight procedures and routines could be very illuminating. Already, I've noticed that the crew went through not just one preflight check, but at least three before we finally took off. That's pretty thorough. They tested the engines and a host of other systems. Everything worked fine, obviously, or we never would have taken off. The same was probably true with Zia's plane. The preflight checks detected nothing out of the ordinary, otherwise they probably would have scrubbed the flight.

But that open cockpit door worries me. It fits with another piece of the puzzle given to us yesterday. Somebody outside the flight deck shouted for the pilot just before PAK-1 crashed. Surely, the radio in the cockpit would not have picked up that voice over all the engine noise if the door had been closed.

Another clue: Somebody had keyed the radio. They had an open mike for at least a few seconds, but neither pilot spoke. What does that mean?

An hour later, we land at Bahawalpur. The cargo ramp drops, and together we exit the aircraft under the tail. The moment we hit the tarmac, we're assailed by heat so intense if feels like we've just walked into an oven. I'm bathed in sweat in seconds.

"Welcome to the Punjab desert," one of the air force guys says.

We are in Nowheresville, the end of the earth. I stop and turn in a circle, checking out our surroundings. There's nothing but a vast and empty sea of sand and reddish-brown dirt in every direction off the runway. In the distance sits a small terminal building, the only sign of civilization on the horizon.

A sudden wind blows across the desertscape, kicking up dust devils in its wake. They dance and spin as the gust slams into us. It feels like somebody's just hit us with a blowtorch.

"It's like a blast furnace here," Brad remarks.

"Be sure to stay hydrated."

"Do you have any water?"

"No."

"Neither do I."

"Well, we'll get some from our hosts."

We walk toward the terminal. Brad nudges my arm. "Take a look at that."

In the distance we can see a bunch of Pakistanis, all dressed in white. They just seem to be milling around on the runway.

"This was the airport PAK-1 landed and took off from, right?" Brad says.

"Yeah."

"Well, what kind of an airport allows civilians onto the runways?"

I stop walking and study the airport's perimeter. No fencing. No security. Not even an outer fence.

"Anyone could have walked in here," Brad says.

"We'll have to find out if the plane was under guard while it was here."

"They wouldn't leave the president's plane unsecured, would they?"

"I hope not."

When we reach the terminal, we're greeted by Pakistani soldiers, who lead us to a collection of beaten and weary World War II–style machine-gun-armed jeeps, a few four-wheel-drive trucks, and a couple of Range Rovers. We load up and soon we're tearing off down a rutted dirt road. An officer riding shotgun talks to us over his shoulder as we bounce along. "It will be dark soon. We will go to the crash site in the morning."

"Where are we going?"

"Our barracks. We have rooms waiting for you."

We drive deeper and deeper into this desolate countryside. Every now and then, we come across a small village. Our convoy sends the locals scrambling away from the road. We see herds of goats with shepherds standing watch over them. A stray chicken here and there runs from our wheels as we pass through these little hamlets. We've driven out of the twentieth century into a scene that could have come straight out of the Bible. Minus our machine guns and gas-powered vehicles, we're bearing witness to a way of life unchanged for thousands of years.

Not a tree or even a hint of green exists in this harsh and sunbaked land. In the small villages, every structure is layered with dirt. I don't see any signs of recent construction. How the occasional farms grow anything out here is anyone's guess.

We slow for another settlement. Locals line the street and gawk at us. They're dressed in traditional Pakistani clothing, which is as filthy as their dwellings. With the fierce winds and dust storms, I imagine it is impossible to stay clean out here. A small boy waves at us. It is the only friendly gesture to come our way. Everyone else just looks at us with a mixture of curiosity and hostility.

On the far side of the village, our rat-patrol convoy slows down. An ancient-looking farmer, his face lined and scarred, blocks the road ahead. He's struggling with a camel who seems to have a mind of its own. The farmer pulls a lead and the camel balks.

We inch past him. The camel eyeballs me as we go by. This is just too surreal.

The air carries a unique bouquet so typical of the Third World. It is a mixture of manure, sewage, and garbage. As we come to the next ham-let along the road, the odor takes on a new pungency. Smoke rises from a heap of trash at the edge of the village where they're burning their garbage. The thick smoke nearly makes us gag.

Just before dark, we reach a Pakistani Army outpost. It is a small gov-ernmental oasis in this barren place. The white stucco buildings look al-most new. We're led into one of the barracks, where our Pakistani officer-host tells us, "You will have to share rooms."

"That is not a problem," I say.

We walk down a long hallway toward a toothless and wizened old man sitting in a chair. As we get closer, the officer points to a pair of Old West saloon-style double doors. "That is for you. A houseboy will remain outside in case you require anything."

Houseboy? That guy looks a hundred years old.

We enter our quarters and find two bare metal bunks, a utilitarian chest of drawers, and a small doorway leading to a bathroom. No air-conditioning. The room smells foul and is sweltering hot. We stow our gear and the Pakistani tells us they're serving dinner at the mess hall.

We make our way to the mess. Inside, we find a buffet waiting for us: mangoes, juice, meat of some sort. The Pakistanis went to great lengths for us, and we try to show our appreciation.

Toward the end of our meal, Cheech reappears and tells us, "We'll leave for the crash site after breakfast tomorrow morning."

We thank him. He gives us a cryptic grin and warns us, "When you wake up, watch your feet."

"Our feet?" I ask, perplexed.

"Yes. Snakes like to get out of the cold during the night. They crawl into the barracks."

"Are they dangerous?"

Cheech gives me a wicked look. "Oh, yes. They are quite poisonous."

"Great. Thanks for the warning."

"My pleasure. Good night, Agent Burton. Sleep well."

What do you know? Cheech can play the game, too.

twenty-four

THE BUFFET AT THE END OF THE WORLD

Brad and I stir shortly after dawn. We spent the night stewing in our own sweat, suffering full bladders, since we were both unwilling to brave the snakes to make a run to the bathroom.

Brad sits up on his bunk, careful to keep his feet far above the floor. He yawns and asks, "How'd you sleep?"

"Didn't. You?"

"Not much. Dreamt about snakes when I did."

"I think Cheech was just getting me back."

"Maybe. But want to risk it?"

The thought of a poisonous snake biting me out in this hellhole does not appeal to me. "No."

"Well, you're the lead investigator," Brad says grandly. "After you."

I look down at the floor. No snakes. I'm not going to take any chances, though. Sitting nearby is a metal wastebasket. I reach over and snag it.

"What are you doing?"

"Scaring the snakes," I answer.

Brad shakes his head. I sidearm the wastebasket across the room. It skids over the concrete, bangs off the doorway, and spins into the corridor. Outside our room, I hear a sudden crash and someone exclaiming in Pashto.

Brad bursts into laughter. "You just scared the hell out of our ninety-year-old houseboy."

"Sorry. Just trying to scare the snakes."

Cautiously, I plant my feet on the concrete floor. No nibbles. I check under both bunks and find them slither-free. Now to clear the bathroom. I step to the doorway and gingerly peer around inside. The place is filthy and reeks. Third World bathrooms are never very pretty. This one looks like a bacteriological experiment gone wrong.

"All clear," I announce.

"Good, 'cause I have to use the john," Brad says with relief.

Twenty minutes later, we're dressed and ready to go. We scarf down some yogurt, mangoes, and juice and head out to the rat-patrol convoy.

Cheech is there, waiting for us. "How'd you sleep?" he asks innocently.

"Oh, very well, thank you," I tell him. I won't give him the satisfaction.

"The crash site is very remote," Cheech explains. "It is a bumpy ride."

He wasn't kidding. Our convoy sets off in a cloud of dust and follows a rutted road through another series of tiny villages. Somewhere along the way, we turn off into the desert and go off-road. We're thrown around in the back of the Range Rover, and by the end of the trip I start longing for the C-130. It was so much more comfortable.

The landscape is flat to the horizon in every direction. The desert exudes hostility. Man should not live here.

A half hour later, several small structures come into view. They look like lean-tos and a few World War II–era army tents. Cheech calls out, "We're here."

We pile out of our rigs, and the smell assaults us. It is a combination of aviation fuel, burned rubber, and burned flesh.

"Keep breathing," I tell Brad. "I've had to deal with this before. You get used to the smell."

"I'll never get used to this," Brad says miserably.

We walk across the sand to one of the lean-tos. It's been thrown together with a couple of metal poles and a makeshift roof of colorful rugs. Inside are a dozen or so folding chairs.

On the other side, I see a blackened scar in the sandy ground. Small chunks of twisted metal dot the scene, all that's left of PAK-1.

Colonel Sowada comes up beside me. "Well, let's go take a look."

We head over, dodging the debris along the way. We come to a small crater, not more than three cars wide lined up door to door, and only about eight feet deep.

"A C-130 made that?" I ask Colonel Sowada.

"Yes. It went straight in. Take a look." He points across the crater. I follow his finger and see a burned outline of the plane's right wing stretching across the desert floor. I look to the left and see another one. Both outlines connect to the crater. "The nose and the fuselage created the crater."

"Where's all the wreckage?" I had expected to see big hunks of aluminum, engine parts, and chunks of the fuselage. But the debris field is very small, only a few yards surrounding the crater, and none of the pieces I see are larger than man-size.

"Aviation fuel burns hot," Sowada's engineer says.

"Could there be parts of the plane elsewhere?" Brad asks. He adds, "Wouldn't that happen if it came apart in midair?"

"Yes, but it doesn't look like that happened. The fireball just consumed the plane."

"Well, let's get to work," Colonel Sowada orders.

As the air force team descends into the crater, I sketch the crash site in my notebook. When I finish, I take photographs with a small push-here-dummy 35 mm camera.

The air force team works dutifully through the morning heat. By noon, we're all baking and I retreat to a lean-to for a break. I notice our Pakistani guests are busy working around another tent. Curious, I watch them. They're setting up lunch. The Pakistanis heap racks of lamb, piles of fruit, and other morsels onto a series of long tables.

Colonel Sowada comes over and sits down next to Brad and me. He looks over at the activity and marvels, "Jesus. It's the buffet at the end of the world."

I pull out my notebook and write "Initial Thoughts" on a fresh page. "Colonel, what do you think so far?"

Sowada's ready for the question. "I can tell you this: No missile hit that plane. It crashed intact, probably at a sixty- to sixty-five-degree angle."

"What about a bomb on board?" I'm thinking of the crates of mangoes brought on board just before PAK-1 left the airport.

"No way."

"Why not?"

"There's no evidence to support a bomb. No blast damage on the pieces we've examined, and nothing fell off the plane before it went down. If a bomb brought it down, the debris field would stretch for miles."

I write all of this down.

"Everything points to control loss," Colonel Sowada continues. "The Herk went in at about 175 to 200 knots indicated. That's below normal cruise, which is about 290. It must not have been very high. It went straight in."

The air force team's pathologist climbs out of the crater and approaches us. He's got horn-rimmed glasses that are spotted with drips of perspiration. "Not a lot of human remains," he tells Sowada. "The Pakistanis already removed most of what was left. Muslim custom dictated that."

I ask, "Were autopsies done on the pilots or crew?"

The doc shakes his head. "No. They were interred within twenty-four hours. The only autopsies that will come out of this crash will be on the Americans. But that's assuming we can find their remains."

He hands Colonel Sowada a charred wallet. The folds appear to be melted together. "Put this with the other personal items. We'll try to identify it later," he tells the pathologist, as he gives the wallet back to him. The doc does as told, then returns to the crater.

Cheech interrupts us next. "We have found a witness to the crash."

That excites me. Right now, I'm feeling like a third wheel. "Can we interview him?"

"Yes. We will take you to him after lunch."

"Thank you, Colonel."

Cheech departs for the crater. Colonel Sowada and I return to our conversation.

"So the plane dove straight into the ground. It was intact before it hit, with no sign of an onboard explosion. A missile didn't hit it. What could have done this?"

"I'm not sure. Maybe mechanical failure of some kind."

"Or somebody killed the pilots," Brad ventures.

If the cockpit door was open or unlocked, it could have happened.

"It would have had to happen fast, before the pilots had a chance to resist," Brad says.

"Or radio a Mayday," I add.

From the crater, we hear the pathologist shout. Standing on the rim, he's holding a charred human femur.

I look over at the buffet. I see a leg of lamb, and my stomach executes a slow roll.

"Let's go see what the witness saw," I suggest.

We climb into the Range Rover with Cheech, a soldier-driver, and a couple other ISI types. After another wild ride, we come to the edge of a small village. We park and wait as the ISI guys go off to retrieve the witness. They return with Methuselah. At least he looks as old as Methuselah. He wears a dirty white robe and frayed sandals. His face reflects the harshness of his homeland. It is furrowed with wrinkles and worry lines.

"This is the shepherd who saw the plane crash," Cheech tells us. "Ask him anything and I will translate."

Methuselah looks terrified. With wide eyes flanked by deep crow's-feet and topped by big, bushy gray eyebrows, he practically trembles with fear—no doubt because of all the ISI interest in the case. The ISI spooks are not known for their gentle demeanor inside Pakistan.

I try to set him at ease. As I offer my hand, I give him a wide, friendly smile. This surprises him, but he takes my hand and tries to smile in return. He doesn't have a tooth left in his mouth.

In a perfect world, we would have an embassy staffer translating for us, and we'd be interviewing this witness far from the intimidating presence of Pakistani intelligence. But we have no control here. We've got to go with what we're given.

"Colonel, please ask him to describe what he saw for us."

Cheech says something in Pashto. The shepherd replies. Cheech turns to us and says, "He was with his goats when he saw the plane. It was low. At first, he says it was flying straight."

The shepherd interrupts and tells Cheech something. "He says it started to go up and down."

"Up and down?" I ask.

"Yes. Just a minute." Cheech starts talking in Pashto again.

Methuselah gets very animated. With one hand, he makes a porpoising sort of gesture. His hand oscillates up and down. It looks like he's describing a roller-coaster ride.

"He says the plane went up and down, up and down. It grew worse and worse until it went nose down and crashed."

"How long did it make those movements?"

Cheech asks Methuselah. "He says at least several minutes."

"Several minutes? Are you sure?"

They have an animated discussion. Finally, Cheech reports, "Yes. He's sure of it. He watched the plane nose up and nose down across much of the sky in his view."

I make the same gesture the shepherd just made with my own hand. The shepherd nods vigorously.

"Ask him if he saw something hit the plane, or if he saw pieces fall off."

The shepherd shakes his head as he answers the question. Cheech tells us, "No. Nothing hit the plane. It was flying along normally one minute. The next it was going up and down. No pieces fell off that he saw."

"Ask him if he saw a missile fired at the C-130."

Cheech does this, then grudgingly reports, "He does not know what a missile is. But he didn't see any streaks of fire or light rising from the ground."

"How high was the plane when it started to go in?"

"He is just a shepherd. He knows nothing of flight."

A stick lies on the ground nearby. I pick it up and point to the sky. "Where between the stars and the ground was it?"

The shepherd does his best to show us. I can't make any sense of it.

How are we going to get an altitude estimate from this man? I scan the sky, mind racing. In the distance, I see a bird circling lazily. That gives me an idea.

"Was the plane flying as high as an eagle flies, or lower?"

Cheech asks him. "About as high as an eagle flies. He says he doesn't see many planes. This one, when it crashed, made his goats panic. They ran away and it took a long time to find them again."

One last question. "Colonel, ask him about the weather. Was there any lightning? Could lightning have hit the plane? What about wind?"

"He says it was a clear day, hot. Little wind. No lightning. He's sure nothing hit the plane."

We thank Methuselah for his time. I'd like to do something for him, give him something for what he's given us, but I have nothing of value on me. We part ways after another round of handshaking.

Cheech slips into the front passenger seat, then twists around to get his eyes on us. "Did you get what you needed?"

"Absolutely. But if we need to talk to him again, can you find him?"

"Of course. We can find anyone in our country. Anyone we wish at any time we want."

No wonder Methuselah was so frightened. We drive back to the crash site in silence.

twenty-five

Back at the crash site, we find Colonel Sowada's team huddled together in a lean-to, absorbed in a discussion. The conversation stops, and everyone listens as we describe the plane's final maneuvers before it went in. When we finish, somebody says, "Hydraulic failure."

Somebody else replies, "That could be it."

Sowada says, "Good work, Fred. You've just given us a huge clue."

"What does it mean?"

"Not sure yet, but it could indicate some sort of control failure." He turns to his team and says, "Okay, let's focus on the hydraulic boost system for the elevators. We need to find whatever we can from it."

The team gets to their feet and starts for the crater and debris field.

"Colonel?" I ask. He stops and waits for my question.

"Let's say the hydraulics do go out. Is there a backup system or some sort of redundancy built in?"

"Yes. There's an auxiliary system, and the pilots could fly on manual control only."

"Could all three systems fail at once?"

"I don't know."

The rest of the day, Brad and I continue to make notes as we watch the crash team sift through the wreckage. We measure the size of the crater and the debris field. We note that the ISI guys can't open the wallet the pathologist recovered. It is too badly burned. Somehow, though, they are sure it belonged to one of the Pakistani passengers.

Later, a few more human remains are unearthed. The doc tell us, "You know, given what your witness described, there could have been enough G-forces to drive the passengers' organs right out of their bodies."

I can't tell if he's kidding or not. During my time as a cop, I came to know some of the medical examiners in our area. They have a penchant for black humor.

Either way, that's not something I needed to know.

Later, Brad and I talk things over. If the plane was pitching up and down so radically, would it have been possible for somebody in the VIP area to come forward and reach the controls? Probably not, especially if the pathologist is right. They'd be thrown around in back or pinned in place.

"All of this points to one of two things," I suggest to Brad.

"What?"

"Okay, mechanical failure is a possibility. The controls could have failed. But it's much more likely the pilots were incapacitated. However it happened, it was fast. Fast enough that both of them had no time to react and no time to issue a Mayday."

"That would explain why the plane flew out of control for so long without a distress call. If an assassin stepped into the cockpit and shot both pilots, they'd fall onto the control columns. Given that, maybe it wouldn't go in right away." Brad's right on the mark here. I write this theory down in my notebook.

Was there an assassin on board who gave his life to the cause? It seems possible. This isn't good news, and it certainly won't de-escalate the geopolitical situation we're in right now. We've got a lot more work to do before we can draw any firm conclusions.

The next day, we return to the crash site. The air force team recovers many key parts, including pieces of the critical hydraulic system, some of the instruments, a piece of the cargo door, and chunks of the flight deck. Colonel Sowada gains permission to take them back to the

United States for testing. By midday, he's amassed a small pile of additional things to take back and test.

Brad and I spend lots of time with the crash team, learning everything we can about what they've found and what it means in relation to the C-130's onboard systems. So far, the team has concluded that the plane's electrical system functioned right up to the end of the flight. The engine-driven hydraulic pumps were also working. That's a possible ding to the theory that hydraulic failure caused the crash. Stateside testing will determine if the hydraulic fluid was contaminated with something. Particles of metal, especially brass, can accumulate in the system and cause valves to stick and controls to jam, which is why changing the hydraulic fluid regularly is important.

If this happened to a valve in the elevator's hydraulic booster system, it could cause the C-130 to suddenly nose up or down. The crew's reaction would be to fight that and regain control. It could explain PAK-1's oscillating flight path before it finally crashed.

What it does not explain is the lack of radio communication during the crisis. Three minutes into the flight, PAK-1 suddenly lost control. For two minutes it gyrated up and down, sending the passengers and crew on a roller-coaster ride. Not once did the Cessna security plane or the Bahawalpur tower hear a Mayday or the pilots giving any sort of indication that something was wrong. In fact, the pilots didn't use the radio at all after the tower cleared PAK-1 for takeoff.

The air force engineer admits that the hydraulic failure theory has some holes. Even if a valve had jammed, the command pilot could have reached down and flipped a switch, shutting the hydraulic booster system off completely. That would be like driving a car down the freeway and shutting off its power-steering system. The driver would still be able to control the car, it would just be a lot harder to turn the wheel. Another recent C-130 crash resulted from a broken throttle cable. I ask if that could happen to the mechanical control lines. Not likely. Even if it did, the pilots could still control the C-130 with its electric trim tabs and the engines.

The trim tabs on the elevators are designed to be able to pitch the nose up twenty-seven degrees and pitch it down seven degrees. The ailerons have trim tabs too, as does the rudder. Working carefully, the trim tabs and the engines can keep a C-130 in the air. In fact, in a worst-case scenario, the C-130 crew can fly and maneuver with its engines alone. The two interior turboprops control pitch in that situation. The outboard engines give the pilots control over yaw, roll, and speed. By adjusting the throttles, a good Hercules pilot can overcome total control failure.

By the end of day two out at the crash site, Brad and I have done all we can. We need to let Sowada's team keep working while we go snoop around some more in Islamabad. For one thing, I'd like to talk to the CIA and see what they know.

Right now, I'm very suspicious. The death of President Zia and his command leadership looks to me like a superbly executed assassination. And if that's the case, the Pakistanis can take it only as an act of war.

In the morning, we fly back to Islamabad and check in with Mel Harrison and Beth Jones at the embassy. We pass along what we've learned. They have precious little information for us in return. The Dark World remains silent on this one. There've been no new leads developed, despite our worldwide search through our intelligence networks.

Tensions between Pakistan and India are still high, but it is looking now like cooler heads will prevail. Unless, of course, we discover that the Indians killed Zia.

A day after our return to Islamabad, Brad and I secure a meeting with the CIA's deputy chief of station (DCOS). The DCOS is not happy to see us when we arrive at his office. He greets us with stony professionalism and doesn't volunteer anything before we start our interview.

I want to learn if the CIA had any information on a planned hit on Zia. Sometimes, the local stations will get a tip or pick up a nugget of intel that they do not pass along to Washington. Getting D.C. or Langley involved in a situation like this usually ends up creating more work for the field operatives. It also causes a lot of second-guessing from armchair generals and bureaucrats who are far from the Dark World's front lines. The agents in the field resent this, and sometimes they hold on to something that should have been passed up the chain.

Sitting across from the DCOS, I ask, "Did the CIA pick up any warnings or threat indicators prior to the tank trials that President Zia was going to be targeted?"

The DCOS looks thoroughly annoyed with the question. I suspect he considers us little better than envoys from the D.C. bureaucracy who are searching for a scapegoat. He eyeballs my notebook, which I've got open in front of me. The CIA inherently doesn't like a paper trail. I think he smells a witch hunt.

"No, Agent Burton. Of course not," he says with barely concealed anger. "If we had, we would have warned the ambassador and passed the information to the RSO."

Standard procedure, standard answer.

"What about the ISI? Did they pick up anything?"

"No. Our sources inside the ISI didn't hear anything." He pauses for emphasis. "If they had reported anything, we would have sent it up the chain of command."

"Could the ISI have held information on a plot and not shared it with us?" I ask.

The DCOS looks at me like I'm a simpleton. "Sure. Look, this is Pakistan. You people from Washington don't get that. You're not in Kansas anymore. Anything is possible here."

We sit in silence. I'm trying to think of a way to continue without annoying him any more. He's obviously not going to tell us much, but maybe there's a way to set him a little more at ease.

Before I can say anything, the DCOS volunteers something extraordinary. "Look," he tells us, "how Zia's plane crashed is irrelevant to the CIA."

What? What did that mean?

"Come on now," I reply, "the president of Pakistan is dead. So's his chief of staff and the head of the ISI. The ambassador and our military attaché are dead, too. All this while you're running a war against the Soviets from here? How can all this not impact the CIA?"

He offers no answer. Instead, he stares tight-lipped at us. The room grows so quiet that we can hear him breathing. He won't break his gaze, and he won't answer the question. What an odd development.

We can't get any more information out of this Agency spook, so we end the interview. He doesn't even shake our hands as we leave.

Brad and I regroup at the U.S. Marine House bar. We sit down and order a couple of beers and some food. While we're waiting, Brad says, "Well, that was pretty weird."

"Yeah. Something doesn't add up with the DCOS."

"Do you think the Agency's hiding something?"

"Maybe. I wonder if it's tied to the station chief's absence."

"What was with that last thing he said? How the plane crashed is irrelevant to the CIA?"

"That really came out of left field," I agree.

Afterward, I call our CT chief back at Foggy Bottom on a secure embassy line. I give him my thoughts and tell him we've done about all we can here. He orders us home on the next flight out, which will also be carrying the pieces the air force team recovered from the crash site. Some of them will go to Lockheed for analysis, others will go to a lab at the Bureau of Alcohol, Tobacco, and Firearms. We'll use the ATF facility instead of the FBI, since the Bureau's cheesed off at being shut out of the investigation. Maybe the lab results will shed some light on all this.

The call to prayer echoes through the darkened capital. Brad and I climb into an unmarked van for a madcap ride to Chaklala Air Base. We race through the city streets, the driver executing an SDR. I keep a lookout on our rear but see nobody following us. We stop at a safe house deep inside the city, where we're told to wait. We'll stage to the airport from here.

Hours pass. Brad and I doze in chairs, our luggage at our feet. Finally, it comes time to leave. Another van pulls up in front of the safe house. We quickly throw our gear inside and pile in. The driver takes us straight to Chaklala and leaves us in a deserted area of the base. We're out in the open, not even a hangar nearby, waiting for our flight in almost total darkness.

We hear our plane before we see it. Its massive turbojet engines whine and keen as the aircraft taxis toward us. I see it as it swings off the runway and recognize it as a C-5A Galaxy, the same giant we flew in on a week ago. It rolls to a stop right next to us. A convoy of vehicles suddenly appears, and U.S. Air Force security troops pour out of the rigs to surround the C-5. As the Galaxy's engines are shut down, a steady stream of vans begin arriving. They line up behind the cargo ramp, engines idling. Waiting.

"What is going on?" Brad asks me.

"I don't know."

A moment later, the cargo ramp door drops. Dozens of wounded men hobble out of the C-5's cavernous interior. Some are walking with crutches. Others limp along, supported by one or two buddies. Heads are bandaged, arms are in slings. It is a parade of battered and injured men. They start loading into the vans, and once full, the vehicles speed away, destination unknown.

Brad and I are utterly bewildered.

From out of the darkness around us, Cheech suddenly materializes. He steps in front of us and says, "Gentlemen, your flight home is here. The items recovered from the crash site will be loaded aboard in just a few minutes. I hope that your laboratories can tell us more about what happened."

"Colonel, who are these men?"

Cheech looks surprised. "Mujahideen, of course!"

When we offer no reply, he continues, "These men were wounded in Afghanistan. Your air force flew them to a hospital in Germany for treatment. They're coming home to continue the fight."

I had no idea we were patching up wounded Afghan freedom fighters.

"Does this happen often?" Brad asks.

"Several times a month at least."

The last wounded warrior deplanes. The vans finish loading them up and race off. A truck arrives, and crates with the critical components of PAK-1 stored away inside are carried into the cargo bay. Just before dawn, it is time to get aboard. We grab our things and start for the ramp. Cheech picks this time to say, "Agent Burton, you were right. Thank you for your efforts here. I hope we were able to get you all the information you needed."

"Yes, Colonel, but we still have a lot of work to do to figure out what happened to PAK-1."

"At least we know it wasn't shot down," Brad injects.

"True, there was no missile hit," Cheech admits.

"But were there really snakes?" I ask. I can't help myself. I've got to know.

Cheech gives me a sly grin. "I'll never tell. Have a nice flight home, gentlemen." Without another word, he turns and disappears into the Pakistani night.

twenty-six

THE PERFECT MURDER

September 1988
Foggy Bottom

The NSC was right: The investigation bought enough time for emotions to calm and tensions to ease. The Indians pulled back from the brink and stood down their military. The surviving Pakistani leaders did not face a coup. Pakistan held a huge state funeral for their fallen leader, and as brutal as he was, they gave him a tremendous memorial. The CIA continues to run the war in Afghanistan out of Islamabad, and the Soviets are still withdrawing their forces from that country. Overall, the world moved on pretty fast, just as it did in 1962.

It takes some time, but the test results finally come back. They stun all of us and cause me to rethink some of the conclusions we drew in Pakistan before we left.

Mechanical failure did not knock PAK-1 out of the sky. That much is clear. Tests were conducted on the surviving parts of the hydraulic boost system to the elevators. The valves did not stick or jam. The pumps functioned normally, even as the plane flew into the ground. The surviving instruments show that the maneuvers conducted as the C-130 porpoised through the sky could only have been carried out if the controls' hydraulic boost system was working. The pilots just wouldn't have had the strength to move the Hercules through those gyrations while under manual control.

The hydraulic fluid itself is the one caveat. It was contaminated with particles, including bits of brass. Analysis could not determine why or how this happened. The fluid had been replaced only fifty flight hours before the crash. Nevertheless, the amount of particles found trended to the high end of acceptable levels. Still, the valves functioned fine. In the final analysis, the crash team determined this could not have caused PAK-1 to go down.

With mechanical failure ruled out, there can be only two remaining answers: pilot error and sabotage.

The pilots were in peak physical and mental condition. Their fitness reports spoke volumes about both how well respected they were and how they were trusted by President Zia. The fact that they did not call a Mayday is supremely unusual. It strongly suggests that something, or somebody, incapacitated them at the controls.

Brad and I had been thinking an assassin shot them both. The findings of the air force crash team do not support that theory. No weapons were recovered from the crash site. That in itself is not damning evidence, as we do know some of the VIPs were carrying weapons. They were immolated in the fire. However, Colonel Sowada's men did not find any evidence of a firefight in the cockpit. At close range, a pistol shot would stand a good chance of going through a human target. The bullet would exit and lodge in the instrument panel or another part of the cockpit. No such bullet hole was found among the pieces recovered from the flight deck.

Although fatal gunshots cannot be ruled out, the possibility looks remote now. But there is another, far more sinister explanation.

The ATF lab results disclose the truth. Their tests discovered traces of antimony, chlorine, and phosphorous in the cockpit and on a recovered mango seed. The rear cargo door tested positive for PNET, a type of explosive compound.

Antimony. Phosphorous. Chlorine. All are ingredients in various types of nerve gas. One of the most deadly, VX, causes near-instant paralysis followed by death within seconds. Somebody planted nerve gas in the cockpit. This can only mean one thing: President Zia and his staff were assassinated.

The autopsy done on the remains of Brigadier General Herbert M. Wassom shows that he had not inhaled any smoke before he died. This proves that PAK-1 did not suffer an onboard fire prior to its crash. It also helps rule out a large onboard explosive as one of the potential causes of the C-130's destruction.

What was PNET doing on the cargo door, then? During their own investigation, the Pakistanis conclude that a small detonator had been aboard the plane. Attached either to a timer or a barometric pressure device, the detonator touched off a very-small-yield explosion, perhaps just big enough to blow the top off a Coke can placed on the flight deck. The interior of the C-130 is so loud that I doubt anyone would have heard such a small pop.

But that's what killed the pilots. When the detonator blew, it released the chemical agent into the flight deck. With the flight-deck door open, the small explosion blew enough particles into the rear of the aircraft to be detected on the cargo door.

The pilots never knew what hit them. The crash team determined that the pilots were not wearing their oxygen masks at the time of the crash. That fits with the low altitude the plane was at when the shepherd saw it oscillating through the sky. That rules out a poisoned oxygen system and lends much more weight to the Coke can theory posited by the Pakistanis.

I think they're right. Now all that's left is to figure out who did it. I spend most of September and early October trying to find a smoking gun that will allow us to name the assassins. In a dime-store spy novel, the hero always finds one critical piece of evidence that ensures the guilty pay for their crime. If the real Dark World worked like that, I would sleep better at night. The truth is, all we can do is assemble the evidence and look at who has the capability to execute such a sophisticated operation.

The Indians have a well-respected intelligence service, but planting nerve gas in Zia's aircraft is well beyond their capabilities. They have no history of pulling off such a sophisticated hit. That doesn't mean they weren't involved on the periphery, but it does rule them out as the actual organization behind the assassination.

The CIA has access to nerve gas and has the ability to orchestrate a covert operation like this. The DCOS acted very strange when we interviewed him, and given some of the rogue operations the CIA has been involved in over the past three decades, their involvement in Zia's death might be plausible if not for one huge issue: motive. The CIA had a good relationship with Zia and the ISI. They worked hand in hand to bring the Soviets down in Afghanistan. Taking him out makes no sense. Zia was our biggest Cold War ally next to Britain.

Scratch the CIA off the list.

What about the Israelis? Tension existed between Zia and Israel for years over Pakistan's nuclear program. The Israelis took out Iraq's nuke program in 1981 with a stunning air raid that signaled to the rest of the Muslim world that Israel was prepared to go to any length to ensure that an Islamic country did not get the bomb.

Could the Mossad, Israel's intelligence agency, have killed Zia because of his nuclear weapons research program? It does make for an interesting motive. But it does not hold up. The Pakistanis already have the bomb. They joined the nuclear club in late 1987. Killing Zia in August 1988 doesn't change the fact that Pakistan now has nukes. The timing of the attack makes the Israelis look like poor suspects. I doubt they had anything to do with this.

What about Pakistani extremists or dissidents? Zia was hated in many circles in his own nation. There had been several attempts on his life, and he'd recently angered the radical Shiite community when one of its leaders was assassinated. Zia's government was blamed for the hit.

That is a good motive for assassination, but the Pakistanis lack the capability to execute such an attack. Only a few countries have such sophisticated chemical agents. The Pakistanis, especially the radical Shiite dissidents, have no access to such a specialized, highly technical weapon.

That leaves the KGB. The Soviets had about fifteen thousand motives for doing away with Zia. That's how many Red Army soldiers have died in Afghanistan since 1979, thanks to the insurgency we've sustained through Pakistan. Zia played a key role in defeating the Soviet juggernaut, something that the Hungarians failed to do in 1956 and the Czechs couldn't do during Prague Spring in 1968. Since World War I, the Russians have not lost a war—until now. They are bitter and angry over the disaster that befell them. And that makes them exceptionally dangerous.

A few weeks before PAK-1 went down, Eduard Shevardnadze, the Soviet Union's minister of foreign affairs, publicly stated that Pakistan would pay dearly for its support of the mujahideen.

Payback. That's a big motive. As the Red Army withdraws from Afghanistan, the KGB took one parting shot at a key enemy. This makes the most sense of all. The Soviet-trained Afghan intelligence service, known as KHAD, has agents operating everywhere in Pakistan. Could the KGB have learned of the tank trials? Yes. The Indians could have picked up on that bit of intelligence and passed it to their Russian friends. That would have given the KGB the time needed to plan the operation. Using a WAD operative, a nerve gas container could have been planted aboard PAK-1. The screening process at Bahawalpur left much to be desired. There was no perimeter fence, and security around the C-130 while it was on the ground turned out to be casual at best. The pilots were supposed to stay with the aircraft but may have walked to the terminal to use the restroom.

A stealthy operative could have sneaked aboard and placed the Coke can somewhere on the flight deck. The detonator, set to explode at either a certain time or a specific altitude, would have barely drawn attention from the pilots as they flew the aircraft at full throttle on takeoff. The engines, only a few feet above their heads and on either side of them, certainly could have masked the sound of the agent being released.

What next? Both pilots inhaled the gas. In seconds, they are either dead or paralyzed. The plane flies out of control. Nose up, nose down, nose up, nose down. The VIPs in back are thrown around, prompting somebody to call out to the command pilot. Of course, he can't respond. Finally, the Hercules pitches up one more time and stalls. The nose drops, but this time there is no recovery. The C-130 plummets to the ground. It explodes, and almost everything is consumed in the fireball.

It is the perfect murder.

The KGB loves to use arcane chemical compounds to kill its adversaries. For proof, one needs only to look at the assassination of Georgi Markov, a Bulgarian defector who died when jabbed by a poison-tipped umbrella in 1978.

The KGB is the only player in this game with motive, opportunity, operational capability, and a history of similar attacks. In the Dark World, you rarely get a complete picture. There will always be missing pieces to the puzzle. All you can do is assemble the pieces you have and draw the most logical conclusion from what you've got.

And in this case, the evidence points to the Soviets.

At the end of September, I write up my report and submit it. A few weeks later, Mel Harrison sends us the summary of the Pakistani crash investigation report. One copy was delivered to our embassy in Islamabad. Mel sends it flash precedence, and the day it comes in I sit in FOGHORN and read it over repeatedly.

The full report runs 350 pages, but all we get is the summary, which totals about 40. The Pakistanis use my report as the basis for theirs, then integrate Colonel Sowada's findings and their own. The report concludes that President Zia and his senior military leaders died at the hands of unknown assassins, who probably planted a chemical agent in the cockpit.

Had this been known in August, I wonder if the news would have pushed the Pakistanis over the edge. Their report does not accuse any nation or organization of the assassination, which is a good thing. But in August, with emotions running hot and the nukes on a hair trigger, these conclusions could have tipped the scales for war. Now, two and half months later, the findings seem to be swept under the rug. Here at home, the Pakistani findings are never made public. My own report vanishes in the bureaucracy. My careful notes from the crash site, including the sketches I made of the crater, disappear from the dead bodies cabinets where I had filed them. State Department officials stick to the hydraulic failure theory. Life is more convenient that way.

One night, just before Thanksgiving, I sit down at my desk and open my moleskin journal. So far, my list contains two names: Imad Mugniyah and his right-hand man, Hasan Izz-Al-Din.

I add number three tonight.

3. UNSUB: KGB assassination team who placed incapacitating IED on PAK-1.

twenty-seven

AUTUMN LEAVES

December 1988
Bethesda

For DSS agents, a quiet Sunday morning is as rare to find as an honest informant. As I pour my second cup of coffee, I'm struck by how serene the townhouse is around me. My wife left a few minutes ago to Christmas shop, leaving me alone with Tyler Beauregard. My loyal dog and I went for our ritual run, and now we're trying to relax in the kitchen. Tyler's taken up station next to my chair, while I try to act like a normal American and read the newspaper.

The problem is I keep waiting for the phone to ring. Something always interrupts a morning like this, and for two years my senses have been tuned to expect it. I know I've got to loosen up my guard, but even as I flip through the front page of the *Washington Post*, I can't help but be tense and alert. I look over at the phone. It sits silent on its cradle. For a moment, I feel trapped. One morning to myself, is that too much to ask?

I try to read the international news, but it is so full of distortions and inaccuracies that I give up for the sake of my blood pressure. The editors at the *Post* will never penetrate the Dark World. The best they can do is shine a pinpoint of light into it here and there. No breadth, no depth, no context. Just a flash, a sliver of an event, served up with little understanding, that's all I see on these pages. I turn to the sports section and get acquainted with the week's NFL matchups. I'd love to catch a game, but I have to check in at Foggy Bottom this afternoon. Perhaps someday.

I polish off my second cup of coffee, toss the paper aside, and wonder what to do next. How do normal people enjoy a quiet Sunday? If this is all you're used to, it must be sublime. For me, I'm finding it very difficult to unwind. Usually, I have so much on my plate that I move mechanically from one event or task to another. There is no end to the conveyor belt of crises; they just pile on and keep coming. If I'm awake, I'm working, getting ready to work, or coming home from work and thinking about it. Call it a perpetual autopilot crisis mode. I can't seem to shut it off after all that's happened.

The phone is silent. That only makes me strain harder to hear it.

I want to relax. I need to. But the more I try, the more I focus on the tension within me. My body's grown used to the constant stress and pressure of my life as a special agent; it has accommodated the sudden adrenaline rushes and the subsequent letdowns. Without those things, I don't feel complete. And that, perhaps, is the most unsettling realization of the day. Physiologically, my life in the DSS has conditioned me to be on a hair trigger.

I find myself in front of the floor safe I had installed when we first moved in. I haven't looked inside it in months. I bend down and open it up. I find the tan leather album that used to absorb so much of my time. I pull it out. This album used to be my passion, my diversion since childhood. But I learned long ago that the DSS and hobbies are not compatible.

I find a chair and slide into it. Tyler Beauregard enters the room and waits for a scratch. Absently, I stroke her head and ears with one hand as I open the album with my other one. Inside are the football and baseball cards I've collected ever since I was a ten-year-old boy.

There are some treasures here. A Joe Namath rookie card occupies a special place of honor. Not only is it worth a small fortune these days, but Namath was my idol as a kid. I loved to watch him play back in the day. And who could ever forget how he knocked the Colts down a peg in Super Bowl III? That bond between this hero of the gridiron and the kid

I once was has never been broken. Perhaps that is the only enduring form of human-to-human loyalty in this world. Everything else seems to be for sale.

But even Broadway Joe had a price. I'll never forget the first time I saw his panty hose commercial. I thought a part of me would die—though I have to admit, his legs did look good in those things.

I turn the page to find my Green Bay Packers collection. I loved the Lombardi era and dedicated many years to finding cards for every member of those great teams. I still have a few gaps, but someday perhaps I'll be able to hit the card shows again and find the ones I need.

The USS Vincennes. *We killed hundreds. The Iranians vowed revenge.*

No. I'm not going to think about work right now. I won't let my brain wander to all the threats and developments of the past few months since I returned from Pakistan. I focus on the cards.

On another page, I find my Shoeless Joe Jackson, the tragic hero of the 1919 Chicago "Black Sox." Dizzy Dean smiles at me from another era, wearing his St. Louis Cardinals uniform. Next to him on the page is the rest of the Gashouse Gang. They were the blue-collar types of their era. They played hard and gritty ball, and weren't afraid to talk about it. Those Depression-era teams gave fans so much hope. They symbolized what we as a country needed to do to get out of that mess.

Operation Autumn Leaves. What did the Germans kick over? Were the Palestinians really going to take down an airliner?

No. Not this morning. This is my time. I've earned it.

Several pages are full of Mickey Mantle cards. At last count, I had almost thirty of them from the '67 and '68 seasons. I traded one years ago to a buddy for a Satchel Paige. Now there was a man who overcame everything thrown his way. He was one of the first African-American pitchers to be named to an all-star team. That was in the early fifties, before *Brown v. Board of Education.* His story made anything seem possible to a kid from Bethesda.

Suddenly, looking at all these relics from my childhood makes me feel a little empty. I'd hoped to share these with my own son someday. But from the seat I'm in now, I don't see how that can happen anytime soon. The DSS is my life. How can I be a father, too?

The phone rings.

Before I even realize it, my body has propelled me across the room. My Pavlovian response brings me to the phone before my brain can catch up.

A pause. It rings again. I take a breath. What is it this time? A bombing? Another clueless academic bagged in Beirut? I want to know. I don't want to know. My Sunday's toast.

"Fred Burton," I say into the receiver.

"Fred! Hey, how are you, buddy?" Fred Davis nearly shouts at me through the phone.

"I'm good, Fred. What are you up to?"

"Well, I'm over at the hangar in Anacostia."

"That explains why it's so hard to hear you."

I hear him laugh. "Listen, we're going to take Eagle One for a little joyride—uh, I mean test flight. Wanna tag along?"

"Heck, yes. Let me get my car keys."

"Don't bother. We'll come and get you."

At noon, Fred Davis arrives in his new ride, a Bell JetRanger helicopter. As he hovers over my townhouse, the rotors acting as the mother of all leaf blowers, my neighbors pour out into their yards. JetRangers are anything but quiet.

I grab my new Sig Sauer automatic and my briefcase. Inside are my earpiece, protection pins, and passport. I never leave home without them, not after all the times I've been shuffled off to foreign lands in the middle of the night. I'm always ready for that now.

The chopper settles into a field behind our townhouse. The blades spin and debris flies. I charge out the back door, looking deadly serious, briefcase in hand, Sig stuffed in my shoulder holster. The neighbors gawk. As I pile inside the bird, I can only imagine what they must be thinking.

"Well, that was subtle!" I shout to Fred. He's in the pilot's seat and turns to give me a face-splitting grin. He's finally done it. My best friend is behind the controls of Eagle One, the Park Service's aerial eyes for the capital. The pride in his eyes over this accomplishment is so clear that I can't help but grin back and shout, "Way to go, Fred! I knew you'd do this."

He motions to the jump seat behind and between the two pilot seats.

As I strap into it, I notice that the copilot is another old friend, Ron Gailey. He was a member of the rescue squad with us back in the day. Ron hands me a radio headset with a microphone and I put them on.

"Let's go do some sightseeing—the right way!" Fred says into the intercom. I key my mike and reply, "Sounds great. Congratulations, my friend!"

"Thanks. Your neighbors are gonna talk about this for weeks."

"Yeah. They probably think we're whisking you away to Camp David or something," Ron says.

We soar over the Potomac River, marveling at the last of the autumn colors. Winter is fast approaching. Today is clear and chilly. The sun's high and the shadows are short. The river is a splendid shade of blue flanked with reflections of the green, gold, and red leaves of the trees that grow along its banks.

I feel at home within this brotherhood of the badge.

"Hey, did you hear anything about a counternarcotics chopper getting shot up in Colombia?" Fred asks over the intercom.

"No, but I can check it out for you."

"Not like we don't get shot at here," Ron interjects.

"What do you mean?" I ask.

Fred banks Eagle One into a turn circle over the Jefferson Memorial. "People over in Anacostia," he says. "They like shooting at the Man's eye in the sky. You know?"

Anacostia is a dangerous place for beat cops, but I didn't know that it is hazardous to fly over as well.

We make another circuit over the Jefferson Memorial. I've never seen it from such a vantage point before, and I'm taken by its perfect symmetry. The grass surrounding it is so lush and green it stands out among all the other colors of this dying fall.

Fred continues, "We were lighting up a crack house after a reported shooting one night. They took some potshots at us, nothing serious."

Part of Eagle One's job is to use the powerful searchlight slung under its nose to illuminate crime scenes and suspects trying to escape. At night, the chopper offers law enforcement in the area a unique advantage. With Eagle One overhead, the bad guys can't escape.

We turn for another run down the river. We come to the 14th Street Bridge.

"I'll never forget that day," I say into my microphone. Both pilots nod but remain silent. The Air Florida crash in '82 was a tragedy that will never be far from any of us who were there.

Fred drops the JetRanger's nose and we speed up. Pretty soon, we're racing along at low altitude, following the course of the river. It is euphoric to be up here, seeing the sights as we talk shop. Already, Fred's seen plenty of action with Eagle One. They've landed on the local freeways to pick up car accident victims and fly them to local hospitals. They've chased car thieves and murderers through the streets of D.C. They've lit up crack houses and vehicular pursuits, only to return to their run-down hangar along the Potomac at Anacostia to take gunfire as they land. What an odd country we live in. From up here, its tranquillity cannot be denied. Yet below that façade, the streets team with conflict.

Forty minutes into the flight, I'm staring out the Plexiglas at the landscape below, listening to Fred as he regales me with another Eagle One story. I feel strange. At first, I can't put my finger on it. Gradually, it dawns on me: Up here with my best friend, I am totally at peace. My mind is clear; I'm not fighting any demons. I haven't felt this way in months. Years. I realize with a start that I'm happy. I'd forgotten how this feels. Happiness pales before the mission of saving lives. It is not a priority. Stopping the next attack is all that matters.

What kind of life is this? When do I get to live it for myself and my family?

Somebody has to do it. But what about the price?

What about the price?

Those are not questions for now. I stow them away in a distant corner of my heart. Right now, I'm just going to focus on the moment and enjoy it.

We skim along the Potomac, and I find it impossible to wipe the smile off my face.

twenty-eight

December 21, 1988
Behind the New Big Blue Door

I reach the office before sunrise on this Wednesday morning, coffee in hand and a few PowerBars in my pocket that'll serve as both lunch and dinner. Though elsewhere in the country most of my fellow Americans are preparing for Christmas, here behind the big blue door, there will be no vacation. We're chasing down dozens of threats that have come in from all sorts of strange nooks and crannies within the Dark World. Things are tense, and the expectation is that sooner or later, we'll get hit again. Ten days ago, the constant tension and pressure had worn me out. Now, thanks to my Sunday flight with Fred, I feel rejuvenated.

I need to be fresh. There's too much going on in the Dark World right now for me to be off my A-game.

Autumn Leaves was the first sign. At the end of October, the West German police launched this operation with the intent of taking out the PFLP–GC terrorists operating around Frankfurt. They raided a safe house used by the Popular Front for the Liberation of Palestine–General Command and took down a cell that may have been planning to blow up an airliner. The police recovered an improvised explosive device built into a Toshiba boom box. About a pound of Semtex, a Czech-made plastic explosive, was hidden inside the stereo. The police also found a Pan Am flight schedule.

Could this have been Iran's effort to exact revenge for last July? Possibly. Rumors circulating since the summer indicate that the Iranians may have given the PFLP–GC's leadership ten million dollars in cash to go after American targets.

On July 3, 1988, the USS *Vincennes,* a *Ticonderoga*-class Aegis missile cruiser, shot down an Iranian airliner, killing 290 people. Exactly what led to the incident is still murky, but the American warship was inside Iranian territorial waters in the Persian Gulf at the time. Needless to say, relations with Iran have been even more inflamed than ever. Their leadership publicly vowed to avenge the deaths of these innocent civilians, which included sixty-six children.

As quiet as the Dark World grapevine was over PAK-1, Iran Air 655 has caused a flood of conspiracy theories, threats, innuendo, and rumor to flow through FOGHORN. We've been inundated with work, sorting through the credible threats and the crackpots. As a result, we've issued travel warnings and have urged American air carriers to beef up their security.

Earlier this month, an anonymous caller phoned the American embassy in Helsinki. He warned that Abu Nidal planned to blow up a Pan Am airliner flying out of Frankfurt within the next two weeks. Given what the Germans uncovered with Autumn Leaves, we took immediate steps. The State Department notified its embassies all over Europe and warned the Federal Aviation Administration. The FAA passed the warning along to all U.S. airlines in hopes that the companies would increase their security. Each carrier has its own private security arrangements, which has been a source of friction between the government and the industry ever since hijackings became relatively common in the seventies and eighties. The cost and delays of additional security are the two biggest stumbling blocks to building a more robust system to protect our planes. Consequently, even though some of the airlines are charging an extra security surcharge to their passengers, the fact is there are plenty of gaps that can be exploited.

Just ask the survivors of TWA Flight 847.

The CT office has grown so large now that we've moved out of the Truman Building. The old rat hole in the basement is gone. Now we've got an oversized, ultramodern cell in the middle of a building across the street on Virginia Avenue. We designed it with security in mind every step of the way. No drop ceilings. No windows. All around the office we have built-in white noise generators. They provide a constant hissing sound that defeats listening devices and directional microphones. Gone are the burn bags. In their place, shredders are scattered all over the office.

I enter our new home and find the perpetual morning chaos in full blossom. We're running multiple security details today, and we've got agents scurrying around between cubicles carrying Uzis and Remington shotguns as they prepare for their day. Others have Sig Sauer automatic pistols strapped to their hips. We have our own secure lines now, and I notice one of our newer agents is on one, looking terribly unhappy. Around him, the traffic flows. Agents move back and forth between their cubes and FOGHORN, which has moved to a new facility right down the hall from us. Radios squawk. Phones ring. The shredders grind. The white noise hiss is almost lost in the cacophony of the CT office at work.

"Morning, Fred!" calls Bob O'Bannon in his languid southern drawl. Bob, formerly a southern Virginia cop, is one of our new agents. He's already proven himself as an outstanding investigator.

"Morning, Bob. What's the word?"

"Looks like a bad episode of *Hill Street Blues* around here."

I start to laugh. Behind me, somebody quips, "More like *Barney Miller*."

As we've grown, we've been fortunate enough to cherry-pick the rest of the DSS for the best and the brightest. We've assembled a group of first-class agents who've done extraordinary work. They've built a tremendous reputation for our group, and now we're turning agents away who want to join us. We rival the Detail as the tour everyone wants.

I reach my cubicle and get to work. I go through the morning cable traffic, then read the Rewards for Justice mail. We get tips via our RFJ address all the time now. Behind me, I can hear one of our agents talking to an informant who seems eager to drop a dime on his buddies. For money, of course.

The phone rings. The Agency wants an update on a case we're involved in, and this absorbs several minutes. As I'm talking, the agent who had been on our secure phone comes over to my cubicle. I hold up a finger and mouth, "Just a minute." He waits until I finish the call and cradle the phone.

"Hi, Stick, what do you need?" Scott "Stick" Stewart is another young agent with tremendous promise. This morning, though, he's looking morose.

"Well, I have an agent in Istanbul on the secure line. He's been chewing me out."

"What for?"

"He sent us some forensic evidence three months ago. He says the Turkish police need answers today."

"Where'd you send it?"

"The FBI lab. You know how they are."

"Did you explain that to him?"

Stick lets out an exasperated sigh. "Yes. But it just made him scream louder."

"When did you get it over to the FBI?"

"Soon as we got it here. He says the ambassador's on his back now, too. Anyway, he wants to talk to my boss now."

I give this a bit of thought. "Okay, give me a minute and I'll be there."

Stick heads back to the secure phone. I take care of a few quick things, then follow him over. I pick up the receiver and say, "Who's this?"

A very irritated voice spits back, "Who the hell are you?"

I ignore this and ask, "What's the problem?"

The voice launches into a diatribe. He's been waiting for months for his evidence results. He needs it now—not tomorrow—and we're all at fault for getting the ambassador on his case.

"Okay," I reply calmly. "I know you think this is your world, but we've got twenty-five major things going on in the office here right now."

That did it. Before I can continue, the agent in Istanbul explodes. A steady stream of shouted epithets and cuss words flows across the transaAtlantic line we're sharing. I hold the receiver away from my ear. As I do, I notice the whole office has come to a halt. Agents are prairie-dogging over the tops of their cubicles to catch a glimpse.

I interrupt him. "Hold on a minute. Hold on."

Miraculously, he goes quiet.

"Okay, you're in luck. I see one of my agents now. He's donning a lab coat. Another one is firing up a Bunsen burner."

Amazingly, the hothead buys it. "They are? Great. I'll wait."

I lay it on thick, "Another one just put on a set of goggles."

"Terrific!"

I reach for a thick book sitting on a shelf nearby.

"Oh my God! Oh no!"

"What? What?"

"No! NO!"

I drop the book on the floor, holding the receiver close. In the quieted office, it sounds like a gunshot. Or a bomb.

We all bust out laughing. The agent on the other end is not amused.

"Look," I tell him once I've regained my composure, "I was making a joke here. I understand this is important to you, okay? Your evidence is over at the FBI lab. I'll send somebody over to light a fire under them and get your results expedited."

"Well, okay." At least he's not yelling anymore.

"The thing is, I do not appreciate you calling up and cussing out one of my guys, screaming like you're out of your mind. Don't ever berate one of my agents again, clear?"

I hear a grumbled apology.

"Good." I hang up. Turning to Stick, I tell him, "Why don't you run over to the FBI lab and tell them to expedite."

"Okay, Fred," Stick says with a big grin. He grabs his keys and heads out of the office. I return to my desk and get back to work.

Early afternoon rolls around, and I start eating a PowerBar at my desk. I've been working on my card-file index of terrorist acts, updating it with all the latest news from around the world. My phone rings.

"Burton."

"Sir," says one of the agents in FOGHORN, "we've just received news that an American airliner has gone down over Scotland."

Oh, God. Not at Christmas.

"Okay. I'll be right there."

I slam the phone down and hurry over to FOGHORN. When I open the door, I find two agents at the console. Both are on the phone. Other phones are ringing in the background. Two TVs are on, one of which is set to CNN.

The U.S. Embassy in London sends us a flash cable. The plane was a 747, the largest American airliner. It belonged to Pan Am.

Autumn Leaves. The PFLP. There was another cell the Germans must have missed.

Over the next hour, details flow in. We can safely rule out a midair collision. The air traffic controllers report that there wasn't another aircraft in the area. Pan Am Flight 103 simply vanished off the radar screen at thirty-one thousand feet, thirty minutes after takeoff from Heathrow Airport, outside of London.

Then Beirut checks in with a stunner. The U.S. ambassador to Lebanon, three agents, and a Defense Intelligence Agency officer were scheduled to fly Pan Am Flight 103 from London to JFK in New York. They were coming home for Christmas to spend the break with their families.

"Okay, we need to get the passenger manifest right away," I tell the crew manning FOGHORN's *Star Trek* console. They start making calls to the FAA, which is already on this one. Pan Am's working on getting the information ASAP.

The minutes tick by. Each embassy has a travel section that makes transportation arrangements for the diplomats at its station. The travel section in Beirut has gone through its records and reports that Ambassador Andrew McCarthy, Major Chuck McKee of the DIA, Matt Gannon, and Ron Lariviere had been booked on Pan Am 103. Matt Gannon is a senior State Department official. Ron Lariviere is one of our own.

Minutes later, our embassy in Cyprus sends a flash cable. Danny O'Connor had flown from Cyprus to Heathrow to catch 103. He's one of our senior DSS officers in Cyprus. I know Danny. He's the son of a Boston cop and a good man.

This is a nightmare.

I step over to one of the STU-III secure phones in the room and call the CIA to find out what they know. When I'm finished, it is clear some catastrophic event took place to knock Pan Am 103 out of the sky. A bomb is the most likely cause.

I go and report all the details to our CT chief. Together, we head up to Clark Dittmer's office. When we arrive, we find him sitting stunned at his desk, watching the live CNN broadcast.

"Sir, Danny O'Connor, Matt Gannon, and Ron Lariviere were aboard. We think the ambassador to Lebanon was, too, though we haven't confirmed that yet."

Our boss looks stricken. He's an honorable man who has steered a steady ship through shoals of chaos and violence for years. But today, this is the worst. Almost three hundred people are dead. And to further compound the tragedy, CNN reports that an entire exchange group from Syracuse University was aboard the flight.

There are no survivors. The plane broke up at thirty-one thousand feet. The pieces fell all around and on Lockerbie. Part of the wing and fuselage hit a housing complex. The fuel tanks exploded with such intensity that nothing in the blast zone remains. The flames consumed everything, including the residents trapped within their dwellings.

Mr. Dittmer's face is long and sallow. His eyes reveal the pain we all feel right now. "Fred," he says gently, "the families. They're waiting. We'll need to put a team together to go talk to them. They may be at the airport."

"Yes, sir. We'll take care of it right away."

Mr. Dittmer adds, "Ron's wife is pregnant."

I can't help but choke up.

"Let's get this done first. Come back in a half hour and give me an update. Fred, after you take care of things, call the FBI and CIA. See what else they've got."

We go downstairs to huddle with the rest of our crew. We send several agents out to find Danny and Ron's families. It is a terrible task, but a sacred one. These families will not be alone tonight.

I return to FOGHORN and check in with the FBI and CIA. While I do, Beirut sends another flash cable. Ambassador McCarthy is unharmed. He missed his connecting flight from Cyprus and wasn't able to get to Heathrow in time to catch 103.

But what if his schedule had been compromised? What if somebody in Beirut passed that information to Hezbollah? I make some calls on the STU-III and confirm that the ambassador was booked under a pseudonym—that's standard procedure these days—but that still doesn't ease my suspicions.

Thirty minutes later, we meet back in Mr. Dittmer's office. I tell him the ambassador is safe, but that this could have been an assassination attempt. Had his travel plans been compromised, only the luck of the draw saved his life.

"That's a good point, Fred. God forbid they went after the plane to assassinate the ambassador. Where is he now?"

I tell him.

Mr. Dittmer asks, "Okay, the CIA seems to be convinced this was a bomb. Who are our key suspects?"

"The Iranians. Hezbollah. Syria if the PFLP–GC is behind this," I reply.

Mr. Dittmer considers this for a minute before saying, "Well, it won't do any good to send a team to the crash site. The Brits and Scottish authorities will handle it. Our embassy in London will coordinate with them. But we do need to find out if this was an assassination attempt."

"Yes, sir. We're working that right now."

"Fred, you're going to need to go to Beirut and run this down."

Our CT chief interjects, "Sir, if Fred goes to Beirut and there's a Hezbollah leak, they'll know what we're doing."

"Good point. You've got a reputation these days, Fred. If you're seen in Beirut, the word could get out we're conducting a CT investigation."

"What about Cyprus, sir?" I ask. "We could set up in a safe house and bring people in through the Beirut air bridge."

"That should work, but we need to minimize who knows you're there and what you're doing."

We talk logistics for ten more minutes. I'll go into Cyprus under a false name and passport. With the help of the RSO, I'll set up in a safe house and bring our agents in one at a time from Beirut. If they don't have answers, we'll quietly send them back to get them.

"You won't be able to tell your family, Fred," Mr. Dittmer reminds me.

"I know, sir."

I'll miss Christmas this year. That's the least of my worries right now, and I have no right to complain. Just ask Ron's wife about that.

I head downstairs to make a few more phone calls. I pack up my briefcase. I've already got an overnight bag with me. I keep it in the office for just this sort of emergency. In thirty minutes, I'm ready to go.

My flight leaves later that night. As we cross the Atlantic, I can't help but think about the people aboard 103. The most recent reports we received before I left FOGHORN included a chilling tidbit. The cockpit, flight deck, and first-class section of the fuselage landed intact. People on the scene reported the pilot's hands were still on the control column. Apparently, the nose section tore off from the rest of the fuselage. It spun through space as the rest of the aircraft fell six miles into the Scottish countryside. Two hundred and fifty-nine names are on the manifest the FAA sent us. Two hundred and fifty-nine victims. Were they alive as the plane came apart around them? Some were. Two passengers were found still breathing on the ground by locals and rescue workers. They both died shortly afterward. Others found passengers still strapped to their seats. One woman was found holding her baby.

Yeah, some of them were alive. And while they may have lost consciousness at high altitude, some of them probably came to as the fuselage hit the warmer, more oxygenated air below ten thousand feet. How long did they have to make their peace and say their good-byes? I do the math in my head.

Two minutes. Those poor people fell out of the sky and knew there was no hope, no survival. No exit but death.

The flight drones on. I can't sleep. I don't even try. A two-minute free fall. Our people. My friends. Children.

Hours later, I arrive in Nicosia, Cyprus, where the RSO, Bill Gaskell, greets me at the airport. Together, we drive through the city to a safe house. While there, Bill and I work out a plan to keep my arrival quiet. I won't come anywhere close to the embassy. I won't be sending anything back to D.C. There will be no paper trail whatsoever. Bill will arrange all the details personally so that our agents in Beirut can be brought out individually and delivered to the safe house with no one the wiser.

Our agents in Beirut are outstanding people. Most are ex–special forces and have long since learned to operate in an environment of supreme chaos and danger. Beirut is still a virtually lawless enclave, and it has long since become a playground for every intelligence agency with a stake in the Middle East. Think of it as a Dark World sandbox. Everyone plays, there are no rules, and there's no adult supervision. It takes a unique spook to thrive in such a place.

That night, a Blackhawk helicopter lands at our embassy in Beirut. It picks up a lone passenger and darts away quickly, its crew on the lookout for shoulder-fired antiaircraft missiles. When the chopper reaches Nicosia, Bill meets it and hustles the agent into a car. He stair-steps through the city, running a surveillance detection route just in case some-body's watching. In a place like Cyprus, you can bet there are spooks out there, lurking, just waiting for us to get sloppy with our field craft.

The car pulls up to the safe house, and the agent slips inside. The dwelling has been swept for electronic surveillance devices and then swept again just to make sure. It's clean. White noise machines hiss in every room, in case somebody's out on the street with a directional mi-crophone.

The posting in Beirut grants these guys some latitude in their dress and appearance. My first visitor sports shoulder-length hair and a big gold hoop earring dangling off one lobe.

The agent and I talk for about an hour. He has not picked up any in-formation that Hezbollah was planning to hit Andrew McCarthy. His in-formants know nothing about Pan Am 103.

Disappointed, I send him on his way. The next night, another Black-hawk sneaks into Nicosia. Another agent arrives at my door, care of Bill's taxi service. He's also got long hair and an earring. I'm beginning to de-tect a pattern here.

During this interview, I discover two important things. First, it is to-tally conceivable that the U.S. Embassy in Beirut has been penetrated by Hezbollah agents. The staff includes a large number of local nationals, and they represent every group within Lebanon. There are Druze, Ma-ronite Christians, and Shiite Muslims all working together to help run the embassy. Chances are, there are at least a few agents in place among the employees. It has happened before.

The other tidbit is more troubling. The embassy uses a private travel agency in the city to make all arrangements for its personnel. Using a local company in a place like Beirut is a huge security risk.

I spend Christmas Day in the safe house, waiting for another agent to arrive. Since this is a clandestine operation, I can't even call my family. For all my dad and wife know, I've dropped off the face of the earth.

Each night, we repeat the interview routine, but I don't learn any-thing new. We cannot prove Hezbollah penetrated the embassy's travel arrangements, but we can't rule it out. There are too many holes that good operatives could exploit.

Ten days later, I've learned all that I can. Bill books me on a flight home.

Before I leave, we head out across the Green Line and drive through Turkish Cyprus until we reach an ancient Greek port called Kyrenia. We find a place overlooking the harbor. Moored boats bob on the water, and couples walk hand in hand along the quay that leads to an amazingly intact Greek castle. Built hundreds of years before Christ, it has withstood the ages. I marvel at it. Its massive turrets and thick stone walls served as a sentinel to the past two thousand years of human history. No doubt, those ramparts will stand watch over the passing of our own era someday. It is a humbling thought and reminds me that all this is just a transient moment in human evolution.

Bill picks this time to give me an update on the 103 investigation. There was a bomb on board. It looks like it was placed inside a suitcase that the baggage handlers stowed in the 747's forward cargo bay. With Pan Am's help, a suspicious bag—a tan hard-shell Samsonite—has been traced to a flight originating in Malta. It was put onto a Malta Air flight that landed at Frankfurt. The ground crew at Frankfurt routed it to Pan Am 103A, a 727 that took it to Heathrow. It was checked through to JFK. It made it through the entire system without getting screened, even though it was an unattended bag. It did not belong to any passenger on any of the three flights.

Somebody studied our security gaps and then exploited them. And that somebody wasn't Hezbollah, Syria, or the PFLP–GC.

It was the Libyans. Some highly classified intelligence just came in that condemns Qaddafi once again. The nature of the intelligence is so sensitive that it can't be released to the public. For now, the fingers will continue to point at Iran and Syria. Meanwhile, the investigators will keep sifting through the wreckage of Pan Am 103, looking for hard evidence that we can use to condemn Libya in a public venue.

It won't be an easy task. When the 747 came apart, pieces fell across eighty-one miles of Scottish countryside. The investigators are combing through some 845 square miles, trying to find every sliver that fell from the sky that night. To do so, the Brits and Scottish police have launched the largest criminal investigation in their history. It is a process that will take months, if not years.

That night, after we return to Nicosia, I pull out my moleskin journal and make another notation. Chances are not good that we will ever catch the intelligence agents or terrorists who planted the bomb in the baggage stream in Malta. The Dark World tends to shield these anonymous operatives from justice. They move through the cracks in society, cause their mayhem, and vanish as silently as they came. Still, I have to believe that some day we'll get lucky.

I leave Cyprus and spend New Year's Eve in the business-class section of a Pan Am 747. The entire flight home, I ponder the ambiguity of my report. I can't rule out an assassination attempt on the ambassador. Could the Libyans, or Hezbollah, or anyone else have targeted the plane because our agents were aboard? It is maddening to have loose ends that cannot be tied up. The neat little Hollywood endings seen in James Bond films just don't exist out here in the darkness.

I return to Virginia Avenue to give my report orally to Mr. Dittmer. As I stand in his office and finish up with my inconclusive conclusions, I can tell he doesn't like it any more than I do.

When I reach my cubicle, I find a layer of cable traffic and other reports waiting to be read. As I leaf through them, I see with dawning horror one question has been answered. The rescue crews in Lockerbie found several passengers among the wreckage whose dead hands still clutched crucifixes. One couple was still strapped in their seats, hand in hand.

These people knew their fate.

The horror of Lockerbie is complete. And it is at times like these that an active imagination is not a blessing for a special agent of the DSS. The nightmares come. Long after midnight for weeks, I cannot help but replay what those final moments must have been like for those people who did nothing wrong but choose the wrong plane to fly home on for the holidays. Night after night, week after week, my imagination becomes a plague. I cannot escape it. I can only try harder, work harder. See more. Do more. It is our job to prevent these catastrophes. My countrymen depend on us to keep them safe. How can I say we didn't let them down?

And what of justice? Even if we do manage to catch the culprits, is that enough? A prison term or death sentence for them seems trivial compared to the horrors they inflicted on innocent men, women, and children. Will justice be enough to comfort Ron Lariviere's child in the years ahead as he grows up without a father?

No. Nothing can rewind the clock and abort this catastrophe. Best case, justice will be but a paltry sop to those whose lives have been devastated by this single senseless act.

But that doesn't mean we shouldn't pursue it. After all, once the last pieces of Pan Am 103 are collected from the Scottish countryside, what else can we do?

PART III: WAR WEARY

twenty-nine

Bethesda Bagels
February 1993

For those connected to Pan Am 103, the nightmare will never really end. The investigation continues, but for me, a deluge of cases come and go since those ten days in Cyprus. The years have started to blur together now that I'm the old man of the CT office. Just as Gleason was once the institutional memory, I have earned that title now, thanks to my seven years on the job.

I'm sitting in a bagel shop in our little D.C. suburb on a cold midafternoon. I came inside for coffee and a cinnamon and raisin bagel. Right now, I've draped my Barbour Beaufort jacket over the back of the small café-style chair I've selected by the window. It has a great view of the street outside.

And I'm studying the street today. People watching is a popular pastime around D.C. Folks will sip coffee and watch the world go by, enjoying the sights. For me, people watching is part of our daily game of survival. We've got to be good at it—my agents and I. Otherwise, we will not survive in the field.

I check my watch. Today's operation started about twenty minutes ago. We'll see who gets burned. I take a long drink from my coffee cup and peer out the window. So far, I don't make out anyone. They're getting better, that's for sure.

I need to be on my toes, but I feel weary. The burden we've carried all these years hasn't changed, it has just evolved. If anything, the world is even more dangerous now, even with the fall of the Berlin Wall. We have new threats emerging from strange corners of the world, leftover consequences from the end of the Cold War. I'm not sure we're prepared to deal with them. Our eyes are elsewhere, as usual.

But at least there have been some moves toward justice. When West and East Germany reunited, we gained access to the Stasi's secret files. The East German police had their hands in all sorts of bloody ops, one of which proved to be the La Belle Discotheque bombing in 1986.

I shake my head. That seems so long ago. I was so fresh-faced and naïve. The world was a big blank slate to me. Now I know its colors and contours. I know just how dangerous it can be. And I'll never forget the victims. It is hard for agents not to get jaded after all we've seen.

The East German files revealed some interesting details. A Palestinian named Yasser Shraydi working for Libyan intel masterminded the disco operation. He worked out of Libya's East Berlin People's Bureau and organized a team that included Musbah Eter, another Libyan intel type, and a Lebanese-born East German named Ali Channaa. Channaa was a Stasi operative who worked closely with Qaddafi's spooks. His wife was the one who actually planted the bomb.

All of them are currently at large, but at least we know who needs to be hunted down and apprehended. That's a big step forward. Such information is usually frustratingly rare.

Across the street, there's a man in a jogging suit loitering at a bus stop. He's wearing a ball cap and sunglasses. He looks cold and underdressed. He's been there since I came into the shop.

I'll have to keep my eye on him.

Do the people around me have any idea of the ruthless depths of the world they live in? Do they have any clue what lurks around them? I certainly didn't eight years ago. Perhaps that ignorance is a good thing. Living life in perpetual fear is not a life at all. In truth, there are moments where I miss that blissful ignorance. Knowledge and a top secret clearance do not equal happiness. I've found that out the hard way.

I have a copy of today's *Washington Times* with me. I open up the front page and pretend to read. My eyes are focused over the top of the paper and on Mr. Jogging Suit at the bus stop.

The end of the Cold War helped solve the La Belle case. Justice has not been served yet, but we have a long memory. If they slip up, we'll catch them. Same with the Pan Am 103 bombers. Two big breaks in 1989 led President George H. W. Bush to publicly point the finger at Libya the following year. In '91, we were actually able to indict two Libyan agents for the crime. We can't get at them. They're somewhere inside Libya, protected by Qaddafi's regime. At least we were able to impose sanctions on the country. Libya does not deserve to be a part of the international community. Not after all the violence and chaos it has caused.

The first break came in the spring of '89. A sliver of the bomb's timing device was discovered and sent to the FBI lab for analysis. It turned out to be an MST-13 device, built by MEBO, a Swiss company with lots of dealings with Libya. We only knew this because the FBI had an identical timer already cataloged in the database, thanks to the dedication of Special Agent Jim Casey, DSS.

In 1986, Casey was assigned to the CT office and was on assignment in Togo, a West African nation where Libyan intel was operating against the regime. After a run-in with some Libyans, Casey recovered a complete MST-13. This was a very sophisticated timer, complete with its own printed circuit board. Jim saw it and thought it looked out of place with the other run-of-the-mill Dark World gear the ESO types were carrying. He palmed it, brought it back to Washington, and sent it to the FBI for analysis.

His thoroughness paid off. The sliver of the MST-13 recovered from Lockerbie became one of the major publicly announced pieces of evidence used to condemn Libya for the downing of Pan Am 103. When investigators checked with MEBO, the company stated that they had sold twenty of these special timing devices to Qaddafi in 1985. The only other customer for that model turned out to be the East German Stasi.

The newspaper at my side, I stand up and walk back over to the bagel shop's counter to get a refill on my coffee. When I turn back to my table, I get a good long look at the street. A metro bus rolls up to the stop that Mr. Jogging Suit is hanging around. When it leaves, he's still there.

How many buses use that stop? I don't know. Not many. We'll see what he does next. Not far away from him, I see a transient moseying along the sidewalk. He's wearing an old green coat and one of those knitted hats with a ball on top. He reminds me of Bob, the U.S. Marshal, who used such a disguise when I met him in '87 atop that partially constructed building. I make a mental note to watch him closely.

No doubt about it, these guys are getting better. I decide to remain here for a few more minutes before taking to the streets. I'll give them a real run for their money then.

The timing device probably would not have been enough to condemn Libya for Lockerbie without also exposing our most classified sources. Fortunately, the forensics teams discovered the bomb had been placed in the Samsonite suitcase. Like the bomb found in Frankfurt during Operation Autumn Leaves, the one reconstructed from the crash site had been built into a Toshiba boom box. One pound of Czech-made Semtex plastique was all it took to take down a massive 747. But the explosive residue the blast left behind gave us the most critical clue. It allowed the forensic investigators to piece together the contents of the suitcase. They found fragments of clothing—a tweed jacket, some pajamas, an umbrella, and a shirt—that had been next to the bomb inside the suitcase when it detonated. They traced those items to Malta, and a check with the stores there uncovered a shopkeeper who vividly remembered selling those items to a Libyan. When shown mug shots, he fingered Abdelbaset Ali Mohmed al-Megrahi, a known Libyan agent.

Okay, enough of the reminiscing. It's time to get out there and play with these guys. I polish off the last of my bagel and drain my second cup of coffee. As I do, I watch the transient wander close to Mr. Jogging Suit. They make eye contact, and I see them chatting.

Big mistake. I make them both. When on a surveillance detail, it is all too common for operatives to wander over and speak to each other after a while. Watching somebody can get boring. It's only human nature to want company. But in this game, in the street dance between target and surveillance team, that can be a fatal mistake.

I toss the newspaper in the trash as I leave the bagel shop. Out on the sidewalk, I snatch a glance at the bus stop. The bum and Mr. Jogging Suit are staring at me. So now I will have a tail. I walk up the street and turn right, glancing back as I do. They're already following me.

Ahead I see a white male, longish hair, beard, and sunglasses, sitting at a window-side table in a "hot shop," a cafeteria-style restaurant. He's eyeballing me over a copy of *The Wall Street Journal*. As I walk past him, I see his gaze following me. I reach the end of the block, and as I turn left this time, I see Hot Shop Man on the sidewalk, looking nervous as he heads my way. Not good. That's three.

There should be one more.

I stair-step up a few more blocks, checking my six at every turn. I see the bum twice. Both times he's watching from a doorway. Mr. Jogging Suit appears as well. Hot Shop Man stays on the opposite side of the street from him, but I catch the two of them trying to communicate as they go.

Bad move. I'll remember that.

The SDR I've run proves that I have a tail. Now I have to shake it. A funnel is a good way to set them back. A few blocks up, there's a footbridge over an expressway. That'll be perfect. I make for it.

Funnels are tough to deal with if you're trying to surreptitiously follow somebody. Things like bridges or escalators or raised causeways force the surveillance team to break cover and move through a narrow stretch of terrain where they are easily detected. About the only thing the surveillance team can do is wait to cross the funnel until after the target is out of its line of sight. It should give me enough time to disappear into the city grid.

I cross the footbridge. The three men tailing me pause on the other side. They mill around and look out of place. They've totally lost both their cover for status and their cover for action. These are critical skills for operatives. I've exposed their weakness here.

A cover for status is nothing more than a reason for an operative to be in a particular place at a particular time. Mr. Jogging Suit was supposedly waiting for a bus. The bum was wandering around aimlessly like bums do. Hot Shop Man was enjoying the morning paper. Those worked. What didn't work is that they lingered around too long. The bus came and went, but Mr. Jogging Suit stayed in place. The bum loitered too near Mr. Jogging Suit. They talked. That looked out of place. Not many people talk to transients. Hot Shop Man blew his cover for status by staring too long at me, following me with his eyes as I went by, then leaving the restaurant too soon.

Cover for action requires more thought and preparation. If an operative is going to move from one place to another, he has to have a clear reason to do so. Perhaps he can cloak his movements by window shopping, or acting like he's looking for something. He could have a bike stashed nearby and once the target's on the move, use it to stay in the vicinity and appear to be nothing more than a cyclist out for a ride.

The best operatives don't stand out. They don't do anything that would draw attention to their actions. They are subtle, and since most people are poor observers, that makes them as good as invisible.

But I'm a trained observer, and I've drawn these three out. They've broken two cardinal rules, and now they're in a tough spot.

I cross the bridge and head deeper into the city. I stair-step at the next block. A cab passes as I cross the next street. I quickly glance at its plates and memorize the number. Two more stair-steps. I've lost my tail. A minute later, I see the same cab parked on the side of the road a block ahead. There's nobody in the backseat. The cabbie's got shaggy hair, a dark complexion, and a bushy mustache. I walk right by his cab.

Two blocks later, he drives past me again. Okay. I've made him. Number four was in a vehicle. The cab was his cover for status and cover for action, but he's overdone it.

Ten minutes later, I'm standing in front of the bagel shop again. I slide my earpiece into place and key my radio. "Team. This is Merlin. Exercise complete."

One by one, my agents congregate back at Virginia Avenue. I explain how I made each one of them. They look sheepish over how easily I burned their cover. "Look," I tell them, "this is going to take time. We'll get it right." I lead the debriefing, and we study our errors and figure out ways to correct them.

Practicing surveillance and tailing techniques right here in town has already given us a wealth of knowledge. Communicating with the rest of your surveillance team, especially on the move, becomes a problem. You don't want to talk with your fellow agent. Too often that blows both your covers. Using a radio or having an earpiece visible is also a rookie mistake. Brief eye contact. A simple hand gesture—subtle, always subtle, of course—these are the ways to speak to each other during this sort of street dance. Clothes make a huge difference. White shirts or pants tend to stand out in the crowd. An agent wearing one or both will usually get made if the target is any kind of observer. Subdued colors that blend into the crowd are the best.

Eyelines are critical components to any successful street dance. Most people keep their heads down as they go about their daily business. Their situational awareness is practically nil. We can exploit that by getting out of typical sight lines and placing agents on balconies, rooftops, around corners, and in other urban nooks and crannies. To avoid typical eyelines takes a light touch and a lot of practice. You've got to be willing to think unconventionally. We're only now starting to really practice this.

A moving target represents a new set of challenges for a surveillance team. How best do you follow your target in that sort of situation? What if he starts on foot but transfers to a car? Clearly, our agents on the street need backup in vehicles. That's a lesson we learned earlier when we first started this training regimen. But where should they be placed, and what happens if the target takes a city bus or goes into the subway system? These are all tactical problems we're working to solve.

Today's exercise was part of a larger plan I've been working on for several years now. The Edward Louis Gallo case, the two Libyan hits in '86 on our diplomats, and the near assassination of President Bush in Kuwait not long ago have all convinced me we need to approach protective security in a new manner. Today's street dance was another test of my new tactics. We'll keep working on it. And when the time is right, I'll take it to Mr. Dittmer and ask that we give it a try. If we do this right, this new concept may just give us the chance to finally get one step ahead of the likes of Imad Mugniyah and Hasan Izz-Al-Din. They're still out there, somewhere, planning their next op. I want to be ready for them this time.

thirty

THE COLONEL'S REVELATIONS

12:25 p.m.
February 26, 1993
Virginia Avenue

"Fred, I've got bad news."

I look up from a stack of recent cables to see Larry Daniele, the best and most incisive analyst we have on our threat-analysis team upstairs, standing next to my cube. He looks grim.

"What is it?" I ask.

"We've had a bombing at the World Trade Center."

I get to my feet. Things are about to get crazy around here.

"They finally did it. They finally hit us here at home."

"Yeah," replies Larry. "We all knew it was inevitable."

Larry and I walk over to FOGHORN. Inside, CNN's blaring on the television. The *Star Trek* console is lit up like a Christmas tree. Each of the duty agents has a phone in both ears. Others ring incessantly in the background.

"Fred?" one of the duty agents asks. "Everyone's calling to see what we know."

"We don't know anything yet. Tell them to hold on."

That's not an answer anyone will want to hear right now.

I watch the scene on CNN. Smoke billows up around the tower. People flee down the street. Emergency response vehicles race to the scene. Except for the New York plates, this could be Beirut or Paris or Berlin.

The first details trickle in. Whoever detonated the bomb placed it in the underground parking garage beneath one of the towers. This strikes me as odd. If Hezbollah pulled this off, they would have left a car bomb on the street in front of the building. That has been their standard MO since Beirut I. Last year, they blew up a car bomb in front of the Israeli Embassy in Argentina, proving they could operate in our hemisphere.

Placing the bomb in the street actually magnifies the destruction the device can cause. The blast blows glass out of windows for blocks, and the shards become flying shrapnel. It always increases the casualties and the carnage.

Maybe whoever planted this bomb isn't nearly as sophisticated as Hezbollah.

The Secret Service operates out of the WTC. Many of its protective security vehicles are stored near that underground parking garage. Could that have been the target? Did somebody go after the Secret Service? I know a lot of those guys from all the times I've been to New York to pull dignitary protection duty. I say a prayer for their safety.

"Okay, guys, call the Joint Terrorism Task Force, the FBI, and the NYPD. See what they need from us. Let's give them whatever support they can use."

"Stick?" I call out. Scott Stewart, who has become one of the best agents in the office, steps forward. "Here, Fred."

"I want you to be our eyes at the blast seat. Take an explosives detector and head on up. Work with the other agencies and check in frequently, okay?"

If Hezbollah didn't pull this off, who did? Mentally, I build a suspect list. The Libyans have been quiet since Lockerbie, but that doesn't mean they haven't decided to get aggressive again. They make the list. Iraq. Saddam Hussein's intelligence service has been up to all sorts of no good since the Gulf War. Between plots to blow up embassies and immolate George Bush with a car bomb in Kuwait, Saddam's agents might very well be behind this.

But then there is the odd group that's coalesced around some of the Afghan war jihadists. They've become more active in the Dark World these past few years and have become virulently anti-American. Just a few years ago, they were our allies against the Soviets. A Saudi Arabian exile named Osama bin Laden appears to be the leader of this group.

By the end of the day, we've learned that over a thousand people suffered injuries from the bomb. Four people are dead. Frankly, I think we've gotten off lightly. Had the bomb been placed on the street and detonated at lunch hour, the casualties would have been catastrophic.

Over the next few days, the pieces start to fall into place. Stick sends frequent updates to us. The bomb's composition included urea, nitroglycerin, aluminum, magnesium azide, and hydrogen. The FBI doesn't have anything on file that fits this profile. This is a new type of bomb, constructed by a new type of terrorist organization. They are aggressive, but their tactics are flawed. For that, I'm relieved.

Stick's there in the blast seat when the investigation turns up a huge clue. The bomb had been placed inside a vehicle. An NYPD bomb-squad tech finds the golden nugget: the metal plate with the vehicle's VIN number intact and readable. A quick check shows it belongs to a Ryder rental truck and that a Palestinian named Mohammad Salameh last rented it.

Within days, arrests are made. Salameh gets nabbed, as do several of his comrades. They all seem to be tied in to a group of jihadists operating out of a mosque in Brooklyn.

Ten days after the attack, I fly to New York to sit down with my contacts in the FBI and JTTF offices. As we puzzle through what's happened, I discover that the FBI had an informant who penetrated the mosque two years ago. He wore a wire and attended planning sessions and meetings with Sheikh Omar Abdel-Rahman, a blind Egyptian cleric who had become the spiritual leader of an entire network of radical jihadists living in the New York area.

I convince my contacts to let me see the transcripts of what this informant recorded. After two pages, I'm floored. After ten, I'm terrified. My mind reels. The informant was a former colonel in the Egyptian military, and he'd somehow earned the sheikh's trust. Abdel-Rahman invited him into his network's inner circle. He took part in dozens of operational meetings.

I cannot doubt the authenticity of what I'm reading. This homegrown group of jihadists have made us out to be fools. And if we don't act fast, somebody else will die for it.

The blind sheikh's minions spent two years preparing target portfolios before they actually launched the WTC attack. Led by a very capable, highly intelligent engineer named Ramzi Yousef, these jihadists planned to blow up landmarks all over New York City. They looked into destroying bridges, hotels, and other fixed targets. But what chills me to the bone is their efforts against the DSS.

For three years, they have been watching us. Their many plans included an operation to assassinate several key leaders, including the UN secretary general and Egyptian president Hosni Mubarak. The planners were especially anxious to take out Mubarak and any other Egyptian diplomatic officials. They had particular hatred for that regime, since the sheikh and some of his followers had been captured in Egypt and tortured during their incarceration.

During one stay, President Mubarak selected the Waldorf-Astoria for himself and his entourage, including his foreign minister, to stay at while they were in Manhattan. Yousef and his operatives scouted out the security arrangements around the hotel. They watched our motorcades and studied our tactics. They knew when we rotated agents, when shifts changed, and where our gaps were in fixed-site security coverage of the hotel. Using local resources, such as taxicabs, they followed our motorcades all over New York. Their operatives became so familiar with us that they not only knew what each vehicle in the formation was for, they could also tell the difference between a DSS motorcade with the foreign minister in it and the one guarded by the Secret Service that included President Mubarak. At times, they could even figure out who was who when our two motorcades operated together. With the Egyptians, we frequently ran joint motorcades with the Secret Service because there'd been so many previous attempts on Mubarak and his government.

As I read the transcripts, I realize that I had been on some of the details they'd been watching. The revelation drains the color from my face. We never even caught a whiff of this sophisticated surveillance operation.

As the meetings unfolded, the sheikh's followers used all of this preoperational surveillance to build brilliantly simple attack plans. For the Waldorf, they decided the most elegant way to defeat our security was also the most direct. Using a stolen van repainted to look like it belonged to Federal Express, they would drive the wrong way down Park Avenue and collide with Hosni Mubarak's motorcade just as it pulled up to the hotel's underground entry point for the rich and famous. We called that vulnerable choke point "the well." A commando team armed with grenades and machine guns would spill out of the van, disable our counterassault vehicles, then take down Mubarak's limo.

Another plan they developed included inserting a team into the UN Plaza Hotel's stairwells, where they would shoot their way to the target's quarters. They also considered planting operatives among the hotel staff. A few waiters armed with automatic pistols could support the hit team very effectively. That was an old Black September trick.

They've studied their history.

More plans and more target profiles come to light on every page of the transcripts. One involved blowing up Marine One while the president's helicopter landed in downtown Manhattan. I'm left utterly speechless. Why didn't the FBI take this cell down months ago?

I can get no answers for that question. My only guess is that they did not take the colonel's information seriously. It was a mistake that cost our country dearly.

The way the sheikh's underlings constructed their target profiles was absolutely brilliant. They are flexible enough to be applied elsewhere. If passed around the Dark World, they could almost function as terror-franchise business plans for other groups.

Why did they elect to launch the WTC bombing first? Only the sheikh and Ramzi Yousef can answer that question. Additional evidence uncovered during raids around New York and New Jersey show that they placed the Ryder truck under the Twin Towers in hopes of knocking one of them down into the other. They weren't looking to maximize casualties on the street, they were looking to totally destroy two icons of American economic might.

Stick and I meet. He tells me that the blast seat was almost ninety feet wide. The bomb, composed of only about a thousand pounds of explosives, tore holes through four stories' worth of concrete. Had it been placed closer to one of the key support pillars inside the garage, Yousef's plan might just have succeeded. Hezbollah would have been happy with hundreds of casualties on the street. This group wanted to kill fifty thousand and destroy an international symbol of American strength. They had the knowledge, the operational skill, and the intelligence to execute any of their planned operations.

Although Ramzi Yousef and the bomb maker, Abdul Rahman Yasin, escaped, the authorities take down almost everyone else in the cell, including the blind sheikh. Incoming intelligence reveals Yasin, who is Iraqi, managed to return to Baghdad. Yousef fled to Pakistan, then disappeared off the grid.

Yousef, the sheikh's key operations man, is out there somewhere on the loose. He knows our tactics. He knows our weaknesses. He knows how to defeat our protective security details. He's also the nephew of bin Laden's right-hand man, Khalid Sheikh Mohammad. This new group in Afghanistan has made it to the major leagues. If we don't make a generational leap forward in how we do business, they are going to hammer us. The smoking hole in the WTC's parking garage serves as a warning for all my countrymen. But the transcripts I read at One Police Plaza are the true lesson to emerge from February 26. It is time to push the panic button.

The day I leave for home, I sit in the terminal at JFK and open up my moleskin journal. I add Yousef and Yasin to my list. We must find them at all costs before they can unleash another attack.

On the flight back to Washington, I can't help but obsess over the plans to hit our motorcades. They followed us without our knowing. They watched us from every angle, both fixed and while we were under way. They never broke cover for status or cover for action. They were ghosts who swirled around us, studying our every move as we unsuspectingly went about our duties.

I run through their scenarios over and over in my head. The FedEx van swings onto Park Avenue, racing for our motorcade. Nobody in the Crown Vic at the head of the column would have expected that. In fact, with the motorcade just pulling up to the Waldorf, we'd all be preoccupied with getting Mubarak out of his limo and into the lobby.

The van screeches to a halt. Bang! The back doors fly open and the commando team launches its assault. AKs blazing, they toss grenades at our unarmored vehicles. For us, it would have been like Custer's last stand. Would we even have been able to draw our weapons in time? I shudder at that question. I don't think we had the correct mind-set to handle such an attack. We've been too focused on stopping the lone nut from walking up to our high-value target and taking a shot, just like John Hinckley Jr. did to President Reagan a decade ago.

It would have worked. Oh, God, it would have worked.

thirty-one

Standing in Clark Dittmer's office later that week, I detail everything that I found in the colonel's transcripts. When I finish, I outline my new ideas. It will take a lot of manpower and training, but we've got to do something new. Fortunately, Mr. Dittmer is one of the most open-minded men I've met in this business.

"Okay, Fred," he says. "You're right. Give your ideas a shot and let's see what happens."

In the days and weeks to come, we develop a new countersurveillance program. When we're running around in motorcades or doing protective-detail duty at events, the agents near our VIP have an immediate situational awareness of not more than fifteen to twenty feet. We operate in that bubble, studying the nearby threats to the exclusion of everything else.

Not anymore. We'll still have the protective agents right there with the VIP, but my group is going to push the perimeter out. We'll go undercover, mix into the crowds, move on the peripheries of the motorcades, and look for anyone or anything out of the ordinary. We'll search out the surveillance operatives, calculating where they'd best be situated, then find perches out of normal eyelines to watch those areas. If we're moving our VIP from point A to point B, we'll send an advance surveillance team to Point B to study the situation.

We'll do it from deep cover. We'll blend in and move among the crowds as one of them. We'll outghost the ghosts who have been following us.

That's a start, but it won't be enough. We're going to videotape every crowd and every speaking engagement involving the VIPs we protect. After each event, we will cull through the tapes, looking for familiar faces, searching for anyone who makes a habit of going to these functions. We'll look for anything out of the ordinary as well. If we see a person acting erratically, we'll get his physical description out to our surveillance teams. If he shows up at another event, we won't just keep an eye on him, we'll talk to him. Agents will mingle through the crowd, make their way to our oddball, and chat him up to determine if he's a legitimate threat. Just a normal conversation, mind you, not an interrogation. This way, we may be able to intercept the Hinckleys and Gallos of the world long before they come into that fifteen-foot bubble around the VIP.

We're going to need to practice our field craft until we are absolutely invisible. No mistakes. No breaking our cover for status or cover for action. We will learn how to follow suspects in every venue imaginable, from large crowds to busy streets to subway systems. We'll learn the best composition of each countersurveillance team; we'll develop the optimal formations that give us all-around visibility. Situational awareness is what we need. It will be our new watchword.

But it isn't enough. Hand in hand with our countersurveillance program, we ramp up another one that I call protective intelligence. When we have a VIP under our care, we're going to do some serious homework. We'll examine every prior threat to that person and draw up a list of organizations or individuals who pose a risk to our VIP. Then we'll study their MOs and look for the ways that these various groups operate so we can develop tactics to counter them. If a terror group likes to kill high-value targets with car bombs, we'll make sure to clear the streets in front of the VIP's hotel and destination points. If a lone nut has sent threatening letters to our VIP, we'll track him down and send a team to sit on him while the VIP's in country. We won't tip our hand. We'll just watch. If the nut makes a move for our protectee, we'll bring him down.

The CT gang loves the new ideas. They're an aggressive, creative bunch, and they throw themselves into the new training program we develop. Some of them get so good that during our surveillance exercises around D.C., they learn to follow suspects, changing clothes along the way to further mask their presence. One minute, Mr. Jogging Suit is two blocks behind a suspect. The next, he sheds his pants and jacket on the fly. Now he's just another guy in a nondescript T-shirt and a pair of shorts. The shoes are the only giveaway, and as we work on our skill sets, we even learn to change shoes on the fly.

To communicate, we use Walkman-style headphones plugged into our radios. Now, instead of having to break cover to talk on a Motorola, or expose our earpieces, we simply look like we're enjoying some good tunes. A hand in the pocket, finger on a button, and we're ready to talk to one another. That innovation alone makes us significantly more effective on the street. We can choreograph our dance without anyone being the wiser.

We wear shoulder and ankle holsters hidden under layers of clothing. Beneath our shirts, our badges hang like St. Christopher medals.

We'll use every asset and department at our disposal. Around D.C., Eagle One will fly sweeps for us along motorcade routes, giving us another perspective in our quest to root out threats. Local police will be used to seal off areas, clear destinations, and design our motorcade routes through their city. They will know the best way to get around their towns, and we'll rely on that skill set.

But that still isn't enough. What if this new group in Afghanistan, which apparently calls itself "the Base"—or al-Qaeda in Arabic—decides to target another embassy or fixed site of some sort? The sheikh's cell in New York City had a long list of monuments, tunnels, and bridges they wanted to hit, so there's no doubt in our minds that such attacks are coming again. How do we get out in front of that?

The colonel's transcripts gave me detailed insight into al-Qaeda's targeting cycle. It starts with preoperational surveillance. They do their homework. They study their targets. They watch our comings and goings to learn the weaknesses of the security setup they'll be penetrating. If we can uncover these preliminary moves, we can defeat them and lives will be saved. We must learn to watch for the watchers. We push out the word to our agents in the field. Extend your situational awareness, look for the unusual. Find the guy who sits too long on the park bench or the garbage-man who never seems to empty any cans. Search for the ghosts, and when they're identified, follow them. See where they go, discover what they're doing. Then develop countermeasures to defeat their plans, and call in the cavalry to bring down that cell.

On that front, we score an early success. One of our best agents, a believer in our new way of doing business, implements our ideas in Beirut. It does not take long for his guys to discover a Hezbollah observation point right by the U.S. Embassy's front gate. The terrorists are hunkered down in a nearby apartment that commands a perfect view of all the comings and goings at the gate. They're obviously studying targets, looking for gaps to exploit. We send in the cavalry to catch this surveillance team, but we're just a hair too late. They vanish into the city. However, we discover they'd leased the apartment after it became vacant. Two can play at that game. We put the manager on our payroll—now we have a watcher in place—and lease all the empty apartments that have views of the embassy gates.

Our situational awareness just helped plug a security gap.

Here in the States, we score other successes. During one weekend in New England, we put a surveillance team out around the security perimeter guarding Princess Diana. One of our guys literally stumbles across a paparazzo who had crawled through a dense forest for over a mile in hopes of getting in a position to use her telephoto lens. A small success, to be sure, but one that I'm sure the royal family appreciated.

The first big test comes in California. We head out to the Golden State to protect Mikhail Gorbachev as he gives a series of speeches around the Bay Area. During one event, our countersurveillance team notices a bearded man in a green jacket acting just a little out of the norm. We study him and peg him as a potential lone nut. During Gorbachev's next speech in San Francisco, our countersurveillance team spots him at the edge of the crowd. We send an agent to talk to him. Disguised as any other face in the crowd, our spook strikes up a conversation with Green Jacket. It doesn't take long for him to conclude Green Jacket's not playing with a full deck. Quietly, we take him down, and discover he's carrying a twelve-inch butcher knife under his coat. He'd been planning to hack to death one of the great world leaders of our era.

When the royal family returns for a visit, we run a full check of all past and current threats against Prince Charles and Princess Diana. The check turns up another kook from Texas, who had actually penetrated security at Buckingham Palace in his quest to get at the royals. We send a team to watch our lone nut in Texas until our visitors depart. The guy never moved, but we'd pushed our situational awareness out thousands of miles. Had he made any attempt to get close to our VIPs, we would have known about it and brought him down long before he got anywhere near them.

Our ideas take off. We share them with other agencies, including the FBI, CIA, and Secret Service. We sell countersurveillance as an outer security ring designed to filter out the threats before they get to the guys with the Uzis standing next to their VIPs. We get almost complete buy-in. The new countersurveillance tactics are used to protect peace conferences and heads of state, dignitaries and fixed sites that have registered threats against them.

But our agents in the field can't do everything alone. We need to have reinforcements. In the months after implementing these changes, we build a fire brigade team stationed out of our Virginia Avenue office. Should an embassy receive a credible threat, our team flies out to it on a moment's notice. They set up shop and start looking for the watchers. At the same time, we change our tactics and timetables to disrupt any planning the local terrorist cells are conducting. Such moves set our foes back to square one in their targeting cycle, and if we find their preoperational surveillance teams, we shove them right out of the game.

We're finally getting ahead of our enemies. Instead of reacting to smoking craters and blown-up airliners, we're scouring the Dark World, eyes open, ready to pounce.

But we're still not to the point we need to be. All these changes make a clear difference in the first year we use them, but gaps remain. Airline security is still a significant problem. In the wake of Pan Am 103, a commission recommended a long list of changes in the way the air carriers protect their passengers. Full searches of carry-on items and screening all checked luggage with X-rays and bomb-sniffing dogs are great ideas, but they are not implemented. The air carriers claim they can't afford it. Our government does not force them. There's little we can do about it; it has become so political and so far above our pay grade that we can only pray another hijacking or Lockerbie does not take place.

I know better. The likes of Mugniyah and Hasan Izz-Al-Din, Ramzi Yousef and Osama bin Laden are out there. And their minions are searching for ways to strike at us.

We pick up the pace, and hone our skills even further. We change our tactics frequently and use increasingly clever covers for our countersurveillance teams. One memorable week, I speed around D.C. as part of the security detail for a delegation of Indian diplomats. Fred Davis pilots Eagle One and covers my back from the air. For just a fleeting moment, I feel like we're working as a team again, like we did when we drove the old rescue squad vehicles back when we were young and eager. So damn eager.

Not long after, we cover the old man, Yasir Arafat, the ultimate terrorist turned statesman. I view it as the supreme challenge. Everyone wants Arafat dead. He's survived so many assassination attempts that he must have more lives than a cat. This is the most dangerous assignment I can give our agents, so I take it myself. The idea of protecting a man who killed countless civilians appeals to no one. He's what I've spent my entire career fighting against. Now my country welcomes him to New York City as an envoy of his people. We must protect him.

As we race around Manhattan, I can't help but think of one of the cold cases I've personally reopened. Back in 1973, when I was still in school in Bethesda, Israel's air attaché assigned to their embassy in D.C. was assassinated in his front yard, mere blocks from my own home. I went to school with his oldest daughter, though I never met her. Yosef Alon died as the Bethesda–Chevy Chase Rescue Squad reached his house and worked frantically to save him.

This case has always been personal to me. The Alon family left our neighborhood the day after the assassination, never to return to the States. When I became deputy chief of the Counterterrorism Division, I made a point of reopening the case. What I found was a long list of errors and cover-ups, FBI mistakes and sinister silence from both the Mossad and the CIA. Using my contacts in the Dark World, I was able to discover who had orchestrated the hit.

The Red Prince. Ali Hassan Salameh was the assassination's architect. The founding father of modern Arab terrorism and the mastermind of the 1972 Munich massacre, he's the man others like Mugniyah, Hasan Izz-Al-Din, and Ramzi Yousef have emulated their entire careers. When

I first started in the CT office, Steve Gleason told me that to understand Middle Eastern terror, I had to understand Black September, Salameh's organization. I'd studied the Red Prince, not realizing that his long reach had once scarred my own neighborhood. Through it all, Yasir Arafat remained one of his closest friends. Salameh became his security chief and even came with Arafat to the UN General Assembly meeting in 1974. I've built a private Red Prince file. In it, I have a photo of his son sitting on Arafat's lap.

My sources say Alon was killed by a two-man hit team. Supposedly, the Mossad hunted them down and took them out years ago. I don't believe that. I think they're still free, out there somewhere in the Dark World. I've added them to the list in my moleskin journal.

As I help protect Arafat, part of me wants to interrogate him. Wouldn't that cause a stir? I want to know what he knows. I want to find out just what the Red Prince was doing when he killed Yosef Alon. Most of all, I want to know if the rumors are true. Time and again, I've had informants tell me that while the Red Prince sowed death all over the globe, he was secretly on the CIA payroll as an informant.

Of course, I never get the chance to grill the old man. Such things are just not done in the nice and tidy diplomatic circles he travels in now. He's gone respectable—at least that's the image he portrays. But at night at the Waldorf, his minions come to pay homage and curry favor. When they arrive, they dump cash into a garbage can sitting outside his suite's door. By the time he leaves for home, his guests have filled and refilled that can many times. Where all that untraceable cash will go is anyone's guess.

Through 1993 and '94, we make great strides in our ability to protect our VIPs. We've developed skills to smell out terror operations, and we continue to work our HUMINT assets in the field. But for every step forward, it seems like the Washington bureaucracy forces us back two more.

A sea change has taken place over at the FBI. Louis Freeh took over the Bureau as its tenth director in 1993. Ever since, counterterrorism investigations have become freighted with huge political baggage. Turf wars between the FBI, the CIA, and the Department of Justice have soured relations across the board. Not only are the agencies not playing well together, but now the priorities have changed. Terrorism is seen less as a national security issue and more like a criminal one. It is a potentially disastrous shift, one that has divided the intelligence community and has segregated those who need information from the information they need. It is the worst catch-22 imaginable.

Let's say you are debriefing a hostage or terrorist. The original notes are taken by the FBI lead case agent and stored as part of the Bureau's ongoing criminal investigation. They end up secreted away in the appropriate investigative file. By law, the agents conducting the debriefing have to be identified for any future federal trial. This effectively ends any spook's career. It outs them, reveals who they are, and ensures they will never be able to work clandestinely in the Dark World again. You can't go overseas and play spook if people know your true identity.

Obviously, spooks are reluctant to be part of debriefings now. This seals off a huge source of HUMINT for us, though we may not have access to it anyway. The debriefing notes, and whatever intel is gleaned from them, is now rat-holed by the FBI. It is rarely disseminated to the other Dark World agencies. We're not talking to one another anymore. Everyone's protecting their turf, and I fear that we'll miss an attack because the right information didn't get to the right people in time.

As far as we've come, we still have many, many gaps. Here in the DSS office, which straddles the FBI-CIA-DIA-NSC-NSA turf wars, we're playing the game without a full deck. It's like hunting for buried treasure with vast pieces of the map missing.

One step forward, two steps back. The bureaucratic wars only grow worse. Meanwhile, out there in the Dark World, new threats loom.

thirty-two

Virginia Avenue

Ramzi Yousef has a two-million-dollar bounty on his head. That's what the Rewards for Justice program has offered for information leading to his capture. The smell of that much cash has brought out the crazies again. For months, we've been dealing with walk-ins who've assured us that Yousef is working at a falafel stand in Algeria or driving a cab in Paris.

Even as we chase him, I spend months trying to glean additional details about his operations from every backdoor source I've got at the Agency and the Bureau. Is Ramzi Yousef an operative of Osama bin Laden's? Is he working for al-Qaeda, or is bin Laden and his organization simply providing support and financial resources? Bin Laden's family is one of the wealthiest in Saudi Arabia. As a result, al-Qaeda is one of the best-financed terror networks we've ever seen.

Al-Qaeda is composed of lots of loose-knit cells working toward common goals. The senior leaders are all Afghan war veterans, men who defeated the Soviet Union with our help, money, and weapons. Most of them are Arab volunteers who we helped get to Afghanistan in the eighties so they could join the mujahideen. Much of their technical know-how came from us. When the NYPD and FBI took down the sheikh's New York cell, we discovered CIA-published bomb-making manuals and U.S. military handbooks. These men helped us win the Cold War, only to turn on us.

Exactly where Yousef fits in with bin Laden's group remains fuzzy. There is obviously an ideological connection, since they're both committed jihadists who seek the destruction of Israel. To do that, they believe the United States must be forced to sever its military and financial ties to the Jewish state. In this, they are not much different from Hezbollah or the PFLP–GC. But those terror groups look absolutely provincial compared to the vision and scope Yousef and al-Qaeda share.

Yousef thinks big. He doesn't bother himself with penny-ante hijackings or bombings. He wants to score body blows against us. Even as he eludes us, he begins a new planning and targeting cycle. We get reports he's in Pakistan preparing attacks against Americans there. Next, we receive credible intelligence that he's been in Thailand and Southeast Asia. His operational security and caution keeps him one step ahead of us. He travels under false names with expertly forged passports. He is the ultimate Dark World ghost.

Chasing Ramzi Yousef highlights the divisions we have here at home. In the eighties, when it was just Gleason, Mullen, and me, we had almost a free hand to do whatever we thought needed to be done. Those days are over. The nineties have seen an ever-increasing bureaucratization of counterterrorism operations. We have layers upon layers to deal with, turf wars to maneuver around or through, and our own internal issues within the State Department that frequently tie our hands. Our own diplomats tend to dislike DSS agents, a sentiment we reciprocate. They consider us alarmist right-wingers at best, John Wayne–style rogues at worst. In return, we call the careerists in the floors above the big blue door the Bow Ties, or Mandarins and Black Dragons. The Black Dragons are the senior diplomats whose career ambitions frequently clash with our own efforts to protect them overseas. These interoffice conflicts have simmered for years. At times, open warfare breaks out. When that happens, everyone loses, especially the American people.

The bureaucracy once cost us a legitimate shot at Ramzi Yousef. One day in 1994, a walk-in shows up at the U.S. Embassy in Pakistan. He's heard about the two million dollars we're offering for Ramzi Yousef and tells our Islamabad agents he can lead them to the master terrorist. To offer proof of his knowledge, he produces a recent photo of Yousef that he has taken. Our men check the walk-in's story. He's on the level, and Ramzi Yousef is indeed in Islamabad. To catch him, all we need to do is take down the safe house he's using. But to do that, our guys on the front line need to get permission.

Dutifully, the RSO, Art Murrell, reports the tip up the chain of command. His report gets routed to over two dozen agencies, from the FBI and CIA to the FAA, the Department of Interior, and even the Department of Transportation. By the time it gets passed around, hundreds of eyes have seen the report. Authorities in Pakistan are notified, which is one of those diplomatic protocols the Mandarins love so much. Unfortunately, in the Dark World, such niceties usually blow operations and sometimes get people killed.

When our guys kick in Yousef's door, they find his safe house empty, a tea kettle brewing on his stove. He's been tipped off. Too many people in Washington and Pakistan seem to know about the pending op and a leak occurs somewhere.

Yousef slips through our grasp and vanishes into the Dark World. We're left searching for clues but cannot get back on his trail.

As for our informant, nobody hears from him again. There is no mercy. In our business mistakes cost lives.

Back to square one. For weeks, we don't get a reliable lead. Then one morning, as I reach the office in my new white Jeep Wrangler, my cell phone rings. There's been an airliner hit in Southeast Asia. I rush through the big blue door and read through the flash cables originating out of Tokyo and Manila.

On December 12, 1994, Philippines Air Flight 434 was en route between Cebu City and Tokyo when a bomb exploded under the seat of a twenty-four-year-old Japanese businessman. Haruki Ikegami's body absorbed the bulk of the blast, which split him almost in half from his crotch to his head. Though damaged, the plane stayed airworthy, allowing the pilots to execute an emergency landing on Okinawa.

Some of our sources suggest Yousef engineered the bomb and planted it aboard the airliner when it was flying from Manila to Cebu City. Others blame various radical Filipino terror groups.

A check of the passenger manifest reveals that an Italian businessman named Armaldo Forlani sat in Ikegami's seat during the Manila to Cebu City flight. He has vanished, and as far as we can tell, no such person by that name ever existed.

I'm not sure what this means. We sit down with our brain trust and discuss the possibilities. If this is Ramzi Yousef, why did he plant such a small bomb? Did he miscalculate its force? What was the possible motivation? The flight had nothing to do with the United States, and Yousef has never advocated attacks on either the Philippines or Japan—at least none that we have picked up anyway.

Perhaps the device itself offers up a clue. The terrorist placed the bomb inside some sort of a plastic container, then stuffed it inside the life jacket under seat 26K. As far as we can determine, the bomb maker used liquid nitroglycerin. If that is true, it would have been invisible to current airline security procedures.

I'm mulling this over while chewing on a PowerBar when an epiphany strikes.

Flight 434 was a test run.

Yousef thinks big. He's also an engineer by training. That means he's methodical, deliberate, and process-oriented. If anything, the target profiles the New York cell worked up reveal a keen attention to detail.

What if Yousef is running experiments? What if he is testing our security systems? If he is, there's a massive attack coming, and we don't even have it on our radar screen.

The days pass. We use every asset we have in every corner of the world to search for the golden nugget that may bring Yousef's intentions into focus. There's nothing, nothing but the crackpots and greedy money hounds who will say anything in hopes of a buck.

Christmas comes and goes. I sleepwalk through time with my precious family, lost in thought at what might be lurking on the horizon. My wife deserves better. So does my four-year-old-son, Jimmy. And as I hold him before he goes to sleep on Christmas night, I wish I could be a more attentive father for him. But right now, my life belongs to my job. The DSS isn't a career, it is a monastic order. There's never enough room for anything or anyone else.

Twelve-hour days stretch to fourteen and sometimes sixteen. When I come home, I try to shut the stress off, but the STU-III right on my nightstand serves as a constant reminder that *something* horrible is sure to happen. I get to the point that I take the regular family phone and place it on my pillow, set to vibrate. My pager and cell phone are never out of reach. I've become a prisoner to modern communication technology.

New Year's comes and goes without another hint of Yousef's whereabouts. My guys work every angle, drill every source. We learn that bin Laden has compartmentalized al-Qaeda's organizational structure to the point that multiple cells simultaneously develop attack plans. What we face is not a terrorist dragon growing in Afghanistan, but a hydra. We can take out one cell, but others are already plotting. Still others are ready to execute. How does one fight such a decentralized enemy? Even if we kill bin Laden, his minions already have their marching orders.

We're going to get hit again. I can't see how we won't, unless a miracle happens that lets us roll up every operational cell. That would be a veritable magic bullet. In the real world, they just don't exist.

thirty-three

Time plus opportunity equals casualties. That is the equation we face right now. The more time we give to Yousef, the more opportunity he has to launch another attack. Frankly, with all the assets marshaled against him out there in the Dark World, I'm surprised he hasn't gone into hiding. Instead, he's demonstrated supreme aggressiveness. We strongly suspect that he executed the attack on Flight 434. To do that at a time when almost any other terrorist would have gone to ground is the signature of someone either totally confident in his own abilities, or a man who is flat-out reckless. Given his past, he doesn't seem like the reckless type. He's got a calculating and logical mind. At some point in his life, he also became a committed jihadist. He received a degree in electrical engineering from a university in the United Kingdom, and before he left the legitimate world for the life of an international terrorist, he worked for the Kuwaiti government as a communications engineer.

We're dealing with a formidable intellect. Fortunately, he tends to surround himself with Luddites whose brainpower leaves much to be desired. That became obvious in '93 when one of his compatriots in the WTC strike returned to the Ryder rental office and tried to recover the four-hundred-dollar deposit he'd put down on the vehicle. A smart operative doesn't make such an amateurish mistake. Yousef's relatively new at the Dark World game. He's good at it, but if we get lucky, he'll make a mistake, and then we'll have him.

We get lucky—almost. In early January, I arrive at work to find my little world behind the big blue door has been thrown into utter chaos.

"What's going on?" I ask Stick Stewart as I come in.

"Fred, the Philippine police almost caught Yousef this morning."

A flare of excitement and relief surges through me. Then I realize Stick said *almost*.

"Tell me."

"He was living in an apartment in Manila. It caught fire last night. The cops and fire brigade showed up. When they got inside the place, they discovered a bomb factory. While they were going through it, one of Yousef's boys came back, apparently to take stuff out of the apartment."

"Who is it?"

"Nobody we know. Calls himself Ahmed Saeed. Not his real name. The Philippine police have him now at a military base outside Manila. They're sweating him, but he's not talking yet."

That won't be pleasant. The Filipinos are not known to be kind during interrogations. Their signature techniques include burning a detainee's scrotum with lit cigarettes.

"Have the Filipinos sent us a list of what they recovered from the apartment?" I ask.

Stick nods and hands me a flash cable from our embassy in Manila. "Here's their preliminary list. There's still more to come. They've got a bomb squad inventorying everything right now. You're not going to believe it."

I sit down at my desk and look at the list. It reads like the contents of a college chemistry lab gone terrorist. Bottles of nitroglycerin were stacked among jugs of sulfuric acid, sodium trichlorate, ammonia, gasoline, silver nitrate, and nitrobenzol. They weren't building pipe bombs with all this stuff, that's for sure.

Sodium trichlorate? Isn't that the stuff used in World War I gas shells? Were they planning to use chemical weapons in their next attack?

The list continues. Beakers and kettles and all sorts of other scientific equipment had been set up inside this apartment. Stick is right. The

Philippine authorities stumbled onto a bomb factory. And the amount of each chemical recovered—sometimes in the gallons—says to me that they were either going to build the mother of all improvised explosive devices, or Yousef was planning to produce a lot of smaller ones.

Yousef and his fellow conspirators fled their apartment as the authorities arrived. In their haste to get away, Yousef made a huge mistake. He left his laptop in the apartment. The files are encrypted, but that won't keep the Filipinos, or us, from getting into them. It is only a matter of time.

Later in the day, we get an update. Yousef was about to launch an assassination attempt on the pope. His Holiness is scheduled to visit Manila in the middle of the month. The Philippine police found detailed maps of his motorcade routes around the city. After the police arrested Saeed, he let slip that he was after the two satans—the United States and the pope.

Ramzi Yousef plotted to kill the pope. Is there a bigger symbol than that in the Christian world? Yousef could have sparked a religious war.

What if this is just the tip of the iceberg? From what I read in the colonel's transcripts, hitting multiple targets at once is an operational objective of these new jihadists. Al-Qaeda's so compartmentalized that Yousef himself might not even know that he's a cog in a larger operation. Are other cells working elsewhere in the world to hit key Catholic leaders, such as bishops and cardinals? There's no way to know, but we need to warn the Vatican.

After the assassination attempt on Pope John Paul II in the 1980s, the Vatican asked the DSS to station an agent there. For years, our service has helped the Vatican plan and execute security procedures for the pope through our agent on the spot.

We warn the American cardinals as well. For now, that's all we can do.

Another update comes in. The laptop's security has been broken. The hard drive is full of airline flight numbers and schedules. There are references to attacks on U.S. nuclear installations. There are also operational plans. The big one is called "Oplan Bojinka."

The attack on the pope is simply meant to be a diversion. In less than a week, Yousef's cell plans to use the chaos a successful assassination would cause to sow liquid time bombs on no fewer than eleven airliners heading to the United States from points across Southeast Asia. Each bomb would be stashed under seats inside life vests—the exact MO in the Flight 434 incident. Using digital Casio watches as detonators, all eleven bombs were supposed to go off simultaneously.

Thousands would have perished, and the damage inflicted on air travel and the airline companies would have been incalculable.

Flight 434 was a test run after all.

We get the word out quickly that we're dealing with a mega-threat, the likes of which America has never faced before. What Yousef's trying to do is nothing short of total war. In case Bojinka is already in autopilot mode, our DSS agents in the field take up stations from Singapore to Tokyo to oversee security procedures and assess potential threats. At the same time, we dispatch one of our agents to Manila. We need to have additional men on the ground out there, supporting the Filipinos.

Where did Yousef go? He fled the apartment building and has not been seen since. Despite his mistake, he still managed to elude the authorities. If his past behavior is any indication, he'll roost somewhere else and immediately begin to plot other attacks. We're racing our intelligence capabilities against his ability to gather operatives and build his bombs. I'm not sure we can win this race.

The days pass. More information emerges from the Philippines. Yousef's group actually set off a small bomb in a mall in Cebu City. The description of the attack sounds like another dry run.

The Filipinos get some additional details on the plot to kill the pope. Again, Yousef's planning was brutally simple and elegant. He'd build an improvised explosive device and strap it to a suicide bomber dressed as a priest. Yousef knew such a disguise would probably get their suicide bomber close enough to the pope to kill him.

Saeed has not broken yet. The Filipinos are probably beating him raw right now, but he's holding out. He's loyal to Yousef.

That isn't surprising. Everything we know about him suggests he possesses remarkable personal magnetism. People gravitate to him. He's a natural leader who has no trouble recruiting foot soldiers when he needs them.

More news flows in over the succeeding days. Yousef's fingerprints are lifted from the apartment, confirming he was there. The police who responded to the scene also saw him on the street. Had Saeed not tried to escape, they might have grabbed Yousef. But in their haste to run down

Saeed, they lost their situational awareness and Yousef bolted into the night.

A thorough list of everything found in the apartment includes a full accounting of the twelve fake passports found hidden in a wall divider, as well as a comprehensive inventory of all the chemical agents the bomb squad unearthed.

We've flown in more help from other Washington agencies. The Filipinos have stumbled across a mint of intelligence information. They need backup, and we need to get into that computer and find out what else resides inside it and the four floppy disks found with it. If the pope was stage I and the airliners were stage II, where does an attack on our nuclear assets come into play? And who is Saeed? What's his role? We need answers, fast.

Discussing the current situation in the office on Virginia Avenue, we conclude that Yousef must know that Operation Bojinka has been overtaken by events, mainly due to the seizure of his laptop. Would he try to execute Bojinka anyway? Doubtful. He's far too smart and cautious to do that. That said, if his past MO holds true, he won't quit, he'll just adapt. This can only mean one thing: He's out there, far out of reach, planning something new. And right now, he's winning the race.

thirty-four

February 1995
Chevy Chase, Maryland

The snow is starting to fall again. Our local radio station, WTOP, keeps warning us we're sure to get hit with a veritable blizzard this weekend. We've already got a good sheen of ice and frozen snow on the ground from a storm that passed through the D.C. area earlier in the week. Bundled up in gloves, hat, and Barbour Beaufort, I'm getting ready by shoveling the driveway.

I don't mind this chore. It gives me time to think, and the outdoor exercise is refreshing. I've spent too much time in the office this winter. As the deputy director for our division, I have more authority and more ability to shape our team, but that's come at the cost of my time in the weeds. I miss it. If I go any further up the chain of command, I'll become purely an administrator. That doesn't appeal to me much.

I clear the driveway and start working my snow shovel across the front walk. It grinds over a sheet of ice, and I have to kick it loose. Once I'm done here, I'm going to finally get to spend some time with Jimmy. We're set to have a snowball fight once the storm arrives. He and Sharon are upstairs right now, getting ready for the day. We moved out of our old Bethesda townhouse not long ago and have gone suburban. We bought this house on Chestnut Street in Chevy Chase in hopes that our family will continue to grow. We both need to work to afford it—my government salary ensures that.

That means Jimmy spends a lot of time in day care, and every time I drop him off there on my way to work, I can't help but feel pangs of guilt. My own dad owned a gas station and dabbled in real estate. He worked harder than anyone I've ever met, but he always made enough to make sure my mom was home to raise us.

Kids and the DSS are not a good mix. Sharon and I knew that when I first joined the service. The life of an agent means children grow up with a largely absent father. We decided to try anyway and find a way to make it work. We have, but Jimmy's still getting shortchanged, at least compared to what my own father gave me.

Tyler Beauregard dashes across the yard, her breath visible in the subzero air. She trots in circles around me, snuffling as she examines my work. She's slowing down, getting old (just like me), and I don't know how much longer she'll be able to keep up our running regimen. I don't want to face that. The problem with dogs is that you outlive them.

I finish up on the walkway and return the shovel to the garage. Inside, I kick off my snow boots.

The phone rings. God, how I've come to hate that noise.

I reach for the kitchen extension. "Hello?"

"Fred? This is Art Maruel."

A surge of excitement swells in me. Art is the RSO in Pakistan. He's an old-school agent with no time for bureaucrats or Bow Ties.

"We need to talk on the other line."

I detect excitement in his voice. Something big is going on, and it doesn't sound like another attack.

"Okay, wait five and call me back." He hangs up. A few minutes later, the phone rings again.

"Fred?"

"Yeah, got ya, Art."

I push the scramble button on the STU-III's console. The line pops and hisses with electronic noise.

"Okay, go ahead," I say after a few seconds.

"Fred, we just got a walk-in who says he knows Ramzi Yousef."

Finally. A break. Art's much too careful to bug me at home over a whack job.

"How good's the source?"

"Miller and Riner grilled him for six hours. They're convinced he's legit."

I know both of those agents. Bill Miller's a redheaded former marine whose performance earned him a tour with the Detail. Jeff Riner is a young agent who I got to know while he was stationed here at the Washington Field Office. He's a good kid, and I trust his judgment.

Art continues, "They've just given me their report. I'm about to send it out."

Alarm bells ring in my mind. We lost Yousef the last time when too many people learned about our other walk-in. We recently picked up information that Yousef was treated in a Pakistani hospital for chemical burns months ago. The Pakistanis never let on. The man has somebody, somewhere, in a position of power protecting his rear.

"Hold up, Art. Let me think about this." If this is on the level, we need to minimize who knows about our informant. We can't be broadcasting the news across twenty-five agencies again.

"Okay, send the report through DSS channels. Eyes-Only Burton. Got it?"

This is not how things are supposed to be done. But the last time Art followed procedure, too many eyes saw our intel, and we blew our chance to get Yousef.

Will Art trust me? I know he will. We're like minds.

"Understood. I'm on it."

"Good. I'm heading for the office."

We click off. I gather up the secure phone and find my briefcase and pistol. After plucking my car keys off their peg, I stand at the base of the stairs and tell my wife I've got to go in.

Jimmy appears at the top of the stairs. I turn for the garage, trying to ignore the guilt attacking my conscience. I have no choice. We have a chance to stop a mass murderer.

Thank God I bought a Jeep. By the time I back it out of the garage, the snow is really coming down. The roads will be a mess. I throw my new rig into four-wheel drive and hit the gas.

My old Jetta never would have made this journey. As it is, my drive turns into a mini-epic. The windshield wipers barely keep up with the snowfall. Sheets of ice and drifts make the roads treacherous. Few people are out, though I do see one hearty bureaucrat on skis, his suitcase strapped to his back, heading for some downtown office with admirable persistence.

When I finally reach Foggy Bottom, I head straight for FOGHORN to wait for the report. It comes in a few minutes later. I take it back to my cubicle, fix some coffee, and sit down to read it.

Art's agents are right. This does look good. On Saturday morning, Islamabad time, the embassy got a call from a frantic wife of one of the staffers who lived in the diplomatic enclave within the city proper. A very agitated Pakistani had forced his way into her house and refused to leave. She needed help.

Jeff Riner and Bill Miller hopped into an embassy SUV and sped over to her house. There, they found the Pakistani inside the house looking practically apoplectic with fear. At first, he was so nervous they couldn't get much out of him. Then he produced a copy of *Newsweek* and showed Bill and Jeff a copy of an article on Ramzi Yousef that included his photo. As he pointed to the picture, he told the two agents that he knew Yousef and where he was staying in Islamabad.

Why did he show up at an American staffer's house and not the embassy?

Bill and Jeff asked him that. He told them he feared detection if he went to the embassy.

Does that mean our embassy is under surveillance? Probably.

He knew the house he selected belonged to an American diplomat because he drove through the neighborhood with Ramzi Yousef, scouting potential targets.

So Yousef held true to his MO. Instead of going to ground after Bojinka was compromised, he's already planning his next op. That drive through the diplomatic enclave was the first step in constructing his next target profile.

Our informant tells us that he had initially been taken with Yousef when they first met. Yousef started grooming him as part of his plan to build a new cell in Pakistan. The informant turned out to be a bad selection. When Yousef took him to Thailand and ordered him to carry out attacks on airliners, the informant could not bring himself to do it. He masked his reticence with plausible excuses that security was too heavy on his flights. Yousef seemed to understand and did not hold his failure against him.

Our man realized he was no killer. In fact, he has a family—a wife and child. Our informant wanted out. Once you join Yousef's cell, though, there is no escape. You remain loyal, or you end up dead.

He heard about the Rewards for Justice program and concluded it offered the only way out of his predicament.

Jeff and Bill disguised the informant and hid him in the back of their SUV. With a blanket covering him, they drove back to the embassy and talked to him all afternoon. The details they gleaned from the informant match much of what the Filipinos found in the Manila apartment.

For two million dollars and a get-out-of-Pakistan-free card, the informant will lead us to Ramzi Yousef.

If it saves lives, that's a bargain. The problem is, how do we pull it off?

thirty-five

I finish reading Art's report. I call him on the office's STU-III and tell him to avoid paper from this point forward. The more that gets written down, the higher the probability this chance gets blown. We'll move fast, for sure, but we'll communicate only via secure phone.

Art's aboard. What we're about to do will be risky. Avoiding the proper channels and blacking out this operation so that only a handful of people even know about it will certainly engender outrage. I'm prepared to deal with that, though. I learned long ago that it is better to act and get chastised later than ask permission and never get the shot.

We will need two teams: Art's in Pakistan and a key group in Washington. Art will use Jeff Riner and Bill Miller as the lead agents, but I know we'll also need Pakistani help. That's going to be very tricky.

First things first. Who do we need here in D.C.? I'll bring in only people I personally know and trust. I make my first call to John Lipka, the chief of the D.C. Joint Terror Task Force.

Despite the storm, John comes over to the DSS office when I tell him we've got something big cooking. After I brief him, he thinks about what our next step should be. "We need to bring in John O'Neil," he tells me.

O'Neil is a legend in the counterterrorism business. An overachieving workaholic in a field full of them, he stands out as one FBI agent who can be counted on to do the right thing. He doesn't play politics; he doesn't rationalize justice. He just wants to stop terrorists and save lives. He is the chief of the FBI's counterterrorism division.

Together, John Lipka and I drive through the storm to the Hoover Building. The halls are deserted, as is nearly every office. But when we reach John's, we find him hard at work. We didn't even need to call ahead. John has a reputation for *always* being in the office.

Together, John Lipka and I outline our plan. When we finish, we can see O'Neil's bought into it. "Sounds good, let's do it."

It takes a few days to get the pieces in place in Pakistan. The informant gives us conflicting information at first, sending our agents off on wild-goose chases to confirm what he's said. Finally, Art's men pin down Yousef's exact location. He's staying in a hotel called the Su Casa Guesthouse.

I give Art the green light to assemble his team. While he's preparing to take down the hotel, we need to get him some support. We need the Pakistanis to help us.

John O'Neil, John Lipka, and I talk this over. There's really only one Pakistani we trust: General Rahman Malik, one of the Federal Investigation Agency's senior leaders. We give him a call, and he joins our little circle of conspirators. He'll provide the entry team, and he handpicks the best of his agents for the mission.

We're ready. To coordinate the op, O'Neil, Lipka, and I meet late Tuesday night at the FBI's ultramodern Strategic Information and Operations Center (SIOC). Nobody is around. It is just the three of us in the room together, standing in front of a bank of three large projection screens surrounded by empty desks and blissfully silent phones. The place is so quiet that I feel like we're inside a submarine.

We've been able to keep a lid on this, which is an accomplishment on its own. O'Neil's briefed one other FBI agent, but that's as far as the news has traveled within the Bureau. For my part, I brought in my immediate superior, Al Bigler. After Beirut I, Al's body was found amid the debris. The rescue crews thought he was dead and dumped him on a heap of corpses. A Lebanese cop who knew him just happened to walk past the dead bodies and noticed Al. The two were friends; when the cop realized

Al was still alive, he got him to the hospital and saved his life. Al is going to join us in the SIOC later this evening. He doesn't want to miss this; he has scores to settle.

Before we can pull the trigger and order the snatch, O'Neil tries to get an FBI agent onto the scene. Unfortunately, there isn't one in Pakistan at the moment. After some running around, we learn the nearest Bureau agent is in Bangkok. O'Neil orders him onto the next plane to Islamabad, but he won't be on the ground in time to take part in the op.

Al Bigler storms into the room. "What have you got?"

"We're just about to link up with Art," I tell him.

He takes up station, leaning against an empty desk. I establish contact with Art through a secure phone and put him on speaker.

"Okay, Fred, what do you want us to do?" Art asks through the electronic pops and hisses of the secure phone.

I look around the room. Every one of us knows what will happen if this goes bad. If we lose an agent, if the man we take down is not Ramzi Yousef, if the Pakistanis make a stink—we will be chum to the office piranhas in our midst. Hell hath no fury like a bureaucrat scorned. We're risking our livelihoods here. And our pensions.

To be honest, I don't care about my career. My ambitions don't revolve around climbing into the halls of power within the State Department. They're focused on winning this war we're fighting that so few Americans seem to recognize even exists. After the World Trade Center, counterterrorism remains at the bottom of our national priorities. Perhaps that's why I don't care about the title before my name or how much power I accumulate. That means nothing when lives are at stake every day. All I want to do is carry the battle home to guys like Yousef so more of my countrymen do not end up free-falling from thirty-one thousand feet. If we don't do it, who will?

There's the rub. Who will?

We will. Looking around the room, I see good men, equally if not more committed than I am. We're the veterans, the men who have waged this campaign against terror our entire professional lives. John O'Neil has made plenty of enemies within his own bureaucracy by doing the right thing. He's given his life to this fight, just as Al and John Lipka have. Maybe the Black Dragons are right. We are zealots. But our side needs zealots, too.

"We ready?" I ask the group.

Nods all around. I look down at the secure phone. "What's the current status, Art?"

Art's warbly, computer-distorted voice replies, "Fred, the target's at the hotel. My team is ready to move."

Time to throw the dice. "Send the guys in."

"Roger that, Fred. Wait one."

Art's at the embassy, where he will stay for the duration of the op. He'll be in radio contact with Bill and Jeff every step of the way and will serve as our link to them.

O'Neil looks grim. The tension in the SIOC skyrockets. We're committed.

"Art," I say softly. "If it's not him, we're all burned."

"Well, you know the old saying: 'Success has a thousand fathers, but failure is an orphan.' "

He adds, "They're en route."

While we wait, I ask Art, "How do you plan to get the informant and his family out?"

He gives me a quick brief. The plan is thorough. Art's done a good job and I know the informant will be safe.

"Fred, everybody's in place. We're ready."

I take a breath, then say a prayer. Please, God, let this be Yousef. Let us get this killer off the streets.

"Go in," I order.

"I can't hear you, Fred."

"Hit the door! Hit the door!"

That did it. "Roger. Stand by." Over his radio, Art gives the "Go" order.

The minutes pass. I can hear Art breathing over the phone, but not a word is spoken.

My imagination sees the Pakistani Inter-Services Intelligence team storming into the hotel with Bill and Jeff. These ISI agents are the best and most trustworthy in Islamabad. At least, I hope they are.

In the background, ten thousand miles away, I hear Art's radio squawk. Through the open phone connection, it is so distorted it sounds like Charlie Brown's teacher talking.

"What was that?" Please, let our men be safe.

Art's voice breaks through my prayer. He's crystal clear. "Fred! Fred!"

"We hear you, Art."

"We've got him. Repeat, we've got him."

"Are you sure it's Yousef?"

Art keys his radio and asks Bill Miller to confirm that the man they've grabbed is indeed the master terrorist.

"Affirmitive."

"Fred, Ramzi Yousef's ours."

thirty-six

November 1995
Bethesda, Maryland

"Hi, Paps, how're you feeling?" I don't need to ask that question. My dad has lost so much weight it looks like he's wasting away. As he zips up his winter coat, I can see his T-shirt underneath hanging on his scarecrow frame. He's pale and wan, and I know he doesn't have much time left.

"I'm okay." He limps to the car. Gently, I help him, holding on to his arm. "Thanks, Freddy," he practically whispers.

I get him to my car and ease him into the passenger seat up front. Jimmy's in back, strapped into his booster seat. "Grandpa!" he exclaims.

"Hey, Tiger," Dad replies. I walk around to the driver's side. For a moment, I pause and look up the driveway. This is the house Dad and Mom bought when I was just a boy. I was raised here. This is my old neighborhood, and the sight of it under these circumstances almost makes me lose my self-control.

I get behind the wheel and turn the motor over.

"Nice new car," Dad says.

It's a BMW 5 Series. I gave up the four-wheel drive for another sedan earlier this year.

I throw the BMW into gear, and we roll past the landmarks of my youth. We pass by the street Yosef Alon's family lived on. Black September operatives killed him right in that front yard over there. The only difference all these years later is that the tree the killers used as concealment is long gone. The FBI tore it out and took it away back in '73. Evidence. Of course, it disappeared.

A soft silence settles over the three of us. Jimmy's content to wait for the adults to say something. Dad stares out the window. This is his home, too. He's been a fixture in the D.C. area since he returned from the war.

"Remember the time you took me to the White House, Paps?"

"Nixon was actually nice to you." Dad laughs. Somehow, this humble man who never quite lost his rough-around-the-edges upbringing made friends on both sides of the political aisle here in D.C. He was a coal miner's son who worked the mines himself before the war, and again for a while after he returned from Nuremberg and the war crimes trials he helped to guard.

His humble origins never held him back, and he wore them like a badge of honor when he received invites to political soirees. That happened a lot when we were all younger. I always marveled at this. He was not a rich man, or a powerful one. But he was respected.

One time, he went to a White House function. Some button-down Ivy League snob struck up a conversation with him and asked, "What do you do?"

Dad didn't brook snobs. "I'm in coal."

"You own your own company?"

"No. I used to shovel it."

The button-down walked away.

Thanks to Paps, I had an extraordinary childhood. He introduced me to presidents. I shook Joe Louis's hand. Dad once gave me a signed photo of JFK that the president had inscribed to me. It is one of my prized possessions and perhaps one of the reasons why I admired President Kennedy so much.

When I used to go on fishing expeditions in the dead bodies cabinets, I read through the assassination file over and over. Within the report, I found the Secret Service had uncovered an interesting fact. When Lee Harvey Oswald was discharged from the marines, he was so bitter that he sent a threatening letter to the secretary of the navy. Who was the secretary of the navy at the time? John Connally. In Dallas that November day in '63, Connally, then the governor of Texas, was riding shotgun in the president's Lincoln Continental. One school of thought inside the Secret Service was convinced Oswald wasn't trying to kill Kennedy. He was trying to kill Connally and settle an old score. He hit the wrong man. I don't know if that's what really happened or not. Only Oswald could tell us that. But it always puzzled me that this bit of information never made the Warren Report.

We come to the rescue squad station. Both Dad and I stare out the window at it, lost in thought. I can almost see Fred Davis and I climbing out of the old rig after a long night's work. The place hasn't changed much at all.

"Dad, look! A fire truck!" Jimmy exclaims happily.

"Your dad used to drive that thing," Paps tells him.

I smile. Jimmy seems impressed. I realize this is a special moment. Three generations of Burton men spending time together hasn't happened in a while. We don't have much time left as a trio.

"Freddy, is all that stuff cleared up at the office? They're not still after you, are they?"

"No, Paps. They're not."

"That was outrageous," he grumbles.

"Yeah. It all worked out, though."

After we caught Ramzi Yousef, the news blitzkrieged through the alphabet soup agencies. The FBI went public and took credit for the capture. Normally, that wouldn't bother the DSS. We like to remain in the shadows. But this time, Al was infuriated. The day after the news broke, he sent me out to host a press conference with the State Department beat reporters. I told the truth of how it went down. This was a Rewards for Justice success, and we were proud of it.

Somebody didn't like the fact that we went public. In the weeks that followed, I was specifically targeted. The State Department's inspector general (IG) opened an investigation on me. So did the Department of Justice's IG office. Rather than celebrating our success, the IG wanted to know why we didn't follow proper procedure. It smelled like a witch hunt, and while the FBI and CIA promoted agents and handed out bonuses in self-congratulatory moves in the wake of Yousef's capture, our guys in Islamabad received nothing. Jeff and Bill didn't even get so much as a letter of commendation.

That made me indignant, and I shook the tree hard until they finally got what they deserved.

"Is the investigation over?" Dad asks me.

Since most of this played out in public, I'd confided in Dad and told him what was going on inside the office. Somebody way above my pay grade was very cheesed off at what I had done. They lost sight of the real point, though. We'd taken a killer off the streets—a killer who was about to go after our own diplomats in Pakistan. That truth meant little to whatever paper shuffler was behind the witch hunt. All he cared about was the process, the bureaucratic niceties that in the Dark World blow ops and get people killed.

I look my dad in the eyes. I can smell his Old Spice cologne and it brings me back to my childhood. He always smelled of Old Spice and Lucky Strike cigarettes. "Yeah, Paps. The investigation's over. Nothing came of it. Everything's okay."

"You sure?" he asks warily.

"Yeah." I break eye contact to watch the road. "Honestly, I think the other agents in the office were more upset about it than I was."

"Well, that just shows they're loyal." Dad reaches into his jacket pocket and produces a blue DSS baseball cap. He flips it up and covers his buzz cut. I'm touched by the gesture.

We hit another stop light. I still have to drop Jimmy at day care. I'm going to be late for work. I can't remember the last time that happened. I realize I couldn't care less.

"Freddy, that Yousef was no different than the Nazis I guarded at Nuremberg. I will never understand what made them do those things. These terrorists are the same."

I look back over at Dad. I can see pride in his eyes. He once guarded the worst criminals in human history. I inherited his sense of moral outrage, his belief in the beauty of righteousness. Ten years in the Dark World hasn't shaken that out of me, and it never will. I had an excellent teacher.

"Thanks, Dad" is all I can manage.

I've seen plenty of gray, way too much of it, in my career. But I've held on to my beliefs. In the end, it wasn't that hard. After all, it's the black and white that defines the gray in between.

We reach the clinic. Today, Dad starts chemotherapy. He's been diagnosed with small cell lung cancer. The doctors give him three months.

"Freddy, I want to be cremated."

No.

I don't want to hear this. I can't deal with it. I want to escape this fate we're both staring down. And I won't lose it. I won't. Not in front of my dad.

I can't say anything. I don't trust myself. He puts a reassuring hand on my arm as I park the BMW. "There's a little creek that runs through Lillybrook."

He pauses. Lillybrook was the West Virginia coal camp he grew up in during the Depression.

"It goes through a little hollow. We used to play there as kids when we had nothing. Nothing."

He's told me about this place before.

"Spread my ashes there."

I force myself to turn my head. I've been looking in the rearview mirror, studying Jimmy, knowing there is no escape from these words. But now, I have to be the man my dad expects me to be.

I face him. Our eyes connect. He looks so weary, so worn down already by this ravaging disease.

"Okay, Paps."

"Thank you, son."

In March, Jimmy and I honor this sacred promise together.

epilogue

BROTHERHOOD OF THE BADGE

Spring 2004
Silver Spring, Maryland

A gentle wind tempers the warmth of this clear spring afternoon. I walk among the shade trees and blooming flowers. The well-manicured lawn is soft underfoot.

"Hey, buddy. I've missed you."

My own voice carries on the wind. I don't come home much anymore, only three or four times a year on business. But every time I do, I come here.

To Fred Davis's grave. I kneel down and pick up the dead flowers scattered around his headstone, thinking about those soul-saving nights at the old house at Brandt Place. That was a lifetime ago. Literally. My closest friend has been dead for almost a decade.

He was the best of us. And not a day goes by when I don't think of him.

I pick away a few upstart weeds and throw them atop the pile of dead flowers I've made.

Being here takes me back to my days as a cop. This cemetery was part of my old beat. I used to push a patrol car up Georgia Avenue right over there almost every night.

And then there were the rescue squad days. Up until recently, those were the happiest days of my life. I think that's why Fred and I were always so close. Life got so much more complex later. We swam in a sea of chaos and just tried to keep our heads from going under. As a cop, as a pilot, and as an agent, personal happiness is always subordinate to duty.

I didn't realize until later just how much of a sacrifice that meant. When Fred finally showed me, I was crushed. Then liberated.

The phone rang one morning in February 1997. I thought it would be FOGHORN with another crisis. It turned out to be Kenny Burchell, an old friend from the rescue squad.

He told me Fred Davis was dead. I remember holding the phone, unable to speak, unable to move. I'd been through so many crises that they'd become old hat to me. I'd just kick into autopilot mode and get done what needed to be done.

Not this time. I'd just spoken to Fred a few days before, his Explorer hit a patch of ice while he was on his way home from work the night before Kenny called me. His rig skidded into a pole. He was taken to Suburban Hospital in Bethesda, where he slipped away.

I brush away a few windblown leaves. I want Fred's grave to be pristine before I leave. It'll show others that this man has not been forgotten.

I remember driving over to the hospital. I knew that I could walk in, flash my badge, and see his body. I could say good-bye. I parked in the lot and couldn't get out of the car. I couldn't even bring myself to reach for the door handle. In the end, I sat in the driver's seat and cried.

I have always been a contained man. I temper my emotions with logic whenever I can. I've never been the outgoing, life-of-the-party type. I'm quiet and slip through the world, comfortable in its shadows. But Fred was my friend.

He was my friend. We'll always be bound together by the brotherhood of the badge. I have never stopped grieving his loss.

The funeral was torturous. I wore a dark Jos. A. Bank suit with black tape over my badge. I hung it around my neck, just like a St. Christopher's medal. Hundreds of cops showed up. The U.S. Park Police helicopters flew overhead in a missing man formation. Bagpipes played, and all I could do was stare at his widow and wonder why this had happened.

Fred never had a chance to have the family he had always wanted. I did. I was the lucky one of the two of us, but my family never came first. My life was all about the job. I started counting up all the missed birthdays, all the Christmases I was overseas or in New York. There were times I was gone for months on protective details and nobody—not even Paps—knew where I was. When I added it all up, I'd already missed some of the most important milestones of my son's life.

That's not how I was raised. I had sacrificed my own children for the greater good.

It became unbearable. Fate stole Fred from his family. I'd squandered mine. I was so busy fighting the good fight, trying to save lives, that I'd lost my own. I didn't own it anymore, the service did. And I realized that I didn't want my son to have a stranger for a dad. Or a widow for a mom.

It was time to pass the torch to the younger guys in the DSS. In '98, I got an offer to go to work for Strategic Forecasting, better known as STRATFOR. It was the opportunity I needed to save myself and my family. I left the DSS with no regrets.

Well, with few regrets. I wish I'd been able to scratch more names off the list in my moleskin journal. But that game isn't over yet.

We moved away from my childhood roots and set up house in Austin. At STRATFOR, I refined my countersurveillance techniques and have helped CEOs and corporations build security plans, both here and overseas. At the same time, I still work in the Dark World. STRATFOR has been called "the shadow CIA," famous for its forecasts of international events. I am part of the counterterrorism team within the company. We watch overseas threats, analyze them, and report our findings to our clients.

Our new life in Texas reinvented my family. My wife didn't have to work anymore. My hours were shorter, and I didn't have to disappear for weeks on end. I had a much more normal job. I was no longer part of a near monastic order with all the demands that were required of me.

It took Fred Davis's death for me to realize what I needed to do with my own life. In a way, it was his last gift to me, this liberation. Since we moved to Austin, my family is my new life.

Fred had always been the one I turned to when the pressure grew too intense. He'd set me at ease, make me laugh. I'd feel reenergized every time we'd get together. I never thanked him. I didn't know how. We never did touchy-feely well. We pretended to be too tough for that.

I reach for his headstone and run my fingers across the letters inscribed in it, clearing away the moss that's grown over the words.

"I wish our kids could have played together, my friend."

I have three now, Jimmy and my two little girls. Together, Fred and I could have tormented their dates when the girls hit high school. That would have been fun: a cop and a spook scaring the hell out of some sixteen-year-old would-be Romeo. The girls would have hated it. But they would've been home by curfew.

The shadows grow long. It is time to go. I stand and start to walk away.

No. Not this time. I stop and turn.

"Thank you, Fred. I just wish you didn't have to die for me to get a second chance."

The next day, I take the Metro from my hotel in Pentagon City, intent on checking in with the STRATFOR office on K Street before I leave for my new home.

Instead, I find myself in a conversation with a World War II veteran. I saw his Pearl Harbor veteran's cap and we began to talk about sneak attacks.

"I'll tell you," he remarks, "I never thought we'd get sucker-punched again."

From my viewpoint, it was inevitable. September 11, 2001, was not a wake-up call for me. It was a reminder.

"It will happen again," I reply.

"What makes you think that?"

"We can't be a hundred percent right all the time."

I almost tell him more, like how the interagency turf wars continue despite the attempt to unify things under the Department of Homeland Security. September 11 prompted many positive changes, like larger budgets for the intel services and more assets to use in investigations. But it also created more layers of bureaucracy, more rules and procedures that everyone must follow. The days of the mavericks making things up as they went along are over.

In my day, we started as three agents against the threat matrix. The world was our beat and we had no rule book. We lived by the seat of our pants and did what we could to stem the tide of carnage. We lacked resources, funding, and technology, but we did have the chance to make a difference. Today's agents can't do what we did. They've got too many restrictions, too many manuals to follow, too many bosses to keep happy. They lack the freedom and the flexibility we enjoyed. I think if I'd stayed in the DSS, I would have suffocated in today's climate.

"You'd think we'd be a hundred percent right about the big ones. Like Pearl Harbor and Nine/Eleven," the veteran says bitterly.

"Well, there are a lot of places where the system can break down. When that happens, we get hurt." Since 9/11, there has been an effort to fix those places, but much work remains. Information sharing is still a problem, and the local law-enforcement agencies who form the front line against terror still do not receive the data they need. They don't have security clearance for most of it. We still lack HUMINT resources in the Sandbox. Coordination between agencies remains touch and go, even during crises. Politics infuses everything, especially after the WMD fiasco in Iraq.

That said, the good guys are holding the line right now. The FBI has done a good job disrupting the operational cells here in the United States. There have been some notable successes since the towers fell. Overseas, we've fared less well. London, Madrid, Indonesia—they remind me that we've still got plenty of work to do.

"Well, maybe it's a good thing then. Maybe this country needs to get hit every few years."

The veteran's comment surprises me. "Why?" I ask.

"We're a complacent people with a short memory. Pearl Harbor. September Eleventh—they were reality checks for the country. They made us wake up and realize the dangers we really face."

"Perhaps," I say. The idea that Americans getting killed could be a blessing in disguise is anathema to me. I've spent my entire adult life trying to prevent that from happening.

At the same time, I realize he has a point. Average people in New York; Washington, D.C.; Chicago; and other big cities are more aware of the threat that terrorism poses than ever before. In these places, office buildings now have evacuation plans and emergency kits and actually run disaster drills. Businesses have prepared contingencies to sustain the continuity of their operations in case their headquarters get hit. Aboard airliners, passengers have better situational awareness, and attacks have been thwarted because of that. In general, we are far more tuned to the dangers lurking in the Dark World than when I was in the DSS.

Before I know it, we've reached the stop for Arlington National Cemetery. The veteran struggles to his feet, grabs his cane, and bids me farewell. As he walks into the station, I can't help but think about my dad.

On a whim, I spring to my feet and edge through the doors just before they close. In a few minutes, I'm walking through row after row of headstones. Heroes. Veterans. They are proof of the blood sacrifice we've given as a nation. Around me, a scattering of Greatest Generation veterans search for lost buddies. I walk past an elderly man on his knees, praying before a grave.

The day is warm. Yesterday's breeze is gone. The stillness in the air lends a serenity to these sorrowful scenes.

Suddenly, I come up short. Did I just see a name I know?

I turn and walk back to the marker. With a shock, I realize that I'm standing in front of Ambassador Arnold Raphel's grave.

March 16, 1943.

August 17, 1988.

He died with President Zia in PAK-1.

Do his loved ones know why?

And what of General Herbert Wassom's family?

They deserve to know to know the truth. And only those of us on the ground in 1988 know it.

Now that I'm out of the DSS, I can do it. I can tell what I know. I owe that to the families.

My time in the Dark World has always been about the victims. Justice is poor compensation for trauma and loss, but it is the best we mortals can do. I kept going and fighting long after I should have stopped, motivated by that desire.

As I leave Arlington, I reach under my suit coat. No longer do I wear a shoulder holster, but tucked inside my pocket rests my moleskin journal. My list. The names within these pages are signposts on the journey that became my life. Some of the names have been scratched off. They're in supermax prisons now, or dead from old age or violence. Abu Nidal is the latest one to go, assassinated by his former allies inside Iraq just before we launched our invasion.

But other names remain. Mugniyah, Hasan Izz-Al-Din, and others still ply their trade of death and violence. Though I'm no longer a government agent, I am still in the game, thanks to STRATFOR. I run my own HUMINT sources from Beirut to Baghdad, Bogatá to Bolivia. I watch. I listen. I do not forget. Instead, I search for answers in the dark corners of the world. My files grow, and cold trails grow warm again. Oh, yes. There will be more names scratched off this list before I'm done.

Bank on it.

Author's Note

Just as this book went to press, in February 2008, Imad Mugniyah died in a car bombing in Damascus, Syria, following a meeting with Syrian intelligence officials. Hezbollah blames Israel for the assassination. Like the Red Prince and Abu Nidal before him, Mugniyah's luck finally ran out.

Acknowledgments

This book recounts the education of a U.S. counterterrorism agent. I have walked you through the world on fire: the assassinations and failures, the lives saved and lost, through the eyes of someone in the arena, when we were greatly outmatched and there were some of us who knew it.

A wise old spook once told me that no operational decision is perfect; you need to manage the blowback. How true. With the benefit of hindsight, which is always perfect, there are some of my past decisions I would love to revise, but amid the shades of gray we operated in, as threats were coming in faster than we could react, we were left with doing the best damn job we could while realizing that some of our decisions might turn out to be mistakes.

Investigating terrorist acts, especially the murky threats, is never easy. Some attacks are simple and others highly complex. Those that involve foreign intelligence agencies are the most complicated because of the merging of two shades of gray and the foggy world of spooks and terrorists, a real nasty combination, one that can get away with murder.

No man goes through life, or a book project, without a lot of help. I needed more than most, I'm afraid. I am sincerely humbled by the efforts of those who saw fit to believe in this project. Jim Hornfischer, my literary agent, set the vision and assembled my team. Will Murphy, at Random House, is owed a tremendous amount of thanks for believing in me, a debt that I can never repay. Lea Beresford at Random House has also been of tremendous assistance. At times, one can't say thanks enough for the tireless efforts of someone who shuns the spotlight but works endlessly to get the job done. John Bruning, Jr., provided the oversight, direction, and tone. He is a patriot, with true character and honor. Those of you with sons ought to want yours to grow up to be like John. Any success this project may have should be his. I'll take the blame for failure.

My current employer, Stratfor, www.stratfor.com, is the finest private intelligence company in the world. Dr. George and Meredith Friedman, Stratfor's visionary founders, strive for brutal honesty but are not afraid to admit when they are wrong. That is quite rare among most intelligence agencies. Most spooks bury their mistakes; at Stratfor, coverups don't happen. Our readers are much too smart to accept errors. Stratfor's analysts, writers, and support staff are the very best of a unique breed of specialists. They make us look brilliant every day. My personal thanks go to Don Kuykendall, Scott "Stick" Stewart, Anya Alfano, Mike Parks, and Susan Copeland.

In the counterterrorism arena, I would like to thank Brad Bryson, John Mullen, Scott "Stick" Stewart, Mike Parks, Bill Armor, Ron Reams, Scott Tripp, Peter Bergin, the late Clark Dittmer, Frank Rodman, Bernard Johnson, Larry Daniele, Mike Posillico, John Taylor, Bob O'Bannon, Bobby Noll, Chuck Hunter, Tom Gallagher, Larry Johnson, Nicholas Smith, Jr., and Fred "Razor" Piry. There was nothing we could not do, anytime or anywhere, despite the naysayers.

A special thanks to Special Agent Steve Gleason. He taught me everything I know about counterterrorism investigations. There has never been a more dedicated or honorable man, pushing boulders uphill or fighting the good fight. I owe you, my friend.

My father, William Harrison Burton, attempted to teach me service, humility, and tenderness. I miss you. For my mother, Helen, and sister, Kelli, thank you for always being there. Jimmy, Katie, and Maddie: Believe in yourselves and strive to make a difference in this world, because you have made a difference in mine. Follow your calling.

Sharon, without your love, patience, and understanding, I would have failed. May God continue to bless our lives.

Fred Burton
Austin, Texas

FRED BURTON is one of the world's foremost experts on security, terrorists, and terrorist organizations. He is vice president for counterterrorism and corporate security at Stratfor, an influential private intelligence company. He is the former deputy chief of the Diplomatic Security Service, the Department of State's counterterrorism division.